Immersion

Manchester University Press

New
Ethnographies

Series editor
Alexander Thomas T. Smith

Already published

The British in rural France:
Lifestyle migration and the ongoing quest for a better way of life   Michaela Benson

Ageing selves and everyday life in the North of England:
Years in the making   Catherine Degnen

Chagos islanders in Mauritius and the UK:
Forced displacement and onward migration   Laura Jeffery

South Korean civil movement organisations:
Hope, crisis and pragmatism in democratic transition   Amy Levine

Integration, locality and everyday life:
After asylum   Mark Maguire and Fiona Murphy

An ethnography of English football fans:
Cans, cops and carnivals   Geoff Pearson

Loud and proud: Passion and politics in the English
Defence League   Hilary Pilkington

Literature and agency in English fiction reading:
A study of the Henry Williamson Society   Adam Reed

International seafarers and the possibilities for transnationalism in
the twenty-first century   Helen Sampson

Devolution and the Scottish Conservatives:
Banal activism, electioneering and the politics of irrelevance   Alexander Smith

Performing Englishness:
Identity and politics in a contemporary folk resurgence
Trish Winter and Simon Keegan-Phipps

Immersion

Marathon swimming, embodiment and identity

Karen Throsby

Manchester University Press

Copyright © Karen Throsby 2016

The right of Karen Throsby to be identified as the author of this work has been asserted by her in accordance with the Copyright, Designs and Patents Act 1988.

Published by Manchester University Press
Altrincham Street, Manchester M1 7JA
www.manchesteruniversitypress.co.uk

British Library Cataloguing-in-Publication Data
A catalogue record for this book is available from the British Library

Library of Congress Cataloging-in-Publication Data applied for

ISBN 978 0 7190 9962 5 hardback

First published 2016

ISBN 978 1 5261 3961 0 paperback

First published 2019

The publisher has no responsibility for the persistence or accuracy of URLs for any external or third-party internet websites referred to in this book, and does not guarantee that any content on such websites is, or will remain, accurate or appropriate.

Typeset in Minion with Futura display
 by Out of House Publishing

*In loving memory of Harry Cornforth,
who taught me to love the water.*

Contents

List of figures	*Page* viii
Acknowledgements	ix
Series editor's foreword	xi
Introduction	1

Part I – Becoming and belonging

1 Becoming	27
2 Unexpected pleasures	45
3 Authentic swimming	63
4 Making it count	81

Part II – The good body

5 Who are you swimming for?	101
6 Gendering swimming	118
7 Heroic fatness	136
8 Failing bodies	152
Conclusion	173
References	179
Index	196

Figures

1 Swimming below the Statue of Liberty
  (Copyright © 2015 Janet Harris) — *Page* 18

2 Greasing up before training (Copyright © 2015 Karen Throsby) — 35

3 Feeding (Copyright © 2015 Peter Anderson) — 35

4 Dover briefing (Copyright © 2015 Karen Throsby) — 37

5 Looking back from the finish (Copyright © 2015
  Deborah Bettencourt) — 48

6 Head stripe (Copyright © 2015 Mark Howley) — 52

7 Emplacement (Copyright © 2015 Colin Hill) — 59

8 Dover training (Copyright © 2015 Karen Throsby) — 119

9 Drinks and snacks (Copyright © 2015 Nick Adams) — 131

Acknowledgements

Both a monograph and a solo marathon swim are credited to individuals but are collectively achieved, and in both domains I am indebted to many.

The book includes material from three publications and I am grateful for the permission to reproduce these publications in revised form here. Chapters 1 and 2 draw on material reprinted by permission of the publishers from 'Unlikely becomings: passion, swimming and learning to love the sea', in *Seascapes: Shaped by the Sea* eds. Mike Brown and Barbara Humberstone (Farnham: Ashgate, 2015): 155–172. Copyright © 2015. Chapters 2 and 6 include material first published in Throsby, K. (2013a). '"If I go in like a cranky sea-lion, I come out like a smiling dolphin": marathon swimming and the unexpected pleasures of being a body in water.' *Feminist Review* 103: 5–22. And Chapter 7 is a revised version of Throsby, K. (2013c). '"You can't be too vain to gain if you want to swim the Channel": marathon swimming and the construction of heroic fatness.' *International Review for the Sociology of Sport*, published online 5 July 2013, DOI: 10.1177/1012690213494080. I was also very fortunate to receive a grant from the Economic and Social Research Council to pursue this research (RES-000-22-4055).

The fieldwork relied upon the sustained goodwill of countless people who shared their time, hospitality, knowledge and experience with me. In particular, I am grateful to Nick Adams, Donal Buckley, Ned Denison, Suzie Dods, Bryan Finlay, Simon Griffiths, Sally Minty-Gravett, Janet Harris, Elaine Howley, Mark Howley, Evan Morrison, Simon Murie, Jen Schumacher and Freda Streeter, who variously facilitated access to research sites and participants, helped me to locate materials and commented on draft chapters, but there are many more without whom the research would have been impossible. I also received swimming support throughout the research period and since from more people than I can name, but I particularly appreciate the support from the beach crew in Dover, the team at Swimtrek, the Jersey Long Distance Swimming Association, the Catalina Channel Swimming Association, the Channel Swimming and Piloting Federation, Chillswim, the Sandycove Island swimmers, NYC Swim, David Barra, Patti Bauernfeind, Emma Brunning, Rondi Davies, Denise Devereaux, Dan Earthquake, Julie Farrell, Paul Foreman, Cliff Golding, Charlie Gravett, Chantelle le Guilcher, Janet Harris, Colin Hill, Neil Morton, Ranie Pearce, Jeff Robbins, Ian Smith, Scott

Stefan, Sam Vincent and Penny Wilkins. I am very grateful for the many hours of coaching, safety cover and crewing that have made my swimming possible.

I have enjoyed the support of colleagues at both the Department of Sociology at the University of Warwick, and the School of Sociology and Social Policy at the University of Leeds, who asked thought-provoking questions, provided moral support when my confidence in the project waned, helped me to carve out the time to finish this book and put up with my occasional absences in search of swimming adventures. Maddie Breeze, Nickie Charles, Rachel Cohen, Bethan Evans, Sarah Hodges, Ruth Holliday, Anne Kerr, Adrian Mackenzie, Louise Mansfield, Maureen McNeil, Celia Roberts, Belinda Wheaton and many others have helped me to think critically about marathon swimming in the course of our collaborations and conversations, reading drafts, listening to endless swimming talk and cheering me on to the finish. I was also invited to present my research at conferences and seminars throughout the country, giving me the chance to further hone my ideas and create new connections. These opportunities are too many to list, but each one was a privilege, and a great help in keeping the book project moving forwards. The team at Manchester University Press have also provided invaluable support, and I am very grateful for their enthusiasm for the project and their expertise in bringing it to fruition.

And finally, to Peter, for all these things and more, thank you.

Series editor's foreword

At its best, ethnography has provided a valuable tool for apprehending a world in flux. A couple of years after the Second World War, Max Gluckman founded the Department of Social Anthropology at the University of Manchester. In the years that followed, he and his colleagues built a programme of ethnographic research that drew eclectically on the work of leading anthropologists, economists and sociologists to explore issues of conflict, reconciliation and social justice 'at home' and abroad. Often placing emphasis on detailed analysis of case studies drawn from small-scale societies and organisations, the famous 'Manchester School' in social anthropology built an enviable reputation for methodological innovation in its attempts to explore the pressing political questions of the second half of the twentieth century. Looking back, that era is often thought to constitute a 'gold standard' for how ethnographers might grapple with new challenges and issues in the contemporary world.

The *New Ethnographies* series aims to build on that ethnographic legacy at Manchester. It will publish the best new ethnographic monographs that promote interdisciplinary debate and methodological innovation in the qualitative social sciences. This includes the growing number of books that seek to apprehend the 'new' ethnographic objects of a seemingly brave new world, some recent examples of which have included auditing, democracy and elections, documents, financial markets, human rights, assisted reproductive technologies and political activism. Analysing such objects has often demanded new skills and techniques from the ethnographer. As a result, this series will give voice to those using ethnographic methods across disciplines to innovate, such as through the application of multi-sited fieldwork and the extended comparative case study method. Such innovations have often challenged more traditional ethnographic approaches. *New Ethnographies* therefore seeks to provide a platform for emerging scholars and their more established counterparts engaging with ethnographic methods in new and imaginative ways.

Dr Alexander Thomas T. Smith

Introduction

Landing

2 September 2010

Stroke, stroke, breathe. Stroke, stroke, breathe – these rhythmic triplets, the soundtrack of swimming.

I had lost track of how many hours I had been going. I had started at two that morning, jumping into the inky-black night-time water, and swimming into a beautiful dawn and through the day; the light was softening, and the cliffs of the French coast had taken on a red, early-evening tinge. Several hours ago – I wasn't sure how many – my boat pilot had come out of the cabin to tell me that it was time for some hard effort now to push through a stubborn tide. I had picked up my stroke rate, searching for the rhythm I had learned in those early morning sprint sessions in the pool over the winter; my crew had stood on deck, clapping and cheering me on. At every feed, they told me I looked fantastic, that I was flying – a generous and welcome fiction. A stiff wind was blowing against the tide, whipping up white-crested waves head on, and in spite of the effort, I could see from the unchanging view of the shore that I was making painfully slow progress. Pushing, pushing. I was getting tired now, and sore; every part of me felt nauseated and grey with fatigue and worry – after all these hours, after all those months of training, perhaps this wasn't going to be my day after all.

Stroke, stroke, breathe. Stroke, stroke, breathe. Trying to keep up the faster pace.

But then – and I don't remember it happening – something had changed. France had been in sight for hours, but I could see clearly defined trees and houses now; we had finally managed to slip out of the pull of the tide and were plying slowly through calm water towards the rocky base of a steep cliff. For the first time that day, when I stopped to feed, I asked my crew 'how much longer?' With only 'one length of Dover harbour' to go, I knew then that I had made it; this final mile was something I'd done hundreds of times in training. Nauseated by tiredness and a day-long diet of blackcurrant energy drink, I refused the offered bottle of feed and kept on swimming.

Stroke, stroke, breathe. Stroke, stroke, breathe. In a more buoyant mood now, my anxiety fading, but still too soon to relax.

The boat was no longer next to me, the water too shallow to go any further in to shore. I heard, or perhaps felt, two distinct, percussive 'thunks' as Peter and Sam, my *crew, jumped in to the water behind me to join me for the final swim to the beach. The backs of my hands and neck prickled with a rush of adrenalin at the sound. The water was warmer now, and the darkness of deep water had given way to a lighter, milkier tone. And then I saw stones on the sea floor, and was taken aback by a sudden upwelling of emotion, tears in my eyes. One last push, arms cycling more slowly now, until my fingertips finally grazed the sea floor, and I was pulling myself in using rocks as hand-holds, like climbing a ladder. Then my chest scraped over the rocks, and I lay, half beached, ready for the very last effort of finishing. With the jubilant shouts of Sam and Peter behind me, I raised myself unsteadily to my feet on the rocky surface, and hobbled awkwardly clear of the waterline, cumbersome, heavy and uncoordinated now, shaking, head and stomach reeling from the shift to vertical. I raised my arms to signal to the boat that I was clear, and was rewarded by a long triumphant honk of its horn.*

I had landed.

In the early evening of 2 September 2010, I landed on the French shore, just below the lighthouse-topped promontory of Cap Gris Nez, sixteen hours and nine minutes after I stepped in the water at Shakespeare Beach in Dover in the thick darkness of the day's earliest hours. In strictly technical, documentary terms, the honk of the horn marks the stopping of the clock. It is the singular point in time, officially at least, when I became an English Channel swimmer – the 1,153rd person to complete the iconic crossing.

But when I think of finishing my English Channel swim, my thoughts rarely jump to that moment of official becoming. Instead, I think of the 'thunks' of Sam and Peter hitting the water, and the sight of the stones on the sea floor. These two brief, innocuous moments are still viscerally evocative for me, reviving the intoxicating swirl of enormous relief, bewildering exhaustion and excited delight that this oddest of days, where I had literally done nothing but swim, had ended as I had hoped it might. Knowing that I was going to finish, it turns out, is more memorable, more evocative, than actually landing. There was more relief in the resolution of uncertainty than the completion of the task, which is fogged in the less pleasant recollection of the bodily discomfort and disorientation of the transition from sea to land.

But these singular moments of landing tell us very little about the processes of becoming. Moving backwards through my own becoming as a marathon swimmer, the start of the swim is its own transitional moment. The ritualised preparations of long swimming enact the transformation from swimmer to marathon swimmer: the smearing on of thick layers of suncream; blobs of Vaseline daubed into armpits, neck folds and under costume straps and edges, applied by the latex-gloved hand of a friend on the half-lit, rolling boat deck; the lowering of goggles over the eyes and the nervously repetitive repositioning of lenses and straps, seeking out the elusively perfect leak-free settlement on the face; a final swig of energy drink; a good luck hug that leaves behind sticky smears on clothes and faces; the leap into the dark water and a short, head-up swim to shore, chasing the circle of light thrown by the boat's spotlight; and a quick hobble up the stony beach to clear the waterline for the start. And then there is the honk of the horn to signal the start of the clock; the first of the two honks that day that form the parenthetical boundaries of this curious day of nothing-but-swimming.

And then, sliding further back in time, there is the training – the work of rendering a body able to do something that it would not ordinarily be able to do: the 5 a.m. pool swims before work; lake swims so cold that I shivered for hours afterwards; six-hour sea swims, putting miles in the shoulders and learning how to endure; gym trips; morning stretching; physio visits and painful hours on the massage table to iron out the knots; eating, drinking and sleeping to maintain an embodied self in training. And before this comes the decision, when the idea, suggestion or dare takes root: long hours at the computer greedily consuming information and drawing up plans; inquiries to the boat pilots; the exchange of money and contracts; medical certificates; 'going public' on social media; the launch of a training blog. These too are all moments of becoming.

But however far back I reach, this is still too linear a narrative to account for my own becoming as a marathon swimmer. Prior to my English Channel swim, I completed two internationally recognised marathon swims (Round Jersey; Jersey–France) as part of my two-year training plan, and in 2011, I travelled to southern California to swim the Catalina Channel. Then in 2013, I swam around the island of Manhattan, and in 2015, attempted the 8 Bridges Hudson River Swim[1] – six marathon swims[2] that punctuate an ongoing process of becoming, with discrete cycles of planning and training rising and falling through wave-like cycles of intensity and embodied transformation. And even within those cycles of training, there are the inevitable interruptions – a busy month at work eating into training time; a lingering chest infection from a winter cold; a much-needed holiday; an injured shoulder. The process of becoming, therefore, is inextricable from periods when that work of becoming either stalls or slides necessarily away from its idealised linear trajectory.

Outside of these episodic interruptions, the endless becoming of the marathon swimmer is also inevitably punctuated by much more calculated, prolonged pauses. In the 2011–12 academic year, for example, I took a complete break from the financial, time and physical demands of long swims. In documentary terms and in the knowledge, skills, techniques and confidence that I had acquired over the preceding three years of training, I was still a marathon swimmer. But this restful year also witnessed a process of palpable *un*becoming as my cultivated long-swim fitness fell away. By the summer of 2012, then, I was a marathon swimmer who couldn't possibly do a marathon swim. After a restful but somewhat bereft year away from long swimming, in the autumn of 2012, I lined up a roster of exciting swims for 2013, and returned eagerly to training, restoring lost fitness, re-embodying the finer details of good technique and putting miles back in the shoulders. But the summer of 2013 was a season where I also learned painful new lessons about yet other modes of (un)becoming: the ignominies and frustrations of two aborted swims, and then a swim-stopping injury towards the end of the season. This latter folded me into a new wave of (un)becoming as I engaged in the frustratingly incremental work of rehabilitating my angry shoulder and re-cultivating my swimming fitness. A year later, I was able to return to training, marking the beginning of another upward cycle leading up to the 8 Bridges swim in June 2015.

These diverse processes and practices of embodied (un)becoming are the first of three key frames for this book, asking: how do you render a body able to swim extraordinary distances? What embodied pedagogies facilitate the production of the marathon swimming body? What are the embodied and social implications, consequences and demands of those processes of transformation?

The second frame for the book is the social world of marathon swimming, the attendant processes of social belonging and boundary negotiation, and the intersecting social and sub-worlds in relation to which that identity work is made meaningful. Social worlds are 'a set of common or joint activities bound together by a network of communications' (Strauss 1984: 123), and are defined not by their relationship to the dominant culture, but by the production of a 'social object' (Crosset and Beal 1997: 81): in this case, marathon swimming. Marathon swimming is a minority practice, but it is also status-bearing, attracting admiration and celebration rather than approbation. The social world of marathon swimming itself is characterised by the rhetorics of distinction, and the boundaries of what 'counts' as marathon swimming are hotly debated and closely policed both in terms of internal coherence and in relation to other intersecting social worlds and sub-worlds. Through these ongoing negotiations and contestations, practitioners of the sport (and related sports) come to define and legitimise themselves and their activities (Unruh 1980; Strauss 1982), maintaining the troubled boundaries of the marathon swimming identity.

Immersion explores the processes through which social world belonging is produced (and contested) among marathon swimmers as well as in relation to its intersecting and sub-worlds. This focus also provides a lens for thinking about the pedagogies through which novices are inducted into the social world and how those boundaries of belonging are policed. This stream of inquiry mitigates against the impulse to conceptualise the endurance sporting body through individualised narratives of triumphant becoming, highlighting instead the inescapably social nature of sporting embodiment. The book asks, therefore: through what norms and values does marathon swimming define itself? How is belonging produced, maintained and contested?

The wider context of neoliberalism provides the third frame for the analysis. Ericson *et al.* describe neoliberalism as 'a prescription for ordering social relations that increasingly pervades contemporary public and private institutions and the lives of individuals' (2000: 532), listing five defining characteristics (532–533): a minimal state, market fundamentalism, an emphasis both on risk management and risk taking, individual responsibility and the conceptualisation of inequality as both inevitable and the consequence of individual choices. With this definition in mind, rather than focusing on the historical or institutional processes that enabled the ascendancy of neoliberalism as an economic doctrine (Harvey 2005), following Vrasti (2013) in her study of volunteer tourism, I'm focusing here on questions of governmentality and the extension of the principles of the market to all aspects of social life (Foucault 2008) – an indirect form of government that 'controls individuals not through explicit forms of domination, but through rationalized techniques and devices which orient action to certain socially useful ends – the "conduct of conduct"' (McNay 1999: 60). Within this framework, the individual is enjoined to become an entrepreneur of the self, managing risk and maximising personal happiness, with social relations redefined not by exchange, but by competition (Lazzarato 2009; McNay 2009; Silk and Andrews 2012).

Sport, according to Miller, is neoliberalism's 'most spectacular embodiment, through the dual fetish of competition and control, individualism and government' (2012: 24; see also, Farred 2012). Prowess in sport is readily attributed to personal investments in human capital – for example, through training and preparation – and the promotion of sport among disadvantaged communities is widely perceived as a means of inculcating those same values of entrepreneurial selfhood among communities suspected of lacking those commitments (Fusco 2006). This reflects both the privileging of competition and entrepreneurial selfhood, both within and outside of sport, as well as its necessary corollary of blame and derogation for those who fail to thrive and achieve distinction (Fusco 2006; Francombe and Silk 2012; Tyler 2013). This is the context through which contemporary marathon swimming is made meaningful, and provides a key frame for the analysis that follows. The book, then, is not a study *of* neoliberalism, but rather, an analysis of a particular practice – marathon swimming – in the context of neoliberalism as a means of interrogating the sport's contemporary inflections. This lens enables me to ask: in what ways is good citizenship produced through the sport of marathon swimming? What can marathon swimming tell us about what counts as the 'good body' in contemporary society? What exclusions and paradoxes does that produce? How are those values contested and/or sustained?

These three frames give structure to the analysis that follows, facilitating both a close exploration of the specific embodied and social processes of marathon swimming, and a critical discussion of the wider social context within which those processes have come to make sense.

Immersion begins with an ending, because while the book draws heavily on my own experiences as a swimmer, it is not a swimming autobiography, which as a genre is dependent on the outcomes of swims for the arcs and turning points in the narrative.[3] There are, therefore, no 'will she/won't she' suspenseful moments in the book, since my focus here is less the long swims themselves and more the mundane processes through which the embodied marathon swimming self is produced, maintained, restored, relinquished and negotiated, and the wider contexts within which those processes take place. Nor is this a 'how to' book for aspiring marathon swimmers. There are many people with far more experience and greater expertise than me who are much better placed to write such a book, and nor was this ever the purpose of this research. The book does, however, draw on the experiences of swimmers – both good and bad – that might offer useful snippets to novices and trigger flashes of recognition among older hands of mistakes made and lessons learned.

Neither autobiography nor 'how to' book, it is, instead, a study of *immersion*, both in the literal aquatic sense of being a body in water, and in the sense of becoming utterly absorbed in and committed to an activity. It is a story of consuming passion – mine, and that of my fellow swimmers – and the material-social possibilities and risks of that immersion. It is not, therefore, a panegyric to marathon swimming, but rather a critical, embodied exploration of both its intense, unexpected pleasures and the values through which it is constituted; values which, at times, leave me riddled with discomfort at their reliance on a mind–body split, a studied apolitical gloss, and the exclusionary rhetorics of individual self-mastery. However problematic I find this framing, my own immersion in the social world of marathon swimming disallows any innocent critique, forcing me instead to consider my own complicity in those values and their associated practices as inextricable from both the intense, consuming corporeal and social pleasures that immersion offers and the social privileges that facilitate those pleasures. The book, then, is a study of the complex relations of immersion and my own tense relationship with a practice that I find simultaneously troubling and unimaginably pleasurable.

In the remainder of this introductory chapter, I begin by explaining the sport of marathon swimming, then describe the research upon which this book is based, and in the final section set out the structure and key arguments of the book.

Marathon swimming

Marathon swimming is a minority sport. To take the iconic marathon swim – the English Channel – as an example, according to the Channel Swimming and Piloting Federation (CS&PF) database, by the end of the 2014 swimming season, 1,538 swimmers (1,061 men and 477 women) had completed 2,025 crossings. The top three nations represented among these are the UK (775 swimmers), the US (400 swimmers) and Australia (163 swimmers), highlighting the nature of marathon swimming as a culturally specific practice (CS&PF 2015). But for all its minority status, marathon swimming has also grown significantly in popularity in recent years. Taking the English Channel once again as the example, while there were 8 successful swimmers in 1960, 15 in 1980 and 25 in 2000, the early twenty-first century saw significant rises, reaching 94 in 2010 and rising to 103 in 2012 (Dover.uk.com 2015). These increases reflect both the improvements in training, nutrition and navigation that have contributed to higher success rates, and the rise in popularity of adventure or endurance challenges, particularly as charitable fund-raising endeavours. The growth in popularity also includes significant cross-fertilisation with other endurance sports such as triathlon, and can also be seen as an effect of the massive rise in popularity of open water swimming more generally. In the UK, this latter is evidenced by the growing popularity of wild swimming (Rew 2009), the introduction of specialist periodicals, a boom in mass participation open water swimming events and a proliferation of swimming holiday companies. This provides the wider context for contemporary marathon swimming, which remains a distinctly minority sport but within a thriving open water culture.

Introduction

The most easily recognised starting point in marathon swimming's history is 25 August 1875, when twenty-seven-year-old merchant naval captain, Matthew Webb, completed the first successful solo crossing of the English Channel, swimming from England to France in twenty-one hours and forty-five minutes. Less than two weeks after his first, unsuccessful, attempt, Webb's successful crossing, which he described in his book, *The Art of Swimming*, as 'the event of my life' ([1876] 1999: 22), rocketed him to fame. Heralded as front-page news, mobbed by crowds, showered with donations and, later, immortalised in A.E. Housman's poem, *A Shropshire Lad*, as well as on matchboxes, in street names, picture books and public statuary (Watson 2000), Webb's achievement gave him heroic status. The swim rendered him a national icon of triumphant masculinity, rebuffing concerns of the era regarding the enfeeblement of the middle classes and the future of the empire (Watson 2000, Ch. 7; see also, Wiltse 2007, Ch. 2). At a celebratory dinner in Dover, he was announced in the introductory address as the man who 'had proved for one thing that the physical condition of Englishmen had not degenerated' (Watson 2000: 158). There is a colonial tone to this declaration, as reflected by Webb himself, who recalled being stationed at 'Port Natal ... on the South Coast of Africa' and having to swim through the surf back to shore after anchoring a boat. He noted: 'I mention this fact, as it has often been remarked that the natives are extraordinary fine performers in the water. In this particular instance, however, not one of them was sufficiently powerful to swim in the surf at the time I mention' ([1876] 1999: 16–17).

There was also considerable national pride that an Englishman had accomplished the feat first. After the crossing, he was presented to the boys studying on his former merchant navy training ship, the *Conway*, as a role model who was 'motivated by the patriotic idea that an Englishman would do more than an American had done' (Watson 2000: 157). This was a clear reference to the American, Paul Boyton, who crossed the English Channel in May 1875 wearing an extravagantly eccentric inflatable rubber suit that was propelled with a double-bladed paddle, and even had an optional sail. Boyton's successful crossing in the suit earned him praise and celebrity, including a telegram from Queen Victoria (an honour denied to Webb) (Watson 2000: 95), and in the public eye the two men were figured as opponents (Watson 2000: 81). As will also be discussed in Chapter 3, this presages the present-day tensions and struggles over definition that characterise contemporary marathon swimming, particularly in relation to the use of wetsuits.

Fifty-one years later, on 6 August 1926, twenty-year-old American competitive swimmer and Olympian, Gertrude Ederle, following an unsuccessful attempt in 1925, successfully swam from France to England in a record-breaking time of fourteen hours and thirty-nine minutes. Only the sixth person ever to swim the Channel, and the first woman to complete the crossing, her record time was broken only three weeks later by German baker, Ernst Vierkoetter, who completed the swim in twelve hours and forty-two minutes. But although several women completed crossings in the years after Ederle's swim, her women's record stood until 1950, when it fell to fellow American, Florence Chadwick. Like Webb, there was a nationalistic fervour to the public celebrations on Ederle's return to the US, including a ticker tape parade in New York, not least in amazement that a *woman* could achieve such a feat, although this was tempered slightly by the need to understate her German heritage in a nation still healing from the First World War (Mortimer 2008; Dahlberg, 2009; Stout 2009; Bier 2011).

Both Webb and Ederle are touchstones for contemporary marathon swimming, and the English Channel remains metonymic of the wider sport. But it is also a sport about which very little is known outside of its own social world, except perhaps for the familiar images of swimmers slathering on layers of grease and fat (a largely defunct practice) or via coverage of celebrity swims such as the successful 2006 English Channel swim by UK comedian, David Walliams (BBC 2006) – the centrepiece for the annual UK fund-raising extravaganza, Sport Relief. However, any attempt to define marathon swimming is to venture into sticky territory (see Chapter 3), so in these early stages of the book, I offer only the lightest touch definition, focusing on how I am using 'marathon swimming' in the framing of the book and its scope.

To summarise crudely, marathon swimming is the practice of *swimming a long way slowly*.

In the 2008 Beijing Olympics, the 10 km marathon swim made its debut, broadly mirroring the running marathon in terms of elite completion times and providing an exciting spectacle with swimmers constantly in sight on the multi-lap, rowing lake course, accompanied by thrilling close-up media coverage. While these swims are impressive and not a little intimidating at the elite level for their ferocious pace, these are not the concern of this book. Instead, my interest here is on what might be described as the ultra domain of open water swimming – those swims that can take ten, and even twenty or more, hours to complete, traversing or circumnavigating predominantly naturally occurring stretches of water including channels, straits, lakes or islands (however marked by human intervention). The iconic marathon swim – the English Channel – provides a useful benchmark for the kind of swimming I am focusing on. It is twenty-one miles across at its narrowest point, with water temperatures of approximately 15–18°C (59–64°F) during the swimming season (usually late June–September). Individual swimmers are accompanied throughout by a dedicated support boat that navigates the swim, liaises with other water users, provides safety cover and serves as a platform from which the swimmer's support crew can provide moral support, sustenance and equipment changes (e.g. fresh goggles or lights for night swimming).

In spite of its iconic status, the English Channel is just one among many in the proliferating roster of global marathon swims that are stored up on swimmers' 'bucket lists' for future adventures, all presenting their own particular challenges in terms of distance, conditions, temperature and wildlife. Therefore, rather than arbitrarily demarcating a minimum definitional distance or time, I conceptualise marathon swimming as relating to swims *on a sufficient scale of distance and/or time for that to be the only thing that you do that day*; in many cases, literally. It is a kind of swimming that requires the capacity to swim at a steady, continuous pace for hours without meaningful rest; it is a distinct mode of being-in-the-water that is fundamentally different from that of the 100 m pool swimmer, or indeed, the

10 km elite racer. However fast or slow that steady pace is, it is this steadiness that I refer to when I talk of swimming a long way *slowly*.

Marathon swimming is not defined by duration alone, but also by the conditions and regulations under which it is conducted, and for the purposes of this book, I'm focusing primarily on what is commonly referred to as 'Channel rules' marathon swimming.[4] These rules nod nostalgically, although somewhat arbitrarily, to the conditions under which Ederle and Webb swam and the contemporary iteration of Channel rules swimming dictates that swimmers can wear only a regular swimming costume (non-buoyant, non-insulating), single cap and goggles and must swim continuously from shore to shore without purposefully touching either the accompanying boat or another person (for example, for support or assistance with propulsion) throughout. With some contextually specific adaptations,[5] 'Channel rules' are a widely invoked benchmark, and these demarcate the *style* of swimming primarily addressed in the book, although always in relation to other modes of swimming and the boundary disputes between them.

The final defining feature of marathon swimming for the purposes of this book is its primary location within the amateur domain. A very small number of elite swimmers from the professional open water racing circuit venture into solo marathon swimming from time to time, generally in order to make an attempt at a record. Australian professional swimmer, Trent Grimsey, who broke the English Channel solo record in 2012 in an eye-wateringly fast 6.55, exemplifies this. These swimmers are highly respected within the marathon swimming community and their swimming feats – unimaginable for a plodding swimmer such as myself – are part of the lore of the sport. But my specific interest in this book is in the *amateur* swimmers for whom the sport is a 'serious leisure' activity (Stebbins 2007), and who make up the vast majority of its participants. For these individuals, who encompass a range of capacities, paces and ambitions, swimming is not a source of income or a full-time occupation, but rather a passionately and often intensively pursued activity that is balanced against a raft of other personal and professional commitments in an ongoing process of producing and maintaining the marathon swimming self.

When I refer to 'marathon swimming' throughout *Immersion*, then, this is how I am using the term: *swimming a long way slowly under a particular set of tradition-oriented rules as a committed amateur.*

With this definition in mind, marathon swimming can be seen as occupying an ambiguous position in relation to other sports. The solo nature of marathon swimming, its location within the natural aquatic environment and the primary focus on finishing rather than winning distance it from what Atkinson describes as 'hyper-competitive, hierarchical and patriarchal modernist sport' (2010: 1250). But it also sits uncomfortably within the domain of what have been conceptualised as 'lifestyle' sports (Wheaton 2004c, 2013). Among the defining features of lifestyle sports outlined by Wheaton (2004a: 11–12), marathon swimming shares the emphasis on grass-roots participation over spectating, the importance of commitment and self-actualisation, a predominantly white, middle-class, Western cohort, a non-aggressive style without body contact (although still embracing risk), and the appropriation of outdoor liminal spaces. However, the sport fails to align cleanly with the relative novelty of lifestyle sports, their ready consumption of new technologies and practices, and the commitment to the adrenalin rush of activities relying upon speed, descent or the risk of catastrophic injury. Indeed, when I described marathon swimming as an 'extreme' sport in an article about my research in the *Guardian* newspaper (Arnot 2010), the readers' comments were awash with protests at my appropriation of the term for a sport like swimming:

> Have the academia of the UK become so chair bound that they consider swimming to be an extreme sport? I thought extreme sports were activities where there was a higher level of risk. The reason people undertake extreme sports is for the adrenalin hit. There you go, can I have me [sic] PhD now?

While by no means risk-free, marathon swimming undoubtedly lacks the hedonistic adrenalin buzz and physical risk of those sports most easily categorised as 'extreme', not least because of the extensive safety procedures required for officially ratified swims (Rinehart and Sydnor 2003; Robinson 2008; Willig 2008; Laviolette 2011). Nevertheless, I have continued to describe marathon swimming in this book as an extreme sport, not because of its relationship to physical risk, but rather, because of its commitment to *excess* and to the testing of bodily limits. Consequently, marathon swimming is perhaps best understood as a form of 'edgework' (Lyng 2005), where the primary risk in the pushing of limits is the failure to complete a swim. Marathon swimming, then, shares the boundary disruptions of other 'post-sport' physical cultures (Atkinson 2010), moving fluidly across the arbitrary boundaries of what 'counts' as sport, and providing novel opportunities for identity formation and self-actualisation.

But these novel opportunities are not open to all, and the marathon swimming social world, while self-defining through earnestly intended narratives of inclusion – of being 'all just swimmers together' – is characterised by a predominantly white, middle-class cohort. Women, too, are in the minority, albeit a significant one; taking the English Channel once again as the exemplar, approximately one-third of all successful swims are completed by women. These demographic trends are not the result of purposeful sexist or racist exclusion, but rather, reflect both the history of swimming and the social and cultural context within which marathon swimming has come to be meaningful.

Historically, both women and non-whites have experienced direct and enforced exclusions from swimming. While public bathing (for men) in open water has been a long-standing part of many Western cultures, and a key site for the demonstration of feats of masculinity (Sprawson 1992),[6] particularly by the nineteenth century, anxieties about public morality and the exposure of the body led to the increasing regulation and containment of bathing and swimming. In Australia (Light and Rockwell 2005), the US (Wiltse 2007; Bier 2011) and Britain (Horwood 2000; Love 2007a; Parr 2011; Ayriss 2012), the customary nudity of male bathing, and the desire to cover and contain women's bodies, led to increasing demands for regulation and control. This led to the proliferation of bathing enclosures and floating baths, which facilitated the regulation of behaviour to account for the demands of modesty, as well as providing grills or pilings which would keep out the debris and human waste that filled many of the rivers and shores. However, while these enclosed swimming spaces facilitated segregation in line with Victorian norms of modesty, access was rarely divided equally, with women confined either to less convenient and more limited hours in shared facilities, or much more confined swimming areas where separate pools were built (Horwood 2000: 656; Parr 2011: 95). Furthermore, even in segregated facilities, by the turn of the twentieth century, women were still expected to swim in hazardously cumbersome clothing or to be covered in a bathing gown on leaving the water, especially in cases of competitive races where men might be among the spectators (Horwood 2000: 657).

In spite of these restrictions, swimming was also conceptualised as a highly appropriate activity for women, albeit in constrainingly gendered terms, as explained in the mission statement for the Women's Swimming Association of New York, which was founded in 1917 to support women's competitive amateur swimming:

> It develops every part of the body thoroughly and symmetrically; produces supple, graceful, well-rounded muscles; makes for ease of deportment and movement; activates functional organs; clarifies the blood and clears the complexion; strengthens and benefits the entire system so generally that its constant use ensures buoyant good health and marked improvement in appearance. It is also an effective normaliser. Its natural tendency is to establish standard body proportions by eliminating superfluous flesh in the stout and building muscle and tissue in the unduly lean. Lastly, it will correct many physical defects and this has often proved a complete cure for nervous and other complaints. (cited in Bier 2011: 103)

In response to growing convictions about the suitability of swimming for women, in the early twentieth century, women's swimming cultures began to thrive, including an impressive roster of headline-grabbing endurance swims. In July 1915, for example, nineteen-year-old Eileen Lee swam nearly twenty-two miles between Tower Bridge and Richmond to wide acclaim, and then, in August of the same year, she repeated the feat, but this time in the opposite direction (Davies 2015: 148). In New York in the same period, a vibrant women's open water and pool competitive scene existed, wherein Gertrude Ederle made her name before going on to become, in 1926, the first woman to swim the English Channel (Stout 2009; Bier 2011). The increased access to swimming facilities, the growing number of path-breaking role models and changing social mores about acceptable bodily display enabled women to engage increasingly with swimming as a sport and leisure activity without the gender segregation that had previously placed so many limitations on them. However, this access was always within the bounds of the social regulation of gender, and marathon swimming (as with contemporary swimming more broadly), while largely free from active exclusions and regulatory constraints, remains profoundly marked by gender relations both within and outside of swimming. For example, as discussed in Chapter 6, the gendered distribution of domestic and reproductive labour impacts upon the time and financial resources available to women for leisure and constrains entitlement to self-investment, effectively delimiting women's access to the sport and its pleasures (and to leisure more generally). The conventional narrative, therefore, of progressive liberation from regulatory exclusions towards participatory equality that characterises the history of women's swimming (Horwood 2000; Love 2007a; Parker 2010; Bier 2011; Davies 2015) is a very partial story that obscures the ideologies of gender that continue to frame the experience of immersion explored throughout the book.

The whiteness of swimming reflects even more sharply the ways in which assumptions, expectations and social context constrain access to the sport beyond actively exclusionary regulation. Contemporary swimming is coded as white, and there is a marked paucity of non-white participants in all dimensions of the sport. An enduring history of biological explanations shores up this racialised profile, particularly in relation to the widely held conviction that black people can't swim because of higher levels of bone density than those of white people (Allen and Nickel 1969). These biological accounts mask the pervasive impact of long histories of exclusion and discrimination through which swimming became a white cultural form. Dawson highlights how many West Africans who were subsequently taken to the Americas as slaves came from thriving swimming cultures; indeed, these skills were actively mobilised by slavers in the fishing, salvage and pearl diving industries, especially at a time when most white people were unable to swim (Dawson 2006). Within the racialised frames of slavery and colonialism, however, these skills were accounted for via the 'animal' nature of non-white others, for whom swimming was seen as a 'natural capacity rather than a learned or intelligent practice (Osmond and Phillips 2004; Dawson 2006) – an assumption that is reflected in contemporary convictions of biologised accounts of black athletic superiority (Hoberman 1997).

As swimming boomed in the US in the early decades of the twentieth century, black people were systematically excluded from municipal pools and beaches through the use of regulation, violence and intimidation (Wiltse 2007). Racialised fears of disease and contamination drove these aggressive exclusions, compounded by shifts in gender relations over the same period that led to the wider acceptance of mixed bathing and increasingly body-revealing women's swimwear. Consequently, pools and beaches became increasingly seen as sexually charged public spaces (Horwood 2000), where white women were deemed at risk from the predatory and uncontrolled sexual desire of black men. As Wiltse argues: 'Gender integration, in short, necessitated racial segregation' (2007: 85). These exclusions were compounded by a lack of swimming facilities in black areas and the growing association of swimming with white privilege through the development of private pools and Hollywood depictions of the glamorous pool cultures of the elite (Horwood 2000; Wiltse 2007).

The legacy of this abbreviated history can be seen in the continued whiteness of swimming long after the elimination of actively exclusionary regulation. For example, in the UK, rates of swimming participation are markedly lower among ethnic minorities, and particularly for women, with participation rates as low as 5 per cent for Pakistani women, as opposed to 17 per cent in the overall female population (Rowe and Champion 2000). Similarly, in the US, the number of black children (aged five–fourteen) dying from drowning is more than three times that of white children of the same age (CDC 2014) – an outcome that is attributed to a range of factors including lack of access and a perceived lack of fit with the sport (Irwin *et al.* 2008). These patterns of swimming ability also map onto class as well as gender, with children in families with less economic and social capital (for example, in the form of higher education) less likely to report themselves able to swim – a trend which is also far more evident among black girls than boys (Irwin *et al.* 2008). The (gendered) whiteness of swimming, then, including marathon swimming, is neither a biological inevitability nor an accident of culture, but rather, the enduring legacy of the racialised practices of exclusion.

I return to these questions of inclusion, access and belonging throughout the book, not to suggest a purposefully racist or sexist social world, but rather, to refuse naturalising or accidental accounts of the demography of marathon swimming, and to disturb comforting narratives of inclusion – that 'we're all just swimmers together'. This approach supports the book's central arguments: first, that however much a minority social world self-defines through distinction, it remains inextricable from the wider social context within which it is made meaningful; and, second, that the narratives of heroism and individual overcoming that attach so easily to a practice such as marathon swimming risk the erasure of the relations of privilege that make swims both possible and exchangeable as capital. It is in this way that *Immersion* both offers an insight into the relatively unknown practices, pleasures and social world of marathon swimming, and mobilises marathon swimming as a lens through which to consider the wider social context within which it is made meaningful.

Aquatic sociology

At first glance, I am an unlikely marathon swimmer, particularly from the perspective of those outside of the sport. I'm a middle aged woman with a very sedentary job as a university lecturer in sociology and a deeply bookish streak; I spend a lot of time reading in my favourite armchair, heating on, hot drink to hand, cat on lap. My build is also far from what would conventionally be recognised as 'athletic'. Outside of the briefest periods of unsustainable diet-induced leanness, especially in my twenties, I have always been varying degrees of fat, and now, in my mid-forties, my hair is greying with decisive speed and my body is relinquishing its life-long pronounced pear shape for the thickening waist of the early menopause. I don't hate my body, or the ageing process; but I am more than aware that a body such as mine – female, fat, middle-aged – is not one to which the label 'athlete' or 'sportswoman' sticks easily. As a relatively successful marathon swimmer, I am something of an imposter outside of the marathon swimming social world; an 'athletic intruder' (Bolin and Granskog 2003) in comparison to the ranks of the youthful, lithe, energetic bearers of national sporting pride and healthful citizenship whose bodies plastered the UK's billboards during the Olympic summer of 2012.

But I can never remember a time when I couldn't swim. I learned at the loving hands of my grandfather, Harry Cornforth (to whose memory *Immersion* is dedicated), and mum, Pam Throsby. Harry was a water polo player in his youth – tall, broad-shouldered, barrel-chested. Poverty, lack of opportunity and inflexible blue-collar employment on the railways meant that he was never able to fully pursue his sport (including a lost opportunity to trial for the Olympics), but he never breathed a word of his disappointment, and through him I learned to love the water. Even now, I have the strongest memory of his hands around my ankles, my own hands gripping the gulley around the edge of the pool for support as he guided my legs through the frog-leg kick of breaststroke. He taught me to dive by placing two-pence coins between my ankles and knees; if I kept my legs tidily together and broke the surface with the coins in place, I got to keep them. I remember my first unaided width, aged five, in a hotel pool on a family holiday in Mallorca, flapping and flailing with graceless enthusiasm to a joyous victory. Later, when I was a little older, I jumped off the three-metre diving board wearing pyjamas, tennis shoes and a thick sweater, smacking the water and then sinking sharply as the oddly assorted clothing filled with water before releasing me to the surface. A little older still, I joined a swimming club, training hard and competing enthusiastically, albeit with limited success. I loved to swim, and I was safe and happy in the water, but I had neither the aptitude nor the appetite for such fierce competition and I dropped training in my early teens and took up the piano instead. But still, I never entirely abandoned swimming, and the chlorinated smell of a swimming pool, perhaps venting unexpectedly into a city street from a basement health club, has always provoked the desire to swim, triggering the embodied memories and pleasures of swimming. In my early thirties, some tentative ventures into the sport of triathlon opened up the world of open water swimming for the first time, quickly becoming the only part of the events from which I drew any real pleasure (or success); and in 2006, a commercially organised swimming weekend in the UK's Lake District led to my first, cautious non-wetsuit swim – a revelatory moment of sensory pleasure from which I never looked back. In the genesis of this research, then, the swimming came first.

Consequently, I brought a long, although unremarkable, competitive and leisure swimming history with me to my nascent marathon swimming career. However, as a fledgling *marathon* swimmer, I still had a great deal to learn and much bodily work to do when, in October 2008, I put down a £250 deposit with a boat pilot for an August 2010 English Channel swim. This book, and the research project upon which it draws, grew out of that first winter of gradually intensifying training, as I began to reflect upon the process of 'becoming' (or trying to become) in which I was engaged.

The book is what I have termed an (auto)ethnography. Using what Wacquant calls 'observant participation' (2004: 6), and alongside conventional ethnographic observation and interview methods, I deployed my own body 'as a tool of inquiry and a vector of knowledge' (Wacquant 2004: viii; Bunsell 2013). This enabled me convictions with respect, even in disagreement, and to take responsibility for my own interpretations as interpretations rather than definitive pronouncements.

Regardless of these compromises, I persisted with my efforts at documenting my own process of becoming, and this corpus of autoethnographic material was intertwined with observational notes about the multiple training and competition sites that comprised the settings for this research: my local lakes and swimming pools in the West Midlands and Dover (UK); Jersey (Channel Islands); Cork (Ireland); Gozo (Malta); and San Diego and San Francisco (US). These fieldnotes documented the everyday routines, practices and interactions between and among swimmers, coaches, crews, supporting family members and curious passers-by in swimming environments ranging from domesticated, sheltered lakes to angry, slate-grey seas; from playful splash-about dips to multi-hour hard training; from the thick grey-green sea of Dover harbour to the clear-blue, wildlife-filled waters of La Jolla Cove in San Diego. In addition to uncountable informal conversations and chance passing encounters, I also conducted forty-five interviews with prospective, successful and unsuccessful swimmers (nineteen women and twenty-six men), during which we discussed in depth their swimming biographies, motivations and experiences of marathon swimming. These were mostly face-to-face (with the exception of two conducted via Skype), either in swimmers' homes or, more commonly, at swimming venues or during post-swim meals. The audio-recordings evoke the locations: the barking of sea lions in the background of interviews at La Jolla Cove; the rain hammering on the roof of my campervan during an interview in Dover; the glugging of a drink being poured or the chinking of plates signalling the arrival of food during a post-swim restaurant interview. This dataset of interview transcripts and fieldnotes is the primary resource for *Immersion*, complemented by textual material from blogs, discussion forums and media reports, gathered more serendipitously than systematically over the course of the project.[9]

The participants were recruited opportunistically via discussion forums, websites, training sites and personal contacts and I never aimed for a fully representative sample – not least because the absence of detailed demographic data for those attempting swims makes it impossible to know with any certainty what would constitute 'representative'. However, as already discussed, and like many other lifestyle, extreme and endurance sports, the marathon swimming community is comprised primarily (although by no means exclusively) of white, middle-class professionals (see, for example, Abbas 2004; Wheaton 2004; Hanold 2010; Thorpe 2011), and this was supported in the sample of interviewees, only two of whom were non-white, and the majority of whom had (or in one case was studying for) an undergraduate degree or equivalent professional training. Four interviewees were retired and one was waiting to start a new job; the rest were employed in a range of professional fields including healthcare, the fitness industry, management, finance, advertising, education, IT, engineering, medicine and the creative industries.

This predominantly middle-class demographic reflects the fact that even though marathon swimming, unlike other water-based sports such as windsurfing (Wheaton 2003), requires little initial capital investment (costume, cap, goggles), it is an expensive sport. Escort boat hire and associated registration fees reach approximately £3,000 for an English Channel swim, and depending on where you live, the everyday work of training quickly becomes expensive as the costs of commuting to training locations and overnight stays mount up. Furthermore, the sport is inherently transnational in nature, demanding the comfort with, expectation of and freedom to engage in extensive travel that marks middle classness (Abbas 2004; Comer 2010; Thorpe 2011).

As a white, middle-class university lecturer, I fit easily into this dominant profile, with the additional privilege of a research grant that gave me both the time and money for a transnational engagement with the marathon swimming world over a relatively condensed time period. This was practically beyond the means of many, especially in economically difficult times, attracting wry comments from both work and swimming colleagues alike about my 'tough' working life as what the *Guardian* pleasingly described as an 'aquatic sociologist' (Arnot 2010). Palmer and Thompson received a similar response from their participants in their study of alcohol-based sporting sub-cultures, who remarked upon their 'cushy' working lives of drinking (Palmer and Thompson 2010: 424). As Palmer and Thompson go on to describe, what appears to be a leisurely research life in fact involved careful impression management and the negotiation of risk, but it is easy to see how others might misunderstand the nature of research into practices commonly

Figure 1 Swimming below the Statue of Liberty during the final stage of the 8 Bridges Hudson River Swim, 2015.

understood as leisure. This is also reflected in the scepticism I encountered regarding the validity of marathon swimming as the subject of sociological inquiry, as in the online reader comment cited earlier. But even though I am now looking forward to being able to swim without the demands of constant documentation and critical appraisal, these years of aquatic sociology have also undoubtedly been an enormous amount of fun, not least because they have led me to swim in exciting locations that I might not otherwise have visited (see Figure 1), and connect with individuals who I would otherwise never have been able to meet in person. The aquatic sociology years have been a privilege and a pleasure.

Immersion

Immersion is a product of those years of aquatic sociology, and this final introductory section sets out the structure of the book and the key arguments with which it engages. The book is divided into two core sections of four chapters each: 'Becoming and belonging' and 'The good body'.

'Becoming and belonging' focuses on the material-social-discursive processes of becoming a marathon swimmer, exploring both the specific embodied work of rendering a body able to swim long distances and the inward- and outward-facing processes through which social world belonging is produced, maintained, resisted and negotiated. The section challenges the prevailing representations of marathon swimming as a site of suffering and overcoming that pitch the swimmer against both the aquatic environment and their own bodily weaknesses. Instead, I offer a more nuanced reading of the social and embodied processes of becoming and belonging, where bodies and environments are not simply acted upon, but also act and change in constant interaction; the experience of becoming a marathon swimmer, I argue, is one that is inextricably emplaced in the social and aquatic environments within which it becomes meaningful. This constitutes a fundamental challenge to the narratives of heroism that attach so easily to extreme sporting endeavours, but which risk the erasure of the social relations and privileged practices that constitute those activities.

Chapter 1 ('Becoming') focuses on the bodily becoming of marathon swimming, with particular focus on the iterative relationship between feeling and doing that constitutes the acquisition of a range of techniques of the body alongside the sensory and material transformations that both facilitate those techniques and are produced by them. I argue that, while embodied work is central to the process of becoming a marathon swimmer, successful becoming is never entirely within the remit of the individual and is contingent on the individual's life experiences, (dis)abilities, situation and social context. This sets the frame for the remainder of the book, for which the relationship between embodied experience and social context is a central theme. Chapter 2 ('Unexpected pleasures') takes the sensory transformations discussed in the previous chapter as its core focus, particularly in the context of the intense and alluring multiple pleasures of marathon swimming. By exploring the socially acquired assemblage of pleasures that work in interaction with suffering and discomfort to constitute marathon swimming, the chapter disrupts the prevailing representations of the sport primarily as a site of suffering and overcoming. This in turn challenges the dominant rhetorics of mind over matter as the key explanatory frame for marathon swimming, with body and mind emerging through the analysis as inseparable inflections of each other. The move away from suffering as the primary focus highlights the central role of marathon swimming's autotelic pleasures in the formation of a collective sense of belonging and distinction – a source of 'existential capital' (Nettleton 2013) that defies articulation and which only those inside can appreciate.

Looking more closely at the demarcation of distinction within the social world of marathon swimming, Chapter 3 ('Authentic swimming') focuses on the ways in which the boundaries of authentic belonging are policed, negotiated, resisted and maintained. Drawing on online debates around a number of contested swims in 2012 and 2013, the chapter argues that attempts to escape the rationalisations of modernity through marathon swimming lead to increased rationalisation within marathon swimming in an effort to preserve its distinction. The evolving rules that characterise this reactive rationalisation are inevitably arbitrary, but their content is less important in terms of the cultivation and demarcation of belonging than the visible performance of allegiance to a set of values around which those debates circulate. The final chapter in this section, 'Making it count', picks up on these authenticity debates to explore the roles of the objects and artefacts of marathon swimming in the production and performance of both becoming and belonging. The chapter argues that marathon swimming has a 'realness' problem, with the swimmer leaving little material trace of a journey that takes place largely out of sight. Marathon swimming's objects and associated practices help to make long swims 'real' as consumable 'things' that can be compiled, displayed or traded as capital in other contexts. This highlights the ways in which quantification does not simply reveal facts about the swimming body and its movements, but changes the nature and meanings of the activity itself. The analysis shows that, in spite of determined efforts to delimit the potentially polluting impact of technology on marathon swimming, the sport is inescapably caught in a technologised consumerist nexus; it is a tradition-oriented sport, but with a strongly contemporary inflection.

The second half of the book is organised around the theme of 'The good body'. This section widens the analytical frame to think about what constitutes the 'good body' in contemporary society and the ways in which marathon swimming both aligns with and poses challenges to definitions of health and good citizenship, and the normative relationship between the two. This section provides both further context for the ways in which an extreme minority sport such as marathon swimming comes to make sense as a status-bearing embodied practice, and deploys marathon swimming as a critical lens for thinking about the normative demands of 'good' embodiment in contemporary society. The analysis in this section highlights the ways in which bodily failures and successes, both within and outside of sport, rarely speak for themselves, but instead have to be discursively managed in order to be brought into alignment with prevailing norms of embodied citizenship.

Chapter 5 ('Who are you swimming for?') addresses the increasingly normative connection between marathon swimming and charitable fund-raising, and asks

Introduction

what is at stake in the public identification of 'swimming for...'. The chapter argues that while 'swimming for...' is a sincere and personally meaningful act, it also risks flattening out the differences between different kinds of suffering that are brought into alliance through charitable swimming. This depoliticises social inequalities and ill health in ways that position the sport (and its social world) as above or outside of politics, while simultaneously reconfiguring what counts as politics. This highlights the comfortable alignment between marathon swimming, charitable fund-raising and the cultural logics of neoliberalism, as well as the opaque and shifting limits to the socially prescribed investment in the self. Chapter 6 ('Gendering swimming') picks up on the apolitical gloss that characterises charitable swimming, focusing on the tension between narratives of gender neutrality and the implicit and explicit reproduction of gender. The chapter explores the ways in which gender is rendered strategically passive or present in ways that sustain a masculine sporting ideal and mask the structural and cultural constraints that refute the claim that 'we're all just swimmers together'. The analysis highlights the importance of conceptualising sporting practice in its wider social and cultural context in order to capture not only specific structures of oppression that limit access to those activities, but also the patterns of oppression that are embedded in everyday life. Nevertheless, the chapter also highlights the contingency of even the most entrenched understandings of the body, creating openings for novel modes of embodiment that directly challenge gendered bodily norms in transformative, albeit highly individualised, ways.

Chapter 7 ('Heroic fatness') extends the argument for contextualisation, this time in relation to the tensions within the sport between the valuing of body fat for its insulating properties and the contemporary repudiation of it as the embodiment of failed bodily discipline. I argue that (some) swimmers are able to negotiate this tension through the mobilisation of 'heroic fatness', which positions purposeful swimming fat as an undesirable necessity, heroically borne in the interests of swimming. However, not everyone is able to position their body fat as 'heroic', revealing the extent to which not all fat is equal either within the marathon swimming social world or in the wider context of a 'war on obesity'. The chapter highlights the habitual elision of fitness, health and leanness that riddles contemporary health and sports policy, while simultaneously demonstrating the deeply entrenched and intractable nature of those assumptions and their enduring effects on the ways in which we understand, evaluate and treat bodies. The analysis suggests the importance not only of opening up sport, but also of rethinking the nature of sport itself outside of its customary utilitarian frames.

Chapter 8 ('Failing bodies') takes up this theme in the context of injury and swim failure, and their intersections with narratives of health, good embodiment and authentic swimming. I argue that pain, injury and swim failure variously serve as markers of progress and 'exciting significance'; provide social distinction and social world belonging; mark out pedagogic opportunities; and always potentially act as material evidence of a body that has failed, both morally and materially. The chapter demonstrates that marathon swimming's bodily failures never speak straightforwardly for themselves, but rather have to be contextualised and accounted for via social world values in order to be rendered forgiveable. As with the case of swimming fat, this highlights the moral nature of 'health' and its symbolic role in determining citizenship, and the uneven affordability of bodily failure. The chapter concludes that the pain and injuries of marathon swimming are ultimately privileged injuries that not only create little deficit in the physical capital already accrued by the marathon swimmer, but also have the potential to increase that capital or facilitate its exchange.

The concluding chapter revisits the key themes of *Immersion*, arguing that marathon swimming is a recreational sporting practice that is intensely meaningful to its participants, constituting a significant and sustained source of identity that literally comes to inhabit the body. However, I argue that the dominant representations of marathon swimming do not always align cleanly with its lived experience, and the chapter explores the disjunctures between representation and lived experience that have emerged in the course of the book. These are not presented as cynical (mis-)representations, but rather, are understood as faithful attempts to make marathon swimming intelligible, both within and outside the marathon swimming social world, using the discursive resources available. I argue that the social world in which marathon swimmers (including myself) become immersed aligns easily with prevailing ideologies, particularly in relation to the celebration of self-efficacy, autonomy and bodily discipline as features of good citizenship, but the repetitive citation of those values, however constrained, also exposes their uncontainability, arbitrariness and contingency. Marathon swimming, then, is always inflected through the norms and values of the wider social and cultural context in which it becomes meaningful, but never entirely determined by them.

In making this claim, though, I do not simply want to go on a hunt for resistance as an attempt to assuage some of my discomfort around my own strategic alliance with values that I resist in other contexts. Instead, following Abu-Lughod (1990), I want to use this observation as a 'diagnostic of power' that allows me to speak not simply about the specific iterations of those relations of power within the social world of marathon swimming, but also to explore what the view from that social world can tell us about those wider social ideologies and power relations. With this goal in mind, the conclusion reflects on the implications of the discussions throughout the book for thinking about what constitutes the 'good body' in contemporary society; how this is inflected through normative discourses of gender, health, citizenship and philanthropy; and how the process of (un)becoming as a marathon swimmer can help us to think both critically and productively about the social, ideological and discursive roles of sport in contemporary society.

Notes

1 The 8 Bridges Hudson River Swim is a 120-mile, 7-day stage swim down the Hudson River, beginning in Catskill and finishing in New York Harbour, with each day starting and finishing at a landmark bridge. See www.8bridges.org for further details of the event.
2 I attempted all seven stages of the 8 Bridges in 2015, but on Stage 2, I was unable to outpace the difficult conditions and fell short of the finish bridge by 2 miles. Although

I failed to complete all 7 stages, I was delighted to finish 6 out of 7 and still consider this swim a success.

3 See, for example, Cleveland (1999), Cox (2006), Humphreys (2013) and Dean (2013).
4 In January 2014, under the auspices of the recently formed Marathon Swimmers Federation (MSF), a small collective of swimmers launched a set of rules for marathon swimming that were designed to standardise practice globally and resist the perceived encroachment of non-traditional practices into the sport (MSF 2014). The concerns that led to the development of these rules are discussed in more detail in Chapter 3.
5 The regulations for the Cook Straits swim in New Zealand allow for a ten-minute 'shark break' following a close sighting, and the Manhattan Island Marathon Swim allows swimmers to be taken from the water during a lightning storm (or other temporarily dangerous conditions) and then to continue the swim once the danger has passed – an occurrence that would signal the end of an English Channel swim.
6 For example, the Romantic poet, Byron, engaged in a number of swimming exploits, famously crossing the Hellespont (between Europe and Asia) in 1810 to reproduce the feat of Leander, who, according to myth, swam the crossing to visit his lover, Hero (Parr 2011: 59–60).
7 There was also a strategic element to this separation, particularly for the funded life of the project, since it was important that the project's feasibility was not dependent on my ability and capacity to keep training. Injury or health problems could have prevented me from swimming at any point in the process, but the possibility of shifting all of my research attention to the ethnographic element of the project meant that the research could continue regardless of my own ability to swim.
8 Since 2009, I have kept a swimming blog (www.thelongswim.blogspot.com) where I engage in the much more informal documentation of my swimming life.
9 Through the book, I have used real names in relation to material taken from websites and blogs that are in the public domain and where the author has published their name on those sites. I have used pseudonyms or generic descriptions ('a female UK swimmer') in all other cases.

1
Becoming and belonging

1

Becoming

I have never lived by the sea, and I loathe boats, succumbing to violent sea-sickness on all but the most fat and stable of ferries on the calmest of days. My earliest ocean memories are from family holidays; of paddling in the shallows or bobbing with my older brother in an inflatable dinghy, tethered to the shore by a long nylon rope held by my dad – a security against the perils of 'being swept out to sea'. As we got older, we played, untethered now and confident swimmers, jumping and body boarding in the breaking waves on Woolacombe Sands, our parents' emphatic warnings to 'stay between the flags' ringing in our ears. The shoreline was our holiday playground; a contained, seductive zone of summer excitement between the dry safety of the beach and the dangerous emptiness of a sea into which careless children could be 'swept'.

Fast forward to the dawn hours of 2 September 2010. I have been swimming for five hours, heading straight out from the pebbly shore of Shakespeare Beach in the pitch dark of night, swimming in a spot-lit pool of light cast from the boat beside me. It is a comforting tether to safety; I remember my dad, ankle deep in water, holding the nylon rope. In the half-light of a beautiful dawn, when I breathe to the left, away from the boat, I see a pinkish sky and a scattering of feathery clouds; a breath to the right reveals the shadowy shapes of Peter and Sam, watching over me from the boat deck, each with a neon light stick dangling from lanyards around their necks so I know they're there, even in the dark. The lights look like two bright green exclamation marks – a surprised commentary on the extraordinary situation I find myself in. I have strayed very far from between the flags now, and my skin prickles with an adrenalin-flooded burst of excitement when the reality of what I am doing hits me through the comforting tap-tap-tap of hands on water: I am swimming the English Channel.

This is a disingenuous way to tell my marathon swimming story – a truncated magic-trick narrative that moves from inside to far outside the flags, flattening out the process through which that transition was achieved. *Ta dah!* And yet, beyond the appeal of the rhetorical flourish of spectacular becoming, there are moments when it feels like this; when behaviours that I have come to experience as mundane flash in sharp relief against the time before immersion, the before-and-after spectacle overshadowing the long, incremental process of becoming that lies between the story's bookends. Nor, as I explained in the Introduction, does this tale of becoming end in the English Channel, but continues to be marked by long, transformative cycles of becoming and unbecoming that neither take me back to where I started nor reach a definitive conclusion. Both this chapter and the next take this 'becoming' as their focus, exploring my own social and embodied transformation into (and occasionally, away from) a marathon swimmer. What had to happen for this landlocked, middle-aged sociologist to become so intimately immersed in the practice of swimming a long way slowly? What embodied work has to be done in order to be able to swim in relative comfort for hours on end, or indeed, for those hours of swimming to make purposeful sense?[1]

Central to these processes of becoming is the understanding of transformation as ongoing work – a self-oriented project of perpetual improvement-focused embodied labour that is accomplished reflexively and iteratively. The marathon swimming body is rendered a project whose finite point is never reached, in a social and cultural context where the body is deemed to be both malleable in the face of vigilance and hard work, and to say something significant about the self (Shilling 1993). As Reischer argues in the context of the exhausted completion of a running marathon, it becomes 'metonymic of one's life' (2001: 30). This is reflected in this discussion forum extract during a debate about the legitimacy of potentially performance-enhancing technologies in marathon swimming:

> [O]nce you've 'walked the walk', you understand that this sport is about stripping yourself down to the most basic aspects of your nature – at 4am in the cold, in the dark, over 3000 feet of water without any shore in sight, you find out if you've got it, and no amount of technology can tell you that. (MSF 2014b)

In spite of the appeal to 'your nature' here, the 'it' of marathon swimming does not conventionally refer to an innate capacity to swim long distances under challenging conditions, but rather, the ability and determination to have *cultivated* that capacity. As one experienced male US swimmer assured me: 'It's all about whether you're prepared to put in the work.' In the dominant self-representations of the sport, marathon swimmers are made via an ethic of work and commitment, not born. This voluntarism and purposefulness simultaneously democratises marathon swimming and provides the basis for distinction: in short, anyone can do it, but the ones who do are the ones who rose to the challenge. This reflects the prevailing ethos of competition that characterises neoliberalism, whereby inequalities are conceptualised not as the result of given appetites and instincts, but rather as having the capacity 'to sharpen appetites, instincts and minds, driving individuals to rivalries' (Lazzarato 2009: 117). The privileged status that attaches to being able to 'walk the walk' relies upon narratives of deserving rather than happenstance; success, here, is earned, not given. As this book will go on to explore across a number of dimensions, the democratic aura of marathon swimming – that anyone could do it if they put in the time and effort – smooths over troubling exclusions around (dis)ability and the intractable limitations imposed by social and economic inequalities. But at the same time, it opens up for scrutiny the process of becoming that might begin to explain how individuals (and groups of individuals) come to be immersed in, and by extension, find pleasure in, an activity that is not inherently or self-evidently pleasurable on the first encounter.

Just as not everyone can become a marathon swimmer for a range of reasons, it is also important to note that not everyone wants to become one. Indeed, for many people outside of the sport, marathon swimming is not only inconceivable but actively undesirable – for example, on the grounds of fear of aquatic wildlife, or disgust at the prospect of pollution or the necessary exercise of bodily functions in the water. Some may simply never have learned to swim, or to swim confidently, rendering marathon swimming literally beyond imagination. And for others, marathon swimming is simply excessive. First, it is physically punishing, and, as discussed in Chapter 8, injury is a perpetual risk and fact of the activity (see also, Turner and Wainwright 2003; Hockey 2005a; Willig 2008; Hanold 2010). Second, like many 'serious leisure' pursuits (Stebbins 2007), marathon swimming is a 'greedy avocation' (Gillespie et al. 2002: 288), consuming time, financial resources and emotional energy in ways which, for some, signify a solipsistic over-investment in the self and a selfishly unbalanced life in relation to domestic and work commitments (Baldwin 1999; Gillespie et al. 2002; Raisborough 2006; Stalp 2007; Dilley and Scraton 2010). And finally, the open water itself is perceived by many as dangerously 'out of bounds' in comparison to the more familiar sanitised spaces of the swimming pool or domesticated beaches, suggestive of risks to life that are out of proportion with a leisure activity. Marathon swimming, therefore, is an out-of-the-ordinary practice whose intensity and extensity positions it as always potentially positively deviant – that is, as too much of a good thing (Ewald and Jiobu 1985; Hughes and Coakley 1991). These all constitute obstacles to the willingness to even imagine marathon swimming as a site of bodily investment.

The ability to imagine and undertake the transformations demanded by marathon swimming does not arise out of nowhere. Writing of triathlon, Atkinson highlights 'the importance of how individual and community tastes and preferences for specific brands of athleticism are patently influenced by the life histories people carry into sport' (2008: 177). He is referring in particular to the disillusioned middle classness of his participants, for whom the 'civilised' bodies of the lean, disciplined triathletes and the structured demands and restraints of training provided routes to social distinction that resist the perceived passivity and apathy of everyday life (Elias and Dunning 1986). But this still cannot explain why a particular sport is chosen, and as Becker notes in relation to becoming a marijuana user, the process of becoming has to be preceded by the willingness to try, perhaps by being around people who are already using the drug and through whom they can gain access to a supply (1963: 61).

The willingness to try, or to imagine, a sport like marathon swimming has a variety of precursors. In my own case, this arose out of a lifetime of pool swimming, and therefore, an existing identity as a (pool) 'swimmer'. The groundwork was further laid by some cautious 'dabbling' in open water lake swimming; first, through my short and unaccomplished ventures in triathlon and then later through commercial swimming holiday companies and organised open water races of gradually increasing length. In the course of my incremental engagement with the social world of non-wetsuit open water swimming – a world I didn't even know existed until I reached my forties – there were several chance encounters with marathon swimmers that triggered me to act upon my interest and growing awareness. This entry into the sport reflects a combination of what Stevenson (2002) describes as 'seekership' and 'recruitment' – common processes through which initial entry into an activity is achieved.

For some marathon swimmers, existing identities as endurance athletes or as charity challenge participants created similar openness to the possibilities of marathon swimming as a plausible new dimension to an existing identity, while for others injury in one sport had led them to swimming as an alternative, less impactful, activity. Some marathon swimmers had simply grown up around the sea or lived near one of the geographical centres (Unruh 1980) of the social world of marathon swimming where a critical mass of accomplished practitioners had normalised the sport. At San Francisco's Aquatic Park, for example, both the Dolphin Club and the South End Rowing Club display impressive rosters of marathon swimmers within a much broader swimming culture across a range of levels and goals; club members, therefore, will not only have witnessed the training of others but also have access to support and informal coaching in their transition into marathon swimming. Consequently, while swimmers' narratives of deciding to attempt a marathon swim often pivot around singular moments – for example, a chance encounter with an encouraging marathon swimmer or a drunken bet among friends – those choices are made possible by the individual's habitus; that is, those values, dispositions and expectations that are acquired in the course of everyday life and incorporated and embodied to the point of appearing 'natural' and inevitable (Bourdieu 1992). The ability to imagine becoming a marathon swimmer, then, always comes from somewhere.

The remainder of this chapter focuses on two iteratively related aspects of the transformational process of becoming a marathon swimmer: techniques of the body and sensory transformations. This echoes the first two stages of Becker's (1963) framework of becoming – learning the techniques and then learning to perceive the drug's effects – but moves away from the linearity of this model, to focus on the iterative and embodied nature of becoming a marathon swimmer. It is this imbricated relationship between doing and feeling that is the focus of this chapter, the development of which lies at the heart of the work of becoming a marathon swimmer and the social world belonging that it enables.

Techniques of the body

In April 2009, I joined a specialist training camp for long distance swimmers on the island of Gozo in Malta. This was not my first sustained engagement with sea swimming; prior to this I had been on organised, leisurely sea swimming holidays in warm, beautiful locations, with stunning swims punctuated by delicious food and sumptuous relaxation. However, the Gozo trip was my first experience of sea swimming in marathon swimming mode and scale. In my mind, this was not holiday; this was *training* and the sea was my proving ground. Already committed to an English Channel swim attempt in August 2010, I had come to see what I could do, how I would cope, and to learn as much as I could in the cool waters of the springtime Mediterranean. I recorded one of the first training swims of the trip in my fieldnotes:

> The boat took us out of the harbour to a spot a couple of hundred metres offshore. We stripped down to our costumes and began the rituals of swim preparation: sun cream first, with its social dance of mutual back slathering, and then standing, arms up and apart, while a latex-gloved guide smeared blobs of Vaseline under our armpits, costume straps and around the backs of our necks to prevent chafing. Already, I had forgotten one of the first lessons we'd been taught on day one – get your cap and goggles on before you grease up so you don't get smudges on your lenses. Absent-mindedly, I straightened my costume straps, getting greasy smears on my fingers before reaching for the goggles perched on top of my kit bag. Beginner's error. I rummaged in my bag for a spare pair, cursing my stupidity and embarrassed at my obviously novice display. Safety boats were untethered, and we were given our orders: a two-and-a-half-hour swim up the coast towards a promontory in the distance and then into a bay, setting off in pace groups marked by hat colour. Then, 'Jump!' Not wanting to appear tentative, I hurled myself off the dive platform and into the air, away from the boat, breaking the surface in an ungainly splash before resurfacing with a horrified gasp. COLD – so much colder than the sheltered, shallower waters of the bay we'd swum in on the first day of the trip. I gave a couple of hyperventilating gasps, straining to catch my breath, but desperately trying to avoid a publicly humiliating display of panic; my skin burned and prickled and my forehead throbbed with an 'ice-cream' headache. Unwilling to be left behind, I started to swim after my fellow yellow-hats, turning my arms furiously to catch up and shake off the shock of cold.
>
> A second problem: the sea was chaotic and choppy, and I was unbalanced and disoriented by the motion across every plane and axis. My months of pool training and careful stroke work seemed useless in the face of this impossibly mobile environment. I mistimed a breath and gulped down a mouthful of sea water, which made my stomach heave; I gagged and wretched, and the tension of coughing creased my face, letting water seep under the seal of my goggles into the corner of my right eye. Cold, nauseous, sore-eyed misery. I was falling behind my group, and each time I fell into a trough between waves, I lost sight of the safety boat and the reassuring cluster of yellow heads in front of me. My fingers felt fat and stiff with cold, and I seemed unable to manage more than a handful of consecutive strokes before being upended by a wave or having to pause to orient myself. Everything I had read told me that I should learn to 'listen to my body' and know my own limits as a marathon swimmer, but I was at a loss as to how to interpret this barrage of unfamiliar bodily signals or where my limits might possibly lie amidst all this novel unpleasantness. All I could think about was how utterly miserable I was and how stupid I had been to think that I could swim the Channel. Self-pityingly, I distracted myself from my suffering and incompetence by drafting a melodramatic letter in my head to my English Channel boat pilot, withdrawing from my 2010 swim.

This extract suggests the wealth of techniques of the body (Mauss 1973) that constitute the marathon swimming habitus – a specific mode of being and doing that prospective swimmers have to incorporate and embody reflexively in order to both be able to swim long distances and belong to the wider community of marathon swimmers. These prescribed modes of being and doing, and their necessary bodily techniques, fall into two separate but interconnecting domains: first, the techniques of swimming; and second, the wide range of preparatory, in-water and post-swim routines and practices that minimise the potential for harm or discomfort for the swimmer and facilitate endurance, as well as signal social belonging through displays of competence and work. These techniques of the body, acquired 'through a process of apprenticeship in culturally specific contexts' (Shilling 2010: 58) are fundamental to the production of the marathon swimming habitus, and their acquisition is a social process of learning by doing.

At the risk of stating the obvious, in order to be a marathon swimmer, you have to be (or become) a competent swimmer. But while there may be a minimum threshold below which marathon swimming becomes untenable, normatively speaking, there is no end point, and even (or perhaps, especially) the most confident and competent swimmers devote at least some training time to ongoing technique work – for example, using repetitive, mindful drilling in order to embody swimming habits that both enhance pace and efficiency and mitigate injury risk. A life-long swimmer, I have always felt comfortable and at home in the water (although not always in the sea) and the act of long swimming came relatively easily to me. But nevertheless, between 2008 and 2014, I underwent four extensive phases of stroke correction to try to fend off injury and find a more sustained and elevated pace than the turgid plod that I so easily fall into. This coaching took place primarily in an Endless Pool – an approximately two by four metre, rib-deep pool with a propulsion unit at one end, creating a moving channel against which to swim.[2] The pool had a mirror on its floor to enable the swimmer to observe their own movements during the process of correction, as well as four video cameras, each recording from a different angle and projecting in real time onto a screen at the back of the pool. This live feed was recorded and edited by my coach, Ian,[3] who also added a verbal commentary to the video for later review. We would pause sporadically to view the footage from the different angles, homing in on technique flaws.

I became a good Foucauldian subject, enclosed, surveilled and willingly focusing on the body's movements in the most minute, repetitive detail in order to increase my swimming productivity (Foucault 1977). Proprioception (the sense of where the body is relative to itself) is dulled by immersion in water, and the sensations of swimming can be deceptive. Like the glass goblet blown by O'Connor (2007), which felt elegantly made but was nicknamed the 'globlet' by her teacher for its squat misshapenness, what can feel smooth and elegant in the water is revealed by video to be distorted and clunky. A hand that feels like it's straight out front can be reaching across the centre line, forcing the body into a banana-shaped arc; a pull below the water can feel like a perfectly executed, high-elbowed 'catch', while the video reveals a straight-armed outward reach, the arm sliding tractionless through the water. We used the mirror and video to help me see/feel the proper movements; the goal is to hold on to those sensations and images in the hope of 'finding' and embodying them in solo practice. As Crossley argues, 'agents can learn to find parts of their body and mobilize them in news ways' (2007: 89).

While new habits form relatively easily, the breaking of old habits takes uncountable repetitions, the body clinging stubbornly to the patterns of movement it already knows. I still struggle, for example, to break the habit of sweeping my arms in an underwater S-shaped pull – a staple of 1970s swimming technique that I imbibed as a child, but which has long fallen out of fashion in favour of a high-elbowed, straight-lined pull down the body. Mauss notes the same point in relation to swimming as a learned technique of the body, recalling how he was taught to swim by 'swallowing water and spitting it out again': 'In my day swimmers thought of themselves as a kind of steam-boat. It was stupid, but in fact, I still do this: I cannot get rid of my technique' (1973: 71). As Spencer notes in the context of training to be a mixed martial arts (MMA) fighter, 'proprioceptive memory is malleable but the "conscious" actor cannot by fiat change it; bodily memories change over time and in and through social working and reworking of bodies' (2009: 132). It is a leap of faith, then, to spend hours each week drilling in the face of the telic demands of a pending long swim, since however persuasive the logic of honing technique, the seductive lure of a long slog in the pool never goes away. This at least has the obvious satisfaction of a direct conceptual connection to a marathon swim that an hour concentrating on my recalcitrant left elbow is unable to deliver in quite the same way.

Beyond the demands of swimming technique acquisition, and even for relatively confident and comfortable pool swimmers, there are also techniques specific to open water swimming, and particularly sea swimming, that have to be acquired. As my swimming apprenticeship progressed, I learned to breathe out slowly underwater to quell the drive to hyperventilate when I jumped into cold water, and although I was never taught to forcefully spit water out of my mouth as Mauss was, like many pool swimmers, I had the habit of allowing water to swill around my mouth while swimming – an embodied custom that is ill-advised in salt water because of the risk of swallowing and the swelling and ulcerating effects of salt water on the tongue and mouth. In choppy water, through instruction from experienced others, careful observation and trial and error, I learned to adapt my stroke to the water conditions: for example, by learning to breathe bilaterally (to either side), enabling me to breathe away from incoming waves, and by increasing the body's rotation along the long axis in rough conditions to help both the mouth and the recovering arm to clear the water more easily. In time and through embodied experience, swimmers learn to take subtle cues from the movement of the water around their hands and bodies as shifts in pressure and density signal the movement and passage of swells. These are techniques, like the act of swimming itself, which can be described and imitated, but can only be acquired effectively through time in the water during which the body acquires the capacity to make the 'fleeting improvisations' (Lorimer and Lund 2003: 142) of habitual movement, especially in an environment that is constantly mobile.

The work of becoming appropriately skilled is never simply a matter of perfect repetition of a carefully honed movement, but rather, demands the ability to constantly adjust and adapt (see, for example, Downey 2005: 49; Throsby 2013a). As Lea argues in her analysis of Thai Yoga Massage (TYM) training, appropriate technique involves being able to 'conjugate with the context' (2009: 467) – a process as much about embodied 'feel' as objective knowledge. As has been documented in other diverse domains of skill acquisition, including becoming a barista (Laurier 2003), piano playing (Sudnow 2001), surfing (Ford and Brown 2006; Humberstone 2011), Capoeira (Downey 2005), glass blowing (O'Connor 2007) and dance (Hahn 2007; Potter 2008), the acquisition of swimming technique is a long, slow passage through various degrees of competence, beginning with the self-conscious watchfulness of the novice and eventually reaching a point where the swimming body seems able to find its own way in the aquatic world. It becomes 'a strategy without a strategist' (Sudnow 2001: x), although repeated phases of stroke correction to incorporate further refinements inevitably return the swimmer to a provisional state of watchfulness.

In a critique of Mauss' analysis of body techniques, Shilling argues that Mauss 'has little to say about the details of how they are actually *taught* or the *experiences* that people go through when acquiring (or failing to acquire) new skills and capacities' (2007: 13, emphasis in original). Instead, Shilling advocates a focus on body pedagogics: 'the central pedagogic *means* through which a culture seeks to transmit its main corporeal techniques, skills and dispositions, the embodied *experiences* associated with acquiring or failing to acquire these attributes, and the actual embodied *changes* resulting from this process' (Shilling 2007). From this perspective, the acquisition of these techniques can never only be the result of what Mauss calls 'prestigious imitation', whereby an individual 'imitates actions which have succeeded and which he has seen successfully performed by people in whom he has confidence and who have authority over him' (1973: 73). Instead, the process of acquiring techniques is fundamentally social in nature, and requires the active input of others – for example, by training partners drawing attention to flaws that the practising MMA fighter cannot see or feel through their own novice movements (Spencer 2009), or a Japanese dance teacher's use of subtle tactile cues to correct a slipping posture (Hahn 2007: 102).

The bodily techniques of swimming are not the only skills that the marathon swimmer has to learn. These additional skills include the rituals of 'greasing up' (see Figure 2); in-water feeding regimens and techniques (see Figure 3); or post-swim changing routines that minimise heat loss (hat first, then the upper body, then the lower half). These regimens can be understood as what Crossley describes as reflexive body techniques, which act back upon the agent in order to modify or manage it in a purposeful way (2004: 38). These techniques are oriented towards neutralising, or minimising, aspects of marathon swimming that would otherwise make it more difficult or uncomfortable, and are therefore essential techniques in the process of successfully becoming. But just as Lea found with the TYM textbook she was given to study (2009: 469), the 'rules' and their limitations only come to life through practice. For example, the preparatory ritual of 'greasing up' involves

Figure 2 Dover beach volunteer Barrie Wakeham helps English Channel swimmer Zoe Sadler to grease up before training.

Figure 3 Feeding.

both a generalisable rule – always use Vaseline (or similar) before even a short sea swim to avoid painful chafing – and a series of idiosyncratic adaptations, including not only favoured products but also an intimate knowledge of likely chafing spots.

This skill acquisition can also be seen as part of what Stevenson (2002) describes as the 'conversion' process during which novices acquire the specialist vocabularies, practices and values of the group or activity as part of their growing 'entanglement' with it. Consequently, attention to these practices also forms the beginnings of social belonging within local marathon swimming communities. Experienced hands expect novices to make 'beginners' errors' and will readily offer advice for future swims; for example, a novice emerging from a sea swim with angry chafing welts will receive sympathy, treatment suggestions and advice about future prevention. Other lessons are quickly learned through trial and error. The 'waterproof' suncreams purchased from the local pharmacy or supermarket are rarely up to the job of a long training swim, leaving novices exposed to the water-intensified rays of the sun and a painfully sunburned back and upper legs. They will soon be online searching for the specialist watersports products they saw in the hands of the more experienced swimmers. And in my first season of sea swimming, even with a specialist sunscreen, I experienced the ignominy of badly burned earlobes, which had escaped my meticulous slathering but which peeked out from underneath my cap. These mistakes are widely understood to be part of the learning process; they are an initiation into social belonging and the subject of some banter and humour among local gatherings of swimmers.

However, other errors are less forgiveable and directly imperil social belonging. For example, a prospective swimmer arriving with inappropriate swimwear such as board shorts, a scoop-backed leisure costume or an elite-style racing suit could expect to receive relatively short shrift, their attire signalling insufficient appreciation of the specific challenges and rules of marathon swimming. Similarly, in a training site such as Dover harbour,[4] which is oriented primarily towards English Channel swimming (and its customary rules), a swimmer turning up expecting to wear a wetsuit is likely to be viewed with suspicion regarding their commitment to the task. Training sites themselves have their own normative cultures and practices, which have to be learned but, normalised through custom and practice, are rarely made explicit until contravened. In the Dover training community, for example, a regime of obedience prevails, and participation in the training culture is conditional on adherence, wherever possible, to the targets and timetables set by the volunteer beach crew (see Figure 4). Freda Streeter – known affectionately as the Channel General to those who have trained under her – sits at the heart of this training culture, assigning to each swimmer the number of hours they should swim each day depending on water conditions and her knowledge of where the swimmer is in their training cycle. For some new to this localised training culture, this is at odds with the demands of autonomy and 'knowing your own body' that constitute the good athlete-subject, and this can lead to misunderstandings that are experienced by the beach crew and other swimmers as an affronting gesture that precludes social world belonging. For example, on his first visit to Dover to train, Chris completed the assigned

Becoming 37

Figure 4 The swimmers gather for the pre-training briefing in Dover harbour.

six-hour swim on the Saturday, and then was allocated five hours the following day – a swim that he was unable to complete due to a commitment at home that meant he had to leave early: 'I got out. The shame [laughing]. But I did not know....' Later becoming aware of his faux pas, Chris emailed an apology and went on to become a highly respected member of the Dover training community, known for a determined work ethic and his support for other swimmers. For others, their misreading of the training culture was experienced as far more alienating. One swimmer, for example, described turning up late for a five-hour swim as a result of train delays, leading him to request more time at the end of the session to complete the day's allotted task. However, the volunteer crew wanted to leave for the day since everyone else had finished, and experienced his request as disrespectful of their contribution, leading to a verbal disagreement. Describing himself as an 'independent person', he subsequently chose to train at another coastal location rather than return to the site of this misunderstanding, later completing a successful English Channel swim.

Writing on the construction of identity in sporting subcultures, Donnelly and Young highlight the importance of socialisation in the development of belonging, arguing that 'members learn to adopt the values and perspectives of the group, taking on new roles and modifying others, and thus establishing valuable new identifications with the politics and symbols of the group as a whole' (1988: 225). This is followed, they suggest, by either acceptance or ostracism, with acceptance 'directly related to demonstrations of appropriate job and/or skill requirements, appropriate roles and identities under specific circumstances, successful socialization procedures and general value homophyly between the actor and the larger group' (Donnelly & Young 1988). The acquisition of the body techniques of marathon swimming, then, can be understood not simply as acquiring the skills and capacities that enable successful long swimming, but also as serving as a *display* not just of appropriate skills and capacities that will facilitate safe swimming, but also of disposition – the willingness to learn, and to work on the body in normatively prescribed ways.

With this in mind, it is also important to note that neither the acquisition of techniques of the body nor the social belonging that specific displays of competence can produce are inevitable. Instead, these are dependent both on the resources available to individuals, and on the extent to which particular dimensions of social identity can be incorporated into the values and practices of the social world. First, and most obviously, those who are unable to swim are unlikely to engage in the extended work of becoming a marathon swimmer. This is significant when it is considered that, in the UK alone, an estimated 9 million adults are unable to swim (ASA 2015) and approximately 45 per cent of all school children are unable to swim twenty-five metres, even though this is part of the national curriculum (ASA 2014). As discussed in the Introduction, there is also a strong racial dynamic to these exclusions. Second, even among those who are able to swim, the work of becoming a marathon swimmer requires resources, as well as bodily capacities, which are inaccessible to many. For example, training requires not only time, but also time-flexibility, as well as financial resources. Furthermore, in spite of the prevailing mind-over-matter rhetorics, some bodies are simply unable to engage in such a practice. As Davis, drawing on work of critical disability scholars, argues, it is increasingly important to think about 'embodiment in terms of its limitations rather than its unbridled capabilities' (2007: 55).

Third, there is a strongly gendered element to the process of becoming a marathon swimmer. In particular, as discussed further in Chapter 6, although marathon swimming displays greater gender equity in participation than many other extreme sports, in common with sport more generally, it remains governed by a masculine ideal that does not always sit comfortably with normative femininity (Throsby 2013a). Magdalinski argues that sport is 'rendered a masculinising ritual, embodying characteristics of strength, power, aggression and confidence. By contrast, female bodies are portrayed as weaker, graceful, flexible and attractive' (2009: 92). When women deviate from these norms, they are easily marked as deviant, effectively constraining women's access to sport (Cahn 1994; Hargreaves 1994). As Young famously observes, 'for many women as they move in sport, a space surrounds us in imagination that we are not free to move beyond; the space available to our movement is a constricted space' (2005: 333). Not only does this make it harder to imagine an endeavour like marathon swimming, but early failures can also be experienced as confirmation of enculturated limitations; my own frustrated despair as I floundered through that first training swim in Gozo demonstrates this gendered confirmation of incapability. Similar doubts are also visible in those whose bodies are not easily coded as 'athletic' by normative standards, particularly in relation to fat, or ageing, often in close conjunction with gendered expectations of the 'good' body (see also, Throsby 2013a, 2013c). For example, one female swimmer who self-identified as 'fat' and who had a long history of struggles with her weight told me that she felt unable to go to see a stroke correction professional because 'he might just take one look and laugh'. These examples provide an important reminder of the normative expectations that frame, and potentially delimit, the work of becoming.

And finally, there are other barriers, which while not inhibiting the mundane processes of acquiring the techniques of the body of marathon swimming, still constitute a potential obstacle to belonging. This was particularly evident in relation to male sexuality, and I met two male swimmers, one in the UK and one in the US, who were out as gay in their non-swimming lives, but were reluctant to come out within the social world of swimming, and particularly in the context of local training sites. As is discussed further in Chapter 6, homosocial bonds among men commonly rely upon collective demonstrations of normative masculinity that shore up both masculinity and heterosexuality of the space – for example, through homophobic and sexist jokes, and the cautious management of touch and bodily display, especially in sport where semi-nudity and public changing is the norm (Wheaton 2004b; Evers 2009). All of these strategies rely on the assumption that none of the group *is* gay, coercing a 'culture of silence' among those who are (Bridel and Rail 2007: 129). Among experienced swimmers, homosexuality can be compensated for by high performance (Bridel and Rail 2007) and I met several openly gay swimmers in the course of the research. But this option is not always immediately open to the novice, for whom coming out may be much more precarious. As a gay UK male swimmer confided in me: 'It's better that they think I'm one of them.' Both the development of a marathon swimming habitus, including the necessary body techniques, and the cultivation of social belonging, then, are highly contingent processes that are inseparable from the identities that individuals bring to the sport (or indeed, which constrain access to it in the first place).

Sensory transformations

Looking beyond the body techniques and social practices that constitute, in part, the marathon swimming habitus, this next section explores another, intimately interrelated, aspect of becoming a marathon swimmer: the sensory transformations that both facilitate technique acquisition and arise from it. As already hinted at in the description of the importance of 'feel' to developing swimming technique, the body techniques of marathon swimming are inseparable from the concurrent sensory transformations that are both necessary conditions of technique acquisition and its outcome. Consequently, novice marathon swimmers have to learn to recognise and calibrate the sensory effects of marathon swimming since, as described in the earlier fieldnotes extract, one of the primary challenges for the newcomer is the unintelligibility of the barrage of novel sensations. This is exemplified by the case of cold.[5] In everyday, non-swimming life, even a modest sensation of cold is usually a prompt to action – closing a window, putting on a sweater, turning up the heating. This reflects Leder's (1990) argument that the body renders itself invisible until pain or discomfort pushes it into the foreground, making it 'dys-appear' in ways that demand action. More overt physiological responses to a fall in body temperature such as goose bumps or shivering are generally experienced as a pressing call for rewarming action. However, in the case of marathon swimming (and much open water swimming more generally), the effect of cold is calibrated on a different scale and while for most non-swimmers or pool swimmers water temperature is measured in wide temperature bands – freezing, cold, warm, hot – regular open water immersion produces a much more refined delineation of temperature, where even a fraction of a degree makes a tangible difference to the experience of being in the water in ways that are inaccessible to the novice or those outside of the community. In 2011, for example, I worked for a short time as a guide for the same training camp in Gozo in which I had participated as a novice swimmer in 2009. During a chilly six-hour training swim, one of the participants broke from the swim circuit in the bay and paddled her way over to the beach, intent on getting out early. She sobbed miserably that she was too cold to continue; she held up her arm, covered in goose bumps, as evidence of her suffering. Another of the guides, a very experienced swimmer who was in the water with the group, headed her off, holding up his goose-bumped arm alongside her own: 'We've all got those. You're fine. Keep swimming!' Thwarted, she slid her body back into the water and headed out into the bay to rejoin the training circuit, going on to safely complete her first six-hour swim.[6] What we usually understand as problematically 'cold' doesn't apply in this context and swimmers have to learn to recalibrate if they are to go on to find marathon swimming pleasurable.

In the weeks following my own first Gozo training camp in 2009, I swam several times a week in much colder water in local lakes, watchfully exploring the effects of cold on my body and trying to identify these new, unintelligible boundaries of safe cold. I described the effects in my fieldnotes: the 'sausage-fingers', clawed hands, ice-cream headaches and numbness at my peripheries as my body held the warm blood protectively at my core. The cold was recorded in my fieldnotes as tingling, biting, burning, searing. Minutes after leaving the water, I learned to recognise the dramatic post-swim shivering of the 'afterdrop',[7] and tense-jawed and fumbling, bundled under layers, I would try to pour hot chocolate from my flask into a cup, slopping liquid over the sides like a drunk. However disconcerting and frightening in the first instance, both to the novice and to the uninitiated around them, all this, I learned, is normal. This is how it's supposed to feel, especially in the early season while the water is still inching out of its winter lows but training can't wait. Occasionally, I pushed the envelope too far and became too cold-addled and thick-fingered to dress myself without help; I tried to remember the feeling of cold that preceded it – the slowing of my stroke and the numbness creeping up my limbs – trying to locate my own boundaries of cold. Like all swimmers, I learned to read the cold based on my body's reaction to it, recalling the connoisseurship described by Becker among his marihuana smokers, who claimed to be able to distinguish between qualities and strengths of the drug based on its embodied effects (1963: 52). In this way, I began to delineate the boundaries of 'safe' cold as an effect of swimming, expanding the safe possibilities of time in the water and the pleasures that it brings.

Experience also affords novices a transformed sensorium, which is both a product of and accessed through swimming. This is significant in the process of becoming a marathon swimmer because reliance upon a conventional land-based sensorium effectively renders marathon swimming an experience of sensory deprivation; indeed, this provides the basis of many of the outward-facing stories of suffering that are told (for example, on charitable fund-raising websites) to illustrate the 'toughness' of the challenge. I also inadvertently reproduced this model of marathon swimming in the funding application for this project, opening the proposal with the claim that swimming requires 'psychological strategies for coping with the sensory deprivations and physical discomforts of marathon swimming'. This rhetorical flourish, which simultaneously denies the pleasures of swimming and reproduces a problematic mind–body split, was no doubt intended to grab the attention of the assessment panel; like fund-raising websites, this was a direct appeal to external negative perceptions of the experience of the sport. But several years on, I cringe at my (melo)dramatic focus on suffering and isolation, which I now see as a very partial representation of my own swimming experience. Instead, I want to reconfigure this claim to argue that marathon swimming is only an experience of sensory deprivation if we continue to rely on the 'classic five' senses (Potter 2008) in their 'land-based' orientation – a configuration that is necessarily re-organised through immersion in water. In short, to learn how marathon swimming feels is to learn to feel differently. As ethnographer of modern dance, Caroline Potter, argues, 'the senses should be understood as an intermeshed web of perceptory apparatuses that direct the body's total attention to its situation in the world, rather than a set of discreet biological pathways that respond independently to physical stimuli' (2008: 446). Specific cultures, therefore, cultivate and transmit what Potter calls a 'shifted sensorium' (459) – in this case, a marathon swimming mode of being-in-the-world that is distinct from the culturally bounded phenomenon of the prevailing Western sensorium (Geurts 2005).

For all of the dulled and diminished sensations of swimming, then, engaging a cultivated 'shifted sensorium' reveals new dimensions of sensory experience that are both the product of and revealed through immersion; these are the illegible experiences of swimming that the novice cannot immediately perceive or appreciate, no matter how good their technical mastery. For example, hearing (in its land-based sense) is dulled by immersion in water; indeed, many swimmers resort to written instruction on white-boards rather than the spoken word during swims (although this is a poor substitute for those, like myself, with imperfect vision that is not amenable to prescription goggle lenses). However, the perception of sound is not dulled, but transformed. As Merchant notes in relation to diving, sound travels faster under water than through air and the viscosity of the water changes the translation of sound waves to nerve impulses, making it hard to tell the origins of noises (2011: 227). The water, then, is far from a silent place, and an unexpected cacophony of new situational sounds gradually becomes audible to the swimmer as they cease to strain for land-based auditory inputs and begin instead to take auditory cues from the aquatic environment: the musical rhythms of swimming as hands tap-tap-tap into the water; the sound-sensation of exhaled bubbles rolling up the cheeks; the watery crackles and ticks of submersion (Merchant 2011); the hiss of pebbles being dragged along the ocean floor; the alarming buzz of an outboard engine, direction and distance distorted by the water. Over time, these sounds become integral to swimming itself, and a brief experiment with custom-made ear plugs in 2011 after recurrent bouts of ear infection failed miserably when I found myself unable to find the rhythms of long swimming *without* the sounds that it had taken me so long to become attuned to.

This 'shifted sensorium' is also necessary to sustain motion and stability while horizontal in the constantly moving aquatic environment – a complex interaction of 'vestibular, somatosensory and visual modalities' that requires the learned integration of breath management (Merchant 2011: 228), as well as sensitivity to the subtle changes in pressure and texture in the water that might facilitate or hinder purposeful movement through it. Like the dancers Potter studied, then, the being-in-the-world of the marathon swimmer, rather than relying on inputs from the land-based 'classic five', is primarily kinaesthetic in mode – 'a heightened sense of constantly shifting one's body in space and time in order to achieve a desired end' (2008: 449).

Learning to perceive, interpret and respond to the effects of being a swimming body in water is therefore a central element of the process of becoming a marathon swimmer, both in terms of recalibrating what counts as a problematic bodily state, and embodying a reconfigured swimming sensorium. This highlights the centrality of the transformation of the body itself to the process of becoming and the inseparability of those transformations from the embodied techniques that facilitate it (Shilling 2010). Writing of marathon running, Reischer argues that cycles of training cause the body to undergo profound changes, including a decreased resting heart rate, increased oxygen capacity, altered blood chemistry, increased metabolism, improved muscle tone and changed body composition; the body, 'from the micro-cellular to the gross anatomical level, is transformed' (2001: 27). These transformations affect how the body experiences the effects of swimming, which in turn contributes to the transformation of the body. As Downey notes: 'Experiences affect how later experiences feel, even immediate sensations' (2005: 33). For example, while the swimmer is learning to perceive and delineate the effects of cold on the body and how to react to them (habituation), the process of regular immersion simultaneously produces physiological adaptations to the cold (acclimatisation) (Hong *et al.* 1987; Makinen 2010), producing marginal but appreciable increases in tolerance. This highlights the dialectic, iterative relationship between the acquisition of techniques of the body, the associated sensory transformations, and the embodied transformations that occur in the course of producing those effects. Training, then, doesn't simply raise the threshold at which swimming becomes too unpleasant or painful to continue, but changes the very sensations through which swimming is experienced and calibrated.

Conclusion

In this chapter, I have argued that the process of becoming a marathon swimmer demands the acquisition of a wide range of techniques of the body that facilitate long swimming. This includes not only those specific techniques of moving the body through water, but also preparatory, in-water and post-swim practices that maximise comfort and minimise harm. These mark out the marathon swimming identity not simply as given, but as produced through purposeful labour. This framing sustains the marathon swimmer as an exemplar of entrepreneurial selfhood, actively fashioning the self and one's own capacities in order to achieve socially rewarded goals. However, the chapter has also argued that, in spite of the democratic aura of marathon swimming, the ability to imagine marathon swimming and participate in it is constrained by a wide range of factors and the status-bearing transformations of becoming are not uniformly accessible. While embodied work is undoubtedly a feature of becoming a marathon swimmer, this is never all there is to the process; successful becoming is never entirely within the remit of the autonomous individual and is profoundly contingent on an individual's life experiences, (dis)abilities, situation and social context. Rather than intending to undermine the satisfactions and pleasures of accomplishment that arise from the work of becoming a marathon swimmer, which are deeply meaningful to many of the swimmers I have met (including myself), I want to mobilise this argument in these early stages of the book as a cautionary challenge to the narratives of heroism that attach easily to displays of physicality such as a marathon swim and to think critically about what social relations risk erasure in those celebrations (see also, Hargreaves 2000).

The second key argument of this chapter is to highlight the iterative nature of the process of becoming, through which new techniques of the body not only transform what the body is able to do, but also the nature of the body itself and the ways in which the (aquatic) world is perceived through the body. Training, then, in both its pedagogic and athletic senses, habituates the body to particular styles and modes of socially contextualised movement, changing the ways that the body feels and functions. Over the six years that I have been actively involved in marathon swimming, I have become a technically more efficient swimmer; my shoulders and upper back have a pronounced muscularity that both enables and is produced by swimming; I know that a black jelly baby will sooth a salt-swollen mouth and that nappy rash cream works wonders on chafed skin; and even in the dead of the UK winter when long, open water swims couldn't be further out of reach, I still have a clear swimming costume mark across my back – irreversible changes at the cellular level from months of sun exposure every summer. My embodied self is literally shaped by marathon swimming; I have inhabited, and been inhabited by, swimming.

The final element of the arguments presented here relates to the question of social belonging and its relationship to the appropriation of the necessary techniques of the body for swimming. In order to achieve social belonging, novice swimmers have to not only acquire (and display) the specific techniques of marathon swimming, but also demonstrate adherence to local and social world values and practices. These too have to be learned, either through watchful imitation or occasionally through reinforcement by confirmed insiders (see also, Donnelly and Young 1988). Social belonging, then, is about more than being able to swim a long way, especially for the novice. This theme is taken up in the next chapter in relation to the sensory transformations of marathon swimming and the opportunities for belonging offered by the pleasures of the sport.

Notes

1 Both this chapter and the next draw heavily on a recent paper in which I tried to make sense of the embodied work of becoming a marathon swimmer (Throsby, 2015a). In that paper, I drew on Becker's famous work on 'becoming a marijuana user' (1963), using his three-step process (learning the techniques, learning to feel its effects and learning to perceive those effects as pleasurable) as a structuring device. However, in hindsight, Becker's model is too constraining to accommodate the iterative and embodied nature of the transformations being addressed here, and I have reframed my original paper in ways that explore many of the same points but which loosen the ties to Becker's analysis to better draw out the specificities of marathon swimming's transformations.

2 The fourth stroke correction took place in early 2014 as part of recovery from a shoulder injury (see Chapter 8), and the coaching took place in a regular swimming pool with the use of video cameras and specialist stroke analysis software, offering a similarly panoptical scrutiny of my stroke.

3 My coach, Ian Smith, died suddenly and unexpectedly in November 2011. He was a consummate professional and is greatly missed by all who knew him.

4 Every weekend from May to September, swimmers gather on the beach in Dover harbour to train under the watchful eye of a team of dedicated volunteers who allocate swim times, assist with pre-swim preparations, provide regular feeds during the swims and act as a source of support and advice for solo and relay swimmers in training, primarily for pending English Channel swims.

5 Not all marathon swims take place in cold water and what counts as 'cold' is a relative judgement. But water temperature is a primary concern for many of the iconic marathon swims (e.g. the English Channel), and the processes of both habituation and acclimatisation are a crucial part of the training process.

6 In order to be eligible to attempt an English Channel crossing, prospective swimmers are required to complete a documented six-hour swim in water at less than sixteen degrees (Celsius). Consequently, the first six-hour swim is a key marathon swimming milestone.

7 After exiting cold water, the body begins to recirculate the warm blood held at the body's core out to the peripheries, driving the cold peripheral blood back to the core, causing a drop in body temperature (the 'afterdrop'). Swimmers learn to use the short window before the afterdrop to change as quickly as possible to maximise heat retention.

2

Unexpected pleasures

When we watch people participating in water-based lifestyle sports such as surfing, windsurfing or kite-boarding, it is not difficult to imagine their pleasures. Adrenalin-fuelled and hedonistic, and acting in spectacular concert with the wind and ocean, it is impossible not to see the joys that might fall to the surfer riding a vertiginous, blue-green wave or the windsurfer careening across the sea's surface. In the cultural imagination, and given the right level of skill and environmental conditions, these activities make sense as potentially pleasurable, regardless (or perhaps because) of the very real risks at stake in achieving that sensory and affective high. Indeed, anyone who has ever ridden even the gentlest of breaking waves in to the beach on a body board will remember the extraordinary pleasures of the sounds and sensations of 'flying' in the grip of a wave. Like any activity, this is not to say that those pleasures are either innate or inevitable; as discussed in the previous chapter, the acquisition of some level of competent technique precedes the ability to find them pleasurable in practice. But even without those cultivated skills, the swooping, flying, plunging acrobatics of the accomplished surfer or windsurfer *look* fun, even to the most uninitiated eye.

Marathon swimming, on the other hand, is much less self-evidently pleasurable. It lacks the spectacle and adrenalin of other lifestyle sports; indeed, most of the 'action' is literally out of general view, and even that which is visible is repetitively unremarkable (see also, Askwith 2013). The imagery of isolation and monotony combines with common perceptions of open water itself as hostile, dirty and unsustainably cold; this is compounded by the enduring images of Channel swimmers being slathered with layer upon layer of grease and fat – a largely discredited practice among swimmers, but one which lingers in the popular imagination for its evocation of disgust. Similarly, even arguably the most spectacular moment of a marathon swim – a successful finish – is hardly a photogenic triumph as the swimmer crawls or staggers out of the water, swollen and unsteady. The impression of endurance sports more generally as fundamentally unpleasant is reinforced by the use of similar practices as punishments in other contexts – for example, in the military or in schools. For example, in February 2014, the UK Department for Education, under the leadership of Michael Gove, issued a report on behaviour and discipline in schools that included as a recommended sanction for poor behaviour, 'extra physical activity such as running around a playing field' (2014: 8). The extra physical activity is not intended as something that might be a welcome distraction or focus for the young miscreants; the shaming monotony of being forced to run around a field is purposefully punitive, and couldn't be further away from narratives of pleasure.

The marathon swimming community itself reinforces the conceptual association of long swimming with suffering, marshalling the rhetorics of mind over matter and bodily mastery and control as markers of social distinction. As discussed in Chapter 5, this is particularly marked in the domain of charity fund-raising, where suffering is actively traded for donations. It is a representation that is not without foundation, since marathon swimming involves a wide range of unpleasant possibilities. In the course of my relatively short swimming career, I have been fearful, nauseous, cold, in pain, hungry, stung by jellyfish, bitten by water lice and exhausted beyond imagination. And yet, like many of my swimming colleagues, I can't stay away; I am captivated by what Wacquant, writing about the experience of becoming a boxer, described as 'the intoxication of immersion' (2004: 4). Similarly, the interview transcripts and fieldnotes are littered with the spontaneous metaphors of intoxication: being 'high as a kite'; 'drunk with joy', 'flying', 'addicted' and 'craving' a swim. So how do swimmers come to find pleasure in a practice that appears at first glance, and certainly via its outward-facing representations, removed from the possibilities of pleasure? And why are these pleasures so representationally understated?

This chapter explores the different kinds of pleasure experienced by marathon swimmers that in turn serve as motivations to engage with the sport. This follows closely from the previous chapter, since the ability to find pleasure in marathon swimming is heavily contingent on successful acquisition of the necessary techniques of the body and their associated embodied transformations. I argue that both the experience of pleasure, and its denial, are markers of distinction, drawing boundaries of belonging both through displays of 'overcoming' suffering and the domination of the body, and the shared experience of inexpressible, visceral pleasures that extend far beyond the more obvious pleasures of an accomplished goal.

Writing of becoming a marijuana user, Becker argues that once the necessary techniques have been learned and the effect of the drug recognised, the final step is learning to enjoy the effects of smoking. In short, he argues that a user has to develop a taste for it if they are to continue using the drug (1963: 52). But for Becker, the pleasures of smoking marijuana are hierarchically ordered, with the individual progressing towards increasing levels of pleasure in the drug as their taste for it develops. But *contra* this hierarchical structure of learned pleasures, I want to argue here that marathon swimming is comprised of an assemblage of socially acquired pleasures that operate in complex relation with suffering and discomfort. This highlights the ways in which the transformations of the marathon swimming body can never be fully accounted for by conventional sporting narratives of mind over matter, opening the way instead for a more nuanced account that emphasises the process of becoming not only as transforming what the body can do, but also how it feels.

Unexpected pleasures 47

The first and most obvious dimension of this assemblage can be found in attempts to reduce suffering through the embodiment and mobilisation of techniques of the body and their associated transformations, as discussed in the previous chapter. Training more generally can be understood as a means of facilitating long swimming by increasing capacity and thereby raising the threshold at which suffering is experienced, postponing its onset. This approach positions pain and suffering as inevitably negative, with swimming pleasure determined by the removal or at least postponement of obstructively negative experiences. However, the nature of marathon swimming makes it impossible to remove pain and suffering from the experience if it is to remain recognisable as the same sport (see also, Willig 2008: 696); indeed, as discussed in the next chapter, attempts to minimise suffering through technological innovation, for example, are generally considered counter to the spirit of the sport. Active mitigation of suffering, then, is only one part of the complex relations of suffering and pleasure, and this chapter focuses on two further dimensions that constitute the 'intoxication of immersion': (1) the recoding of suffering as pleasure; and (2) the novel pleasures of swimming.

Recoding suffering as pleasure

> You know the great sort of personal development quote about 'it is not necessarily the destination, it is the journey that matters' and I was sort of like … it is not for me [both laugh]. … It is all about the destination. (Simon, UK English Channel swimmer)

> When I am in there I spend the entire time thinking what the hell have I done here and how the hell did I get myself into this and when can I get out and that is the one enduring thought throughout the swim – when the hell can I get out of this, you know. And what I do it for is the sense of achievement. (Stephen, UK multiple English Channel swimmer)

Marathon swimming has an obviously telic orientation: the successful completion of a long swim. In the case of some marathon swim events such as the Manhattan Island Marathon Swim (MIMS) or the Rottnest Channel swim in Australia, the goal of completion is sublimated for a small minority of swimmers to that of winning (or placing high up the final rankings), but even in these competitively oriented 'race' events, finishing still remains the primary goal for the majority of participants (see also, Atkinson 2010; Hanold 2010). This is not to say, of course, that individuals don't have aspirations in relation to finishing times, but particularly for swims where conditions are highly unpredictable, such as the English Channel, finishing is the fundamental measure of success (see Figure 5). Pleasure, from this perspective, lies in the sense of achievement on completion – 'the destination' – and suffering ('the journey') is the price that is paid.

Exemplified by the popular exercise mantra 'no-pain, no-gain', this is a common trope within the field of sport and physical training, where the 'burn', however unpleasant at the time, is experienced as evidence of progress towards a goal, and where sacrifices in time, money and sociality are made 'worth it' by a successful outcome. A hard pool session or a long, cold open water swim can be notched

Figure 5 Looking back after swimming the Catalina Channel, July 2011.

up as more 'miles in the bank' in preparation for the target swim that may be months or even years ahead. In an overt example of the use of 'economic terms to decipher traditionally non-economic behaviours' that characterises neoliberalism (McNay 2009: 60), I often overheard swimmers talking about 'cashing in' their training in order to get through a long swim or of 'drawing down' on banked miles. Suffering both in training and during a marathon swim is figured here as a hard-earned currency to be traded for the sense of achievement that comes from reaching your 'destination'. This is the frame within which both Simon and Stephen in the opening quotes to this section make sense of marathon swimming, mobilising an archetypal mind-over-matter account of their engagement with swimming. Success, as the conventional wisdom of marathon swimming goes, is '20 per cent physical and 80 per cent mental'.

But the situational utility of suffering also becomes an acquired taste, and those sensations that may have previously been experienced as unpleasant or frightening are recoded and recalibrated to constitute a source of pleasure. This is distinct from the active trading of suffering for pleasure – a 'no-pain, no-gain' construction that maintains the construction of suffering *qua* suffering as a tradable object that serves as a foil to the pleasures of finishing. Instead, the 'burn' of training comes to be appreciated and actively sought, not as the price exacted in exchange for swimming, but as an integral part of the activity itself. As Aalten notes in her work with ballet dancers, in an activity whose telos is to push at the boundaries of bodily possibility, pain and discomfort are not only inescapable, but also central to definitions of success (Aalten 1995, 2007).

But while pain and discomfort are central elements of marathon swimming, this is not to say that engagement with the sport constitutes a direct seeking of pain *per se*. Simplistic assumptions about relations of masochism, where pain and suffering are sought as sources of pleasure in their own right, are insufficient to explain marathon swimming, even though this explanation is often self-deprecatingly used by swimmers as a shorthand means of making sense of the sport to doubtful others. Instead, rather than being gluttons for punishment, swimmers become connoisseurs of suffering, delineating between degrees and qualities of suffering along sport-specific scales, judging not between pain and its absence, but rather, which qualities and degrees of pain and suffering will facilitate progress in the sport, or constrain present and future participation.

Writing of ultra-marathon running, Hanold describes how her participants offered three categories of pain: discomfort, good pain and bad pain (2010: 172). The latter of these – bad pain – is experienced most directly in relation to the pain of injury, which signals a threat to ongoing activity in ways that preclude it as a site of pleasure. This is taken up in detail in Chapter 8 in the context of swim-stopping injuries. But both 'discomfort' and 'good pain' can be understood as a positive part of the experience of swimming; indeed, they are actively sought as evidence of hard training that pushes at the borders of capacity, producing immediate and longer-term physiological impacts that are coded as desirable (Atkinson 2008; Hanold 2010). For swimmers, the discomforts of tired shoulders, for example, are routine and constitute a desired outcome that signifies an effective swim; the fatigued muscles are an embodied sign of progress in the cumulative capacity-building process of training. And alongside these longer-term benefits, a hard training session, as signaled by muscle soreness, might also be a harbinger of a sumptuous night's sleep, or generate a hearty appetite that gives gustatory pleasure. As such, as Crossley argues in relation to cross-training in the gym, 'sensations that would in most contexts be experienced as uncomfortable and painful, and as such would tend to terminate activity, must be (within a range) welcomed' (2004: 53–54). This is not the same as trading pain for pleasure, but rather, of recoding those experiences themselves as the defining normality of the practice. Recalibrated as 'normal' and no cause for concern, these sensations and discomforts also come to serve an informational function. As Spinney notes in the context of mountain road cycling during a difficult climb: 'pain becomes simply the bi-product of ascent; a barometer of how the ascent is progressing, whether the goal can be achieved and the feeling that must be endured to achieve the goal' (2006: 726). Similarly, Hockey describes the ways in which respiratory rate and leg cadence become part of a 'spectrum of bodily indicators' through which distance runners develop a sense of pace (2005b: 188).

'Good pain', on the other hand, can be understood more clearly as 'pain' than 'discomfort', but in ways that are coded positively, particularly around both being able to push the body towards its limits and being able to make it 'actively absent' (Aalten 2007). This can be seen in the duress of endurance – for example, by sticking it out in very cold or rough conditions or persisting over longer periods of time than anticipated. Like Aalten's ballet dancers, swimmers have to render the pain actively absent in order to continue; to refuse to 'hear' it in the face of the conventional wisdom to 'listen to your body' (Aalten 2007). Unlike the 'discomforts' of swimming, which are the 'normal' features of the practice, these are more notable moments of (temporary) pain for meaningful purpose; for finishing or, at least, pushing to the very edges of capability before being forced to abandon a swim. This experience of 'good pain' is entirely situational; the same sensations while sitting working at my desk would be a sign to pack up and go home to bed, but during a swim are experienced as productive and facilitating, not least because they are both temporary and voluntary. However unpleasant in the moment, 'good pain' is also the stuff of 'war stories', providing material for heroic tales of triumphant overcoming or humorous accounts of the ridiculous misery of self-inflicted, but ultimately benign, suffering (Kane and Zink 2004). In a sport where very little of note happens over long periods, these tales of suffering provide narrative turning points that enliven an otherwise unremarkable tale.

This process of recoding and recalibration depends upon the minimisation of the seriousness of unpleasantness. Like the swimmer in Gozo who had to re-evaluate her goose-bumped arm, swimmers have to learn that what might be considered serious and intolerable in one context (aching or shivering while sitting at my desk) is not serious in a swimming context. While particular sensations may be experienced as unpleasant or disgusting, once they can be categorised as no immediate threat to either well-being or ongoing training and swimming, then the body's 'dys-appearance' (Leder 1990) is stripped of its affective call to action. And in its place, an opportunity for collective humour opens up that is a core site of social world belonging. The archetypal illustration of this can be seen in the dramatic shivering that swimmers often experience post-swim. This is the result of the 'afterdrop', which occurs when the cold blood held at the peripheries during immersion begins to circulate back to the core once the swimmer leaves the water, causing a small and temporary drop in body temperature. This shivering is a thermogenic response, and not shivering after having become cold can be an indicator of dangerous levels of hypothermia; but to novice swimmers, or to uninitiated onlookers, the spectacle of an aggressively shivering body can be a distressing cause for alarm. The face takes on a rigid, palsied appearance, the voice quavers, teeth begin a cartoonish chatter and hands lose both dexterity and stability, making it difficult to hold a warm drink without slopping it uncontrollably over the sides or manage a button or zip fastening.

Noticeable shivering of this kind, combined with what is often an eccentric piling on of thick, ill-matched clothing and hats on days when others may be walking around in jeans and a T-shirt, make the post-swim body unreadable to uninitiated others. I was told many tales of stopping off at petrol stations for a hot drink or nipping in to supermarkets for post-swim snacks while still bundled up and shivering, leading the individual to be misread by sales staff or security guards as drunk, on drugs or as a possible shoplifting 'hoodie'. These experiences echo those of people with disabilities affecting speech and motor skills, whose movements and speech patterns are experienced by others as illegible and potentially threatening (Clare 2003; Chandler 2007, 2010; St. Pierre 2012). There is a racialised dimension to these misreadings too, as illustrated by Leroy Moore, founder of the Krip Hop movement, whose poetry describes being profiled and stopped by police four times in a single month:

> Black Disabled Man
> Must be a drunk
> Slur speech drugging feet
> Must be begging for money (cited in Hills 2012)

But while these misreadings are dangerous and shaming, for the marathon swimmers, the misunderstandings are easily dispelled; as discussed in relation to fat in Chapter 7, the abjection of the post-swim body is never 'real', and these misunderstandings can be retold as humorous anecdotes of distinction rather than as angry testimonies to discrimination and abjection.

Once collectively acknowledged as harmless, shivering becomes an entertaining opportunity for in-group hilarity in recognition of the absurdity of a cluster of shivering, heavily clad bodies trying to pour out hot drinks or raise a cup to their lips whilst trying to dodge the slops and splashes. It is a ludicrous spectacle that offers unique possibilities for group belonging. The post-swim shivers are often videoed on smartphones and posted online; there is even a Facebook group called the 'Shiver Club', which serves as a shared repository for the recordings, which are usually brief and unsteady and filmed to a soundtrack of howls of laughter as a shivering swimmer struggles comically to eat or drink. The videos, and their sharing, reveal the rich sociality of those moments. Swimmers help each other to dress and, informed by the learned connoisseurship of cold, make sure that everyone is safe and well; they share food and hot drinks; good swims are celebrated and encouragement, advice and reassurance offered to struggling novices who are still learning their own safe boundaries of cold and what this absurd spectacle of shivering might signify.

A second example of this sociality is the taking and online posting of pictures of some of the collateral effects of marathon swimming that are as unintelligible to those outside of the sport as the effects of cold, but which are also more enduring than a post-swim bout of the shivers: for example, sharply marked head and body stripes, or thick, furry tongues from exposure to salt water. Even with the sturdiest sunscreen, marathon swimming exposes (some of) the body to the water-intensified rays of the sun over long periods of time, producing a distinctive set of bodily markings, both around the shape of swimwear and on the face, where the swim cap leaves a horizontal pale band across the top of the forehead and white goggle-rings around the eyes. These bodily markings draw furtive and occasionally overt stares that can spill over into direct queries, or even advice about the use of fake tan or creative hairstyling to cover the marks. In playful defiance, photos of headstripes and thick tongues are posted on social media and enjoyed as a shared currency among marathon swimmers (see Figure 6).

The pleasures in these collective celebrations are rooted in distinction. The furry tongues, eccentric dress and illegible body markings all function as visible badges of honour; as embodied proof of swimming. And this in turn marks the

Figure 6 Elaine Howley displays a head stripe at the end of her English Channel swim, 2009.

swimming body as out of the ordinary. Every bewildered glance or comment, or every disbelieving stare from onlookers as swimmers march down the beach into the water, shores up the construction of marathon swimming (and therefore, the swimmers) as extraordinary. And this too is part of the pleasure of the sport; as Willig argues in relation to 'extreme sports', being seen by others as different is a source of enjoyment in itself (2008: 696). It is an uncomfortable, egoistic truth, but especially for those like myself whose bodies and public performances rarely stand out or surprise people, these moments of distinction are a (guilty) pleasure and a moment of status-bearing difference (Niedzviecki 2006).

A further dimension of the assemblage of suffering and pleasure that constitutes marathon swimming is its status as what Cohen and Taylor (1992) call 'escape attempts'– to flee the press of mundane routines and seek out meaning, novelty and a sense of identity. This reflects Atkinson's (2008) analysis of a group of Canadian triathletes who, he argues, were seeking the 'exciting significance' of the sport as an antidote to the perceived social fragmentation of society and its descent into mundane, predictable habits, stripped of risk and excitement (see also, Elias and Dunning 1986). In a mundane world of work and carefully managed risk, the challenging aspects of training can become inextricable from a pleasurable sense of escape that many swimmers value both for the break in routine and the exciting sense of difference that it offers. A salesman and father to young children, Robert, articulated this directly as he described his experience in 2009 of a training camp in Cork, Ireland. The camp is renowned for its intensity, offering a relentless roster of twice-daily cold water swims organised by the thriving marathon swimming community based at Sandycove Island – one of the 'geographical centres' (Unruh 1980: 284) that comprise the social world of marathon swimming:

> I think the best thing about it was it gave me an insight into what it would be like to live the life of an athlete. Because we'd get up at 4.30 in the morning, not every morning ... get down to Sandycove for 5 a.m., do a few laps because this gave the locals the opportunity to do their swimming [before work]. Get back to the B&B, shower, get a great cooked breakfast – because you deserve it! – fall asleep watching terrible TV in my room, wake up, meet up for lunch, eat – you deserve it, because you are going to burn it off later in the day, maybe have a nap in the afternoon then go for another swim in the evening. I just absolutely loved it. And then again, not having a knee in my eye at 6.30 in the morning was refreshing.

Robert's imagined life of the professional athlete is unrealistically leisurely, but nevertheless, his pleasure hinges on the (temporary) suspension of ordinary routines in order to centralise swimming and the freedom to focus on the intense bodily work of training. This recalls Wacquant's fantasy of giving up his academic career and becoming a full-time boxer (2004), or McKibben's decision to take a year out to train full time as a cross-country skier: 'a one-year extravaganza, the kind of self-indulgent solipsism that could be justified by someone in training for an Olympic medal but not for someone trying to come third in his age group at the local race' (2010: 1).

For Robert, who had taken holiday from work to join the camp to prepare for an upcoming English Channel swim, the post-swim hours became spaces of recovery and leisure rather than exhausting work hours around which he usually had to fit his training – time to eat a hearty breakfast, sleep, watch bad TV and chat with fellow swimmers. He also enjoyed the (guilty) pleasure of a break from the daily demands and interruptions of his young children; a knowing and temporary suspension of normality that compounded the fantasy of life as an athlete. However unpleasant the early morning or the cold water, then, it is framed within a satisfying narrative of both escape and distinction; the imagined life of the athlete is figured here as an extraordinary life – a rare luxury in a context where leisure ordinarily has to compete with the more mundane demands of work and family life.

These pleasures of escape are the pleasures of privilege. The freedom to escape is contingent on the presence of others to cover caring responsibilities, on employment conditions that allow for paid leave and flexible schedules, and on access to a disposable income that can accommodate such resource-hungry leisure. As discussed further in Chapter 6, it is also profoundly gendered, since for a woman, transferring the care of young children to others in order to pursue a self-directed leisure activity is a socially precarious act that can imperil her status as a good mother in a way that doesn't attach so easily to men (Dilley and Scraton 2010).

But nevertheless, these escape attempts speak to the social privileging of individuality and distinction, and of sport as a key vehicle for achieving that through its displays of individual responsibility, bodily discipline and self-efficacy. The unusual pleasures of the freedom to 'live the life of an athlete', to bear the unusual markings of athletic endeavour in ways that only those inside can fully appreciate or to experience the purposeful 'pain' of socially valorised athletic effort or indeed the longed-for pleasure of a completed marathon swim – all these both facilitate belonging within the social world of marathon swimming and mark out the boundaries of distinction between the swimming and non-swimming worlds (Fusco 2006; Miller 2012).

Novel pleasures

As discussed above, these acts of recoding reconfigure suffering *qua* suffering as a tradable, valued asset, and provide the ground for novel forms of belonging. But as discussed in Chapter 1, we can also see new sensory modes and capacities that are nurtured through immersion (in both senses of the word) that are particular to marathon swimming and only accessible through enduring engagement with the sport and the embodied transformations that it produces. These in turn open up possibilities for novel pleasures that are particular to immersion. This can be seen in this autoethnographic extract from July 2011, which attempts to capture the learned embodied and affective comforts of the water:

> It is midnight, and after a three-hour crossing into rolling five-foot swells, our boat, the *Outrider*, has moored in a dark cove on Santa Catalina Island while we make the final preparations for my swim – a twenty-one mile crossing to the mainland, landing just south of Los Angeles. I am standing on the edge of the boat, my body slick with suncream and with globs of Vaseline smeared in my armpits and costume straps. Seasick from the boat ride over, the mingled odours of marathon swimming – boat diesel, sea salt, cream and grease – trigger another wave of nausea and disorientation. I look down at the inky black water, and suddenly, something on the peripheries of my goggle-restricted vision breaks the surface and slaps quickly back into the water again. The nausea retreats, superseded by a fear-filled rush of adrenalin; my heart pounds, my seasick stomach knots coldly, and the back of my hands, head and neck prick sharply, like the skin is lifting up from the muscle and bone. Even though I accept the crew's reassurances that it was only a flying fish drawn in by the boat's lights, all I can think about – irrationally, disproportionately – is sharks, and I am more viscerally frightened than I can ever remember being before a swim. The crew is waiting for me to jump, and I feel momentarily trapped and full of despair – another wave of nausea from the rocking of the boat and a fresh prickle of fear. I know that I have to go, that for me, being in is always better than being on the water. I count to three under my breath and jump outwards, away from the boat, dropping vertically downwards with my arms pressed to my sides, allowing the momentum of the drop to drive me well below the dark surface. And then there is a moment of familiar, restorative calm; the water stops my descent and I hang still for a few brief seconds, held by the dark, warm sea, and hearing and feeling the bubbles

from my trickling exhalation roll up my face to the surface. My heart is no longer pounding in my ears or my skin crawling with fear. It is thickly quiet after the busy noise of the boat, and the flashing green safety light clipped on to my goggle straps casts a ghostly intermittent glow from behind me. Feeling the buoyancy of the salty water start to push me towards the surface, I reach up with both arms, tilt my hands to feel for the water, and then drive them downwards propelling myself upwards with a stabilising fluttery kick to break the surface and take a deep breath. It all took just a matter of seconds, but finally, I'm ready to start.

At first glance, the familiar rhetorics of (rational) mind over matter offer the beginnings of an explanation for this moment of transformation. I appear to have dominated my fears and bodily disturbances in order to continue the swim, quelling both the nausea of seasickness and my shark paranoia by jumping in. But while this can, perhaps, account for my decision to jump, it has little effective explanatory power for the calm that followed. Instead, and to read this phenomenologically, this can be understood as evidence of the affective, sensory and bodily transformations that are enacted through the process of becoming a marathon swimmer and the novel possibilities for embodied pleasures that these open up.

Writing about adventure climbing, Lewis cites climber Bill Murray, who recounted a post-war return to the sport after a six-year absence:

> At the very instance my hands and feet came on the rock six years rolled away in a flash. The rock was not strange, but familiar. At each move I was taking the right holds at the right time – but no, I did not 'take' the holds – of their own accord they *came* to me. Hand, foot, and eye – nerve and muscle – they were coordinating and my climbing was effortless. (Murray, 1951, cited in Lewis 2000: 75–6, emphasis in original)

Like Murray's return to the rock face, I felt at home in the water – the feel of the water and bubbles on my skin, the sounds, the sensations of the water movement, resistance and buoyancy. The waters off Santa Catalina Island became 'not strange, but familiar', like Murray's rock. Self-evidently, the cooperative qualities of rock, or water, are not innate to those environments (even while inseparable from them). Instead, these two pleasurable moments can be understood not as the outcome of intellectualised technical mastery or overcoming, but rather, as examples of cultivated, contextualised 'corporeal knowing' (Lewis 2000: 71), with the body as the subject rather than the object of knowledge (Merleau-Ponty 1962) and via sensory modes that transcend the 'classic five' (Potter 2008). This is not to write out the mind from swimming experience, but rather, to argue that 'the mind is necessarily embodied and the senses mindful' (Howes 2005: 7). As Howes notes, 'a focus on perceptual life is not a matter of losing our minds but of coming to our senses' (Howes 2005).

In line with the observations of the previous chapter, it is kinaesthetic sensations – jumping, sinking, floating, moving, reaching, propelling – that govern the moment of immersion off Santa Catalina, and provide the comforting familiarity that I experienced (see also, Straughan 2012). The experience of swimming, then, is only one of sensory deprivation (and of overcoming that sensory deficit) if the primary sensations of swimming are those that are dulled by the practice. If, however, swimming is characterised by *heightened* kinaesthesia, then a more positive, sensorially enhanced space opens up.

This sensory transformation is founded upon the transformations described in the previous chapter, but these novel pleasures are more than the sum of their parts, constituting instead a constantly shifting assemblage of experiences and sensations that come to comprise what Nettleton describes in the context of fell running as 'existential capital' – a mode of capital that 'comprises visceral pleasures, corporeal resources and a novel form of sociality' (2013: 209). It is not tradable for other forms of capital that might bring financial rewards or symbolic status (as the pleasures of finishing a marathon swim might) but rather, 'cements the sociality' of the runners (or swimmers). It is experienced by those within the sport as simultaneously inexpressible but communally known and understood, to the exclusion of those outside of the sport who can never really know what swimming feels like. One swimmer I met described it as a 'precious secret' that she carries around with her in her everyday life.

The comfort that I felt on jumping in to the Catalina Channel is a small taste of this existential capital; indeed, the ways in which people enter the water can be read as a potent indicator of belonging. Novice or under-confident swimmers tend to lower themselves into the water gently or hesitate at the shoreline; when they submerge, they surface quickly, snatching breath, holding their heads uncomfortably high above the surface while they get their bearings. Experienced open water swimmers, though, tend to leap or plunge whole-heartedly, lingering in the initial immersion, feeling for the water, exhaling gently before rising to the surface. They are happy to find themselves 'at home'; their bodily disposition exudes comfort and an absence of urgency.

My fieldnotes reflect the constant tension between the desire to articulate and represent these visceral pleasures and their inexpressibility. This next extract is one such attempt – a six-hour swim at the end of the 2010 iteration of the same training camp where Robert was able to revel in the life of the athlete. The swim took the form of one-mile laps around Sandycove Island, supported by volunteers based on one corner of the island who passed us our pre-prepared drinks and snacks as we beached ourselves hourly at their feet:

> The first two hours were nothing but slog. The week of hard swimming had left me tired and vulnerable to the cold; I felt disjointed and awkward in the water, like a wind-up bath toy, and I had already resigned myself to a trudging swim, counting down each lap towards the finish. But into hour three, at last, my body seemed to 'find' the water, whole-bodied now. I relaxed downwards, like someone finally settling into a chair they hadn't trusted to bear their weight. I let myself be held there, suspended between the opposing forces of gravity and buoyancy, between air and sea. Every movement felt smooth and powerful, as if I were sliding on a gentle downhill slope. Imagine a big tub of ice-cream left out in the sun momentarily to soften, and then running a scoop gently down the surface to expose a long, smooth furrow. Swimming felt like travelling, frictionless, down that ice-cream furrow. On the outside of the island, facing out into the Atlantic,

large swells started rolling in, churning up the water when they hit the island's shallows. The more chaotic movement of the waves, combined with the sight of the swaying, drifting ribbons of seaweed on the sea floor, stirred the familiar nausea of seasickness. I moved further out, lengthening the circuit but where the water was too deep to see the weeds, and where the sea had a steadier rhythm into which I could fold myself. It was a clear, sunny day, and the light travelled down through the water in shafts; shoals of tiny fish zipped across my field of vision. I saw the occasional jellyfish suspended a couple of metres below, ghostly beautiful, happily out of reach. The time between feeds gradually collapsed, and for a few brief hours I felt like the best swimmer in the world; like I could swim forever; like the water was all mine.

As explored further in Chapter 6, there is an inescapably gendered element to this experience and my pleasure in it, in both the extraordinary feelings of physical competence and ownership and the seductive pleasures of such extended self-oriented practice. But this also begins to capture the existential capital of marathon swimming – a shared, but elusive, visceral pleasure. One swimmer described it to me as 'a comforting euphoria'; for another, it is 'stretching, reaching, gliding bliss'; it is 'effortless'; like 'flying and running across the surface'. As one US swimmer noted: 'it feels like the feeds are coming every five minutes and time just speeds up. … People assume that the time just drags, but the opposite is true.' Then, tellingly, he paused, struggling to find the words, before appealing to shared experience: 'Well, you must get this too.' Unlike 'finishing' or 'overcoming', these autotelic pleasures have no currency outside of marathon swimming, but are potent markers of distinction within – only fellow insiders are seen as able to appreciate them.

These experiences are often articulated by swimmers themselves through the language of 'the zone' or of 'flow': 'a state of experience where a person, totally absorbed, feels tremendous amounts of exhilaration, control and enjoyment' (Hunter and Csikszentmihalyi 2000: 2). Access to this cultivated merging of action and awareness (Hunter and Csikszentmihalyi 2000: 15) depends on having already acquired the technical skills and sensory capacities to move coordinately and unselfconsciously through a shifting aquatic environment that has already been rendered familiar through training. And while there is nothing inevitable about flow, and it is an outcome of 'feel' rather than 'will' (Game 2001: 8), when it occurs, the rewards are great and constitute a significant incentive to continue in the sport.

Writing in relation to windsurfing, Humberstone argues that flow is too specific a concept in its focus on 'physiological changes and sharpened awareness' (2011: 505) to express the more exhilarating moment of nature-based sport. Instead, she argues that the concept of 'flow' fails to incorporate 'the specific juncture of embodiment, senses, nature and practice-in-nature' (Humberstone 2011: 507). In Howes' terms, it is not sufficiently 'emplaced' to fully capture embodied experience and the 'sensuous interrelationship of mind-body-environment' (2005: 7). Instead, Humberstone proposes grounding those experiences 'in the embodied affective of the practitioner' in order to access the 'spiritual', connective dimensions of those experiences (2011: 505). Among the swimmers, this is commonly expressed through feelings of 'oneness' with the open water, as in this passionate account from San Francisco marathon swimmer, Elizabeth:

> But every time you're out there, it's different, and I feel like ... I know this is a little hokey, but you're very aware that the world is much bigger than you. I live in this incredibly urban city, and then you go out into the bay and it's very clear that there is a natural world right there. And that kind of world of nature is huge. I mean, you just ... the water is really, really big. And it's alive. And so when you swim in a pool, it's like a puddle. Like a dead puddle. And it's good – you can get fitness out of it. But when you go out here, you're stepping into something that's very much alive.

For Elizabeth, and almost every open water swimmer I have ever met (including myself), the 'dead puddle' ('concrete prison', 'chlorine box') is a useful training device, but a poor, utilitarian substitute for 'real' swimming; as Straughan reports in relation to diving, the open water is experienced as 'the antithesis of terrestrial living' (2012: 24). Similarly, distance runner Allen-Collinson, rejects the treadmill as 'a dire last resort', arguing instead that 'my body as part of the elemental world is a fundamental component of my running experience' (2011: 290). This elemental world seeps into my own fieldnotes and swim memories: the texture and movement of the water; biting hail stones; rolling fog; glistening sunshine; the taste of saltwater; the warm sun on my shoulders; the angry honk of a territorial goose; the underwater chink of pebbles being pulled across the sea floor; the sighting by my crew during my Catalina Channel swim of a blue whale – the world's largest mammal – that rolled itself quietly through the water's surface, offering a flash of its tail flukes before disappearing again. The sensory and affective pleasures of swimming, then, are 'environmentally specific, produced in concert with water and the properties of this element' (Straughan 2012: 26). This understanding is at odds with the customary representations of marathon swimming as 'a man and woman against whatever elements God or Mother Nature has decided to challenge you with on a given day' (Zornig 2011a), replacing the rhetorics of 'conquering' with a much more collaborative, emplaced understanding of the relationship between the swimmer and the water (see Figure 7). As English Channel swimmer, David Clarke, told a journalist, 'when I got out of the ocean, stood on the shoreline in France and looked back across the Channel, it did not look defeated to me' (Rodgers 1999).

One of the unique aspects of marathon swimming through which it becomes 'emplaced' is the presence of aquatic wildlife, and aside from the respiratory movements of ebbing and flowing water that render it 'alive' to the swimmer, the open water is literally full of life. Much of this is microscopically invisible to the human eye and most aquatic life keeps sensibly out of sight, the surface splashing, the dark shadow cast by the body and the idling of the engine from an accompanying pilot boat signalling an uncertain threat to be avoided. But swimmers will inevitably have direct encounters with wildlife in ways that can be experienced as intensely pleasurable and exciting, or occasionally as moments of fear or pain.

In the UK, the possibilities for wildlife encounters are relatively limited, with the occasional excited report of a dolphin sighting, a stand-off with an angry swan,

Figure 7 Emplaced swimming in Windermere, UK, 2013.

an encounter with a curious seal, a stinging brush with a jellyfish or a 'fish-slap' from a startled carp. In southern California, however, I encountered wildlife on an altogether different scope and scale, and particularly in the protected wildlife reserve of La Jolla Cove in San Diego. The shores are home to a colony of sea lions, birdlife abounds and the waters are teeming with life that to my British sensibilities was hopelessly exotic. Just metres from the shoreline, scores of bright orange, hand-sized Garibaldi fish live among the weed and rocks in the cove, forming a glorious welcome committee for a visitor more accustomed to the dark, quiet tones of the fish that live in the domesticated, manufactured lakes where I did most of my training at home. Further out into the bay, on my first swim in the cove, a formation of bat rays 'flew' gracefully below me, and I found myself hanging in the water, face down, arms and legs spread for stability, able to do nothing but stare. And then, from my local swimming companion, an invitation: 'Let's go and see the sharks.'

For anyone brought up in the 1970s, as I was, even the mention of sharks triggers the pulsing signature music from the films in the *Jaws* franchise, or perhaps a flash of the 1977 James Bond film, *The Spy Who Loved Me*, in which sharks serve as the executioners for the arch villain, Karl Stromberg. The cinematic memories, the primal fear of being eaten alive and the unseen, shadowy depths of the ocean make the shark metonymic of 'risk' in swimming. I had never seen a shark until this trip, but even so, like everyone, I felt like I 'knew' them and certainly feared them, especially in waters where sharks are known inhabitants. Several marathon swimming locations are home to potentially dangerous shark populations, including southern California, Florida, Hawaii, New Zealand, South Africa and Australia, with a few infamous locations known for seasonal concentrations of Great Whites, such as False Bay in South Africa and the Farallones in northern California (Casey 2010). Various concessions are made to their presence, including the use of devices that repel sharks using electronic pulses, crew acting as dedicated shark spotters and the use of non-standard regulations such as the ten-minute shark break allowed on swims of the Cook Straits (New Zealand). Most swimmers, however, rely on the noise of the boat engines and the unlikely odds of an aggressive encounter to keep them safe. In reality, the objective risk of being taken by a shark while swimming, especially with a boat, is very low, but they still maintain a special place in the swimming imagination as 'the landlord' or 'the man in the grey suit' – gendered and anthropomorphised euphemisms that acknowledge our place as visitors in a domain to which the shark belongs and in which it is an apex predator. But the shark is also a greatly maligned creature; they do not predate purposefully on humans (unlike humans who predate mercilessly on sharks and virtually every other sea creature), and sharks only take a very small number of people each year, usually mistaking them for customary prey such as seals. And nor are all sharks Great Whites, although they continue to dominate the popular imagination of 'the shark' as a result of their life in film.

And so it was that my companion (an experienced local) and I went to 'see the sharks'. Leopard sharks use one part of the bay as a nursery, and after just a few minutes of scanning the sea floor, several metre-long, benign, but distinctly 'sharky' shapes drifted lazily below. A dark, flat stingray hustled along the sea floor, and my friend warned me to keep my feet up, since they lie concealed in the sand and will give a painful sting if accidentally stepped on. It seemed ridiculous to be worrying about the threat from another sea creature whilst watching sharks swim by.

The following day, and out in the bay with a group of regular local swimmers, I felt a distinct 'bump' on my thigh. It was a moment of complete terror; one of the only things I knew about shark behaviour was that they would sometimes 'bump' people to try to work out what they were or as a prelude to a test bite. Bump, bump. The swimming body is, in one sense, constantly both touched by and touching the water, but this produces a sense of flying, of being untouched. Consequently, any unexpected physical contact – for example, with wildlife, or a piece of flotsam or jetsam – is a jarring and sometimes frightening interruption. Awash with floods of adrenalin and my heart pounding, I sat up in the water, looking for my companions, who were pointing and laughing; a juvenile seal, wide-eyed and puppy-faced, popped up in front of me. It flipped away playfully and I ducked underwater to watch as it turned back and we hung vertically below the water, looking at each other. It eventually swooped gracefully away and after some excited laughter, we continued our swim, graceless compared to its effortless flight through the water. Even the most experienced local swimmers, I learned during my stay there, never become jaded by these encounters with aquatic wildlife; no matter how many times they've seen a passing convoy of bat rays or come face to face with a seal, they always stop to watch and social media updates are awash with accounts of sightings and encounters.

Writing about diving, Merchant notes that novices are often disappointed with the aquatic wildlife they encounter (or fail to encounter), since it is more elusive and less plentiful than both nature documentaries and dive school marketing materials would suggest (2011: 223). But while for divers, encounters with wildlife are a key goal of the activity, for marathon swimmers, this contact is far more incidental and unpredictable, constituting one element of the environment within which swimming is 'emplaced' without being the reason (or at least the primary reason) for entering that environment in the first place. These creatures, then, join the assemblage of experiences and sensations that comprise the existential capital of marathon swimming.

Conclusion

This chapter has explored the pleasures of marathon swimming. Some of these are easily imaginable – for example, the joy, excitement and relief of completing a long swim, or the satisfying 'burn' of training that signals progress towards a longer-term goal. But other pleasures are less easily imagined, especially from outside a sport whose dominant self-representation is one of suffering and struggle. These autotelic pleasures – the pleasures of long swimming for its own sake – are the product of an assemblage of environmentally emplaced sensations and encounters that rely upon the cultivated techniques and embodied transformations of the process of becoming a marathon swimmer. These pleasures comprise the 'existential capital' of marathon swimming – the shared, inexpressible pleasures that are treasured as knowable only to those within that social world (Nettleton 2013). This constitutes one means of shoring up the distinction of marathon swimming, but these pleasures are also sought for their own sake, and for many serve as a key motivation for continuing with the sport. This is not to posit a hierarchy of pleasures within the sport. For some, such as Simon and Stephen who I cited earlier, the sought-after pleasures are those of finishing (the 'destination' rather than the 'journey'); for others, it is the euphoric moments of 'flow' or the temporary escape from terrestrial boundaries of mundane existence; and in any one swim, it may be all of these things and more, either simultaneously or episodically. It is this socially acquired assemblage of pleasures, working in complex interaction with suffering and discomfort, that constitutes the pleasures – both expected and unexpected – of marathon swimming.

This aspect of marathon swimming is noticeably absent from the dominant representation of the sport, and this reflects habitual and entrenched ways of thinking about sporting embodiment, where the body is figured as subject to the control and demands of the mind ('20 per cent mental, 80 per cent physical'). This effectively precludes any discussion of pleasure except for that inherent in defying and overcoming suffering in order to triumph. This framing aligns cleanly with the contemporary valorisation of the strong, autonomous individual who is able to exercise control over the body (and by extension, Nature) in order to achieve status-enhancing, capital-accumulating goals.

As an alternative to this constraining mind–body split, I have argued that the swimming body not only undergoes the obvious muscular, cardiovascular and metabolic changes in the course of training, but also changes the way it *feels*. It is this 'shifted sensorium' (Potter 2008) that enables the swimmer to feel 'at home' in an environment to which it does not 'naturally' belong. This focus on the sensory transformations of marathon swimming facilitates a move away from habitual and entrenched ways of thinking about embodiment, although it is also important not to overstate the sensory pleasures and transformative capacities of swimming. Access to them is mediated by material and social constraints, and nor are they necessarily enduring or inevitable. Indeed, while I experienced a calming 'at-homeness' when I jumped into the waters off Santa Catalina Island, this was by no means a cure-all, and within ten minutes of starting the swim, the lingering bodily disturbance of seasickness from the boat-ride got the better of me and I vomited violently and repeatedly. This set off a chain reaction of burning acid reflux and the regurgitation of feeds that lasted for the next seven hours – a condition of bodily dys-appearance (Leder 1990) that precludes a euphoric or spiritual engagement with the water. It is in such moments that the 'kernel of truth' that Leder observes in the mind–body split makes sense (Leder 1990: 107). Indeed, as I struggled with nausea and acid reflux, there was some comfort in bracketing off my body as a problem to be managed, rather than experiencing my failing, rebellious body as integral to my sense of self.

Nevertheless, the focus on the unexpected pleasures of swimming offers an antidote to the reflexive resort to mind-over-matter explanations; it is never the action of one to the exclusion of the other, even if that is what it feels like. The cultivated marathon swimming body, then, is one that has been transformed – physiologically, functionally, sensorially – in ways that cannot be accounted for via a mind–body split. Instead, to appropriate Grosz's metaphor of the 'inverted three-dimensional figure of eight' of the Möbius strip, these swimming pleasures show 'the inflection of mind into body and body into mind, the ways in which, through a kind of twisting or inversion, one side becomes the other' (1994: xii). The suffering body is made 'actively absent' (Aalten, 2007), but like the strip, mind and body are inseparable inflections of each other.

Using Nettleton's (2013) concept of 'existential capital', I have argued that the autotelic pleasures of marathon swimming, although very subdued in outward-facing representations of the sport, are a valued aspect of a collective sense of social belonging and distinction through swimming – a 'precious secret' that only those already inside can fully appreciate and that cannot be articulated easily. Indeed, this inexpressibility in part explains its absence from outward-facing representations. The next chapter maintains this focus on social belonging, but this time in relation to the fervent boundary disputes around what 'counts' as authentic marathon swimming – boundaries that, unlike the inexpressible pleasures of swimming, *have* to be articulated both within and outside of the marathon swimming social world if they are to be made meaningful.

3

Authentic swimming

> We must be loud and our voices must be heard. We cannot let up until our sport is purified and distanced from the sports which cause confusion.
>
> (Zornig 2011b)

Writing about the controversies surrounding 'bolting' in climbing, Lisa Bogardus cites climber and author, Joseph Taylor, who suggests that 'no sport has had an issue that matches climbers' fixation with bolts' (cited in Bogardus 2011: 286). Clearly, neither Bogardus nor Taylor have spent much time with marathon swimmers, among whom debates about what constitutes (il)legitimate assistance are an endless source of debate and contestation that easily match those of the climbing world for their vociferousness. This passion manifests itself most overtly in relation to the use of wetsuits, which have become emblematic of the perceived threat from outside to the presumed purity of 'Channel rules' marathon swimming. Neoprene full-body suits provide performance-enhancing buoyancy and insulation and are standard equipment in mass participation and elite open water swimming as well as triathlon, but for many marathon swimming devotees they diminish the challenge of long open water swimming in ways that pose a fundamental threat to the sport itself. This is reflected, for example, in the relentless jokes at the expense of wetsuited swimmers, or affective displays of disgust if asked to assist in zipping up a wetsuit. While the wetsuit remains a lightning rod for the ire of a community ever ready to defend itself against the perceived threat of dilution and erosion, it is also metonymic of a diffuse constellation of technological, social and practical innovations that threaten to seep through marathon swimming's ineluctably porous definitional boundaries. The attempts to manage the troubled boundaries of 'authentic' marathon swimming in the face of both innovation and cross-fertilisation with other sporting social worlds are the subject of this chapter, providing a platform for exploring the processes of social becoming and belonging that frame the embodied transformations discussed in the previous two chapters.

Social worlds are a 'set of common or joint activities bound together by a network of communications' (Kling and Gerson, cited in Strauss 1984: 123), and they are defined by the production of a 'social object' (Crosset and Beal 1997: 81) – in this case, marathon swimming. These social worlds are not geographically defined, but are formed and maintained through the shared language, practices, channels of communication, values and perspectives that arise from a common interest (Unruh 1980; Crosset and Beal 1997). Three key processes characterise social world formation and maintenance: intersections with other social worlds, segmentation in to sub-worlds, and processes of legitimation and authenticity (Strauss 1982, 1984; Bogardus 2011). Consequently, unlike approaches that focus on subcultures in opposition to the mainstream (Crosset and Beal 1997; Hodkinson 2002), a social worlds perspective focuses on social change; of 'groups emerging, evolving, developing, splintering, disintegrating or pulling themselves together, or parts of them falling away and perhaps coalescing with segments of other groups to form new groups, in opposition, often, to the old' (Strauss 1978: 121).

Marathon swimming fits this model well. It is 'spatially transcendent' (Unruh 1980: 274), even though it also has a number of 'geographical centres' (Unruh 1980: 284) where concentrations of both local and transiting swimmers gather either seasonally, as in Dover harbour, or year-round, as in San Diego's La Jolla Cove or San Francisco's Aquatic Park. Instead of geographical boundaries, contemporary marathon swimming as a social object is coordinated via networks of primarily online communication, including the websites of local marathon swim governing bodies, discussion forums, blogs and other social media. It is through these interactions that the troubled boundaries of marathon swimming are iterated, maintained and resisted within the social world itself, across the slippery boundaries between intersecting social worlds and in relation to mainstream culture. This discursive work is oriented primarily towards narratives of distinction – the marking out of what makes marathon swimming particular – but also towards establishing a hierarchy of social worlds, with marathon swimming at its apex. The rhetorics of purity that characterise much of this boundary talk, as in the epigraph to this chapter, speak directly to this hierarchical vision, positioning marathon swimming as *the* social world against which other forms of open water swimming are measured. It is this status that is perceived as at stake in the management of the troubled boundaries of marathon swimming.

The bodily work of becoming a marathon swimmer, as discussed in the previous two chapters, is inextricable from the production of the social object 'marathon swimming', but significantly, successful swimming accomplishments in themselves do not constitute social world belonging. Indeed, while no one wants to fail at a swim, if everyone succeeds, the currency of success is devalued. Instead, belonging is determined by overt and explicit allegiance to a set of values that circumscribe the act of swimming itself. In their contemporary manifestations, these align strongly with those of the neoliberal present, celebrating moral individualism, autonomy, responsibility and bodily discipline, and are translated into a cluster of practices through which authentic marathon swimming is performatively enacted. This moral-code-in-practice is tradition-oriented but ultimately arbitrarily defined and unstable in its details, and the shoring up of this shifting ground is a key target of the discursive traffic across the marathon swimming networks. However, as I argue in this chapter, the very attempts to sediment that moral-code-in-practice through detailed explication and repetitive citation (to use Judith Butler's (1990) term) provide their own undoing, exposing the arbitrariness and porosity of that which appears momentarily fixed. This catches the marathon swimming social world in a paradox whereby ever-decreasing circles of rationalisation produce and accentuate irrationalities that in turn necessitate further rationalisation. But I want to argue that the impossibility of pinning down a definitive set of rules is not an obstacle to social world belonging any more than is the absence of a record of successful marathon swims; instead, it is demonstrable allegiance to the values that provide the rationale for those rules that 'counts' rather than the purity of the rules themselves.

In making this case, I find myself somewhat at odds with many of my fellow swimmers for whom these debates are profoundly serious and meaningful. While I have always found these discussions to be a fascinating insight into the social world of which I am a part, as well as a manifestation of the intense passion and pride that the sport ignites in and among individuals (including myself), I have never been able to bring myself to feel strongly about them. Indeed, I am uncomfortable with narratives of heroism and purity that I find both exclusive and as overstating the importance of swimming as a voluntary leisure activity. My first impulse, then, is to resist the discourses of heroism that often run through these debates, as well as the inevitable focus on suffering (and the refusal to lessen it), and instead to soften the boundaries of swimming to draw more people towards the sport. My desire has never been to adopt an 'anything goes' approach to marathon swimming which remains a very particular way of engaging with the aquatic environment, but rather, to challenge the hierarchies of accomplishment that this boundary work produces.

But this too is not an innocent position, since I choose to swim by what can be broadly categorised as 'Channel rules' – a position that holds the hierarchy in place, however inadvertently – and I undoubtedly benefit from the work performed by others in confirming and protecting the boundaries of authenticity and the status that attaches to it both within and outside of the swimming community. It is also a reflection of my own considerable social and professional privilege that I can choose to treat marathon swimming as leisure – a position that has some disturbing echoes of the privileged rhetorics of amateurism in the nineteenth and early twentieth centuries (Love 2007b; Bier 2011). This chapter, then, comes with a caveat, with my own cautious partiality unquestionably forming the lens through which I view these debates (as it must with all of the analysis, but which perhaps becomes more evident here because of my disjuncture with the more mainstream view within the community).

This is also the least autoethnographic of all of the chapters, because to see that boundary work in action requires a different kind of data and analytical mode. The chapter, then, draws primarily on textual data gathered from online debates in blogs, discussion forums and other media, supplemented by observational and interview data. I take a discourse analytical approach to the data, treating talk and texts as actions (Potter and Wetherell 1987; Gill 1996, 2000; Wood and Kroger 2000), and asking how language is being used to construct and resist positions in relation to authenticity in swimming. This discursive work illuminates what is at stake in those debates and for whom.

The main body of the chapter begins by introducing two case studies,[1] both from the summer of 2012, which were springboards for vigorous debate not only within the marathon swimming social world but also between that and other intersecting worlds about what constitutes authentic marathon swimming. Drawing on the online discussions that followed these two cases, the analysis sets out what I see as the defining discourses both of the social world of marathon swimming and of authentic belonging to that world. After setting out the case studies, the chapter focuses on two key themes: first, the necessary arbitrariness of the rules; and second, the centrality of 'respect' to the construction of authenticity.

Brittany King

On 8 October 2012, *Shape* magazine published a blog posting as part of its 'Motivation Monday' series under the headline: 'Meet the woman who swam the English Channel' (Nuñez 2012). The blog post tells the story of twenty-nine-year-old Texas veterinarian, Brittany King, who attempted a solo English Channel crossing in September 2012. In question and answer format, King's narrative is one of hard training leading up to the swim, and brutal suffering during the event itself, all framed within the project of raising money for an animal charity. Toward the end of the post, King notes that 'it's okay to adjust your goal if you have to', before explaining that the swim was completed in a wetsuit. An italicised editorial note records that this means that 'her accomplishment hasn't been officially recognized by the Channel Swim Association [sic]' because of the wetsuit use.

On her blog, King (2012) elaborated on the decision to use a wetsuit, explaining that during her training swims in Dover harbour while waiting for a swimmable day, she repeatedly struggled with the cold. She reported that her pilot suggested that she cross in a wetsuit instead, and although she was reluctant to do this, she eventually decided to start the swim without the wetsuit, but to have it with her as an option. At some point during the swim, she put the wetsuit on and completed the swim. She explained:

> I found that sometimes you have to adjust your goal to reach your dreams. I never planned to wear a wetsuit, but I had to face reality that I am not a penguin. My body just couldn't handle the hypothermia. Every person is different. But the end result was still the same.

On 17 January 2013, the Channel Swimming and Piloting Federation (CS&PF) president, Nick Adams, added some corrections into the 'Comments' section of the *Shape* blog, pointing out that King had, in fact, swum under the auspices of the CS&PF rather than the Channel Swimming Association (CSA)[2] and that, in addition to using a wetsuit, she had also used fins – something that was never mentioned in either the *Shape* article or King's personal blog.[3] On 22 January 2013, the *Shape* blog posting was picked up by open water swimming commentator, Steven Munatones in his blog, *Daily News of Open Water Swimming*, under the headline,

'Fit for a king, but not for the Channel community' (2013a). 'What we find surprising,' Munatones argued, 'is that she had a wetsuit on board her escort boat in the first place, especially one that fit her. That is not something that the usual English Channel aspirant does, no matter how honorable their charity channel crossing is.' He concludes: 'There is no shame in calling it a day. But calling for a wetsuit rubs the channel swimming and marathon swimming communities the wrong way, especially when so much publicity is the result.'

Munatones' post found its way onto the discussion forums of the Marathon Swimmers Federation (MSF) under the thread title, 'Who earns the title "Channel swimmer"' (2013a) and fiery debates ensued about what constitutes an authentic claim to the title, responsibilities to charities, publicity-seeking, the media, the regulation of Channel swims and the values of amateurism.

Diana Nyad

On 16 August 2012, sixty-two-year-old US swimmer, Diana Nyad, began her fourth attempt to complete the 103-mile crossing from Cuba to Florida. Her first attempt was in 1978 using a shark cage – a feat subsequently completed by twenty-two-year-old Australian swimmer, Susan Maroney in 1997. Nyad returned to the swim in the summer of 2011, when two separate attempts, both without the drafting advantage of a shark cage, failed as a result of difficult conditions, her relatively slow swim speed, injury and painful jellyfish stings. Nyad's 2012 training and the actual attempt, promoted via her Xtreme Dream brand, was the subject of considerable press attention as well as being extensively reported and promoted on her website and other social media. The ambitious swim was a hugely expensive operation – the *New York Times* estimated a cost of $500,000 for the attempt in July 2011 (Alvarez 2011). In response, Nyad signed up commercial sponsors, raised funds through public speaking events, and visitors to the site were invited to 'support the dream' by direct donation or by purchasing Xtreme Dream branded goods such as T-shirts, jerseys, caps and wrist bands.

The marathon swimming community watched rather uneasily as the Xtreme Dream operation gained momentum. The publicity and commercialisation sat uneasily with many, as did the growing entourage of up to sixty support crew, but at the same time, the audacity of the venture was captivating. Watching and waiting for the swim to begin, and especially following Penny Palfrey's unsuccessful attempt at the same swim at the end of June 2012 (Palfrey 2012), several technological innovations became the focus of intense debate: a 'necklace' device designed to drip warm water down the neck and chest during feed breaks; a full body 'stinger suit' to protect against the dangerous jellyfish that rise to the surface at night; and an underwater directional streamer, trailed from a pole attached to the pilot boat, to keep the swimmer on the most efficient line.[4] These innovations triggered debates both on Nyad's blog, where supporters of Nyad clashed with marathon swimmers in the 'comments' below the relevant blog posts, and on marathon swimming discussion forums and blogs about the nature and boundaries of (non-)assistance in marathon swimming and the benefits of local versus global swim standards and governance (MSF 2012a, 2012b). These debates reached a much more furious pitch during the swim itself; first, when news footage showed Nyad holding on to the pilot boat during a feed (a move that would end an English Channel swim); and, second, when it became clear that she had exited the water during a fierce storm and then resumed the swim once the storm had passed. These debates continued to rage after the swim, which Nyad was unable to complete, particularly in relation to a perceived lack of clarity about the length of time spent out of the water mid-swim because of the storm, and an unexplained post hoc revision of the total time spent in the water (Nyad 2012a).

In the summer of 2013, Nyad made her fifth attempt at the swim, walking triumphantly up the beach in Florida over fifty hours after jumping into Cuban waters. Given the events of the previous year, many marathon swimmers raised questions about the conduct of the swim, leading both to the longest and most commented on thread (MSF 2013b) in the forum's history and an unprecedented engagement with the mass media demanding answers from Nyad and her team about key details of the swim that many felt were unclear. Comprehensive answers were unforthcoming and the moment passed leaving Nyad and her brand largely untarnished and the marathon swimming community frustrated.

The arbitrariness of rules

As described in the Introduction, the social world of marathon swimming is governed by a broad allegiance to 'Channel rules', with some localised exceptions; the outcome of swims is measured and recorded against this set of rules under the surveillance of an appointed independent observer. While the professional marathon swimming racing circuit is governed by international regulations under the Fédération Internationale de Natation (FINA), there is no national or international rule-making or governing body for solo marathon swims, with most established swims working to locally-declared regulations.

In January 2014, a small collective of experienced marathon swimmers and organisers under the auspices of the MSF (2014a) launched a set of rules that were intended as a globally applicable resource primarily aimed at those attempting new swims for which no local governance exists. But the MSF is not a governing or accrediting body, and while the new rules have some authority through collective community consent, marathon swimming still has none of the overarching national or international rule-books of professional competition of other more mainstream sports such as cricket or football (soccer). As such, as with traditional climbing (Bogardus 2011), compliance with rules for specific swims is largely voluntary, with the obvious exceptions of those points where the governance of swims intersects with national and international laws around maritime safety or immigration. It is for this reason that it is perfectly possible, as in the case of Britanny King and a growing number of others, to complete a swim using a wetsuit or other aids. Local governing bodies would not recognise the swim (or it might be acknowledged with a special 'wetsuit' annotation), but it would not be an illegal act. As such, the rules take the form of an evolving ethics and style-based moral code against which the 'ability, courage and character' of swimmers (or climbers, for Bogardus) are presumed measurable (Borgardus 2011: 288). This voluntary moral code – and it must be voluntary for the moral accomplishment to attach to the individual – is the axis upon which debates around the slippery boundaries of authentic swimming turn.

One of the defining features of marathon swimming as a social world is its tradition-oriented nature. Unlike many alternative or lifestyle sports, for which innovation and creativity are integral (Wheaton 2004a), one of the cornerstones of marathon swimming identity is the idea of consistency over time. This sentiment is embodied in the figure of Captain Matthew Webb. Both the CSA and the CS&PF explicitly cite Webb's swim as the historical and ideological pioneer of English Channel swimming:

> The swimmer Capt Webb is the original pioneer who inspires successful and aspiring Channel swimmers to this day. (CS&PF n.d.)
>
> The Sport of Channel Swimming traces its origins to the latter part of the 19th century, when Captain Matthew Webb made the first observed and unassisted swim across the Strait of Dover swimming from England to France in 21 hours and 45 minutes. (CSA n.d.)

The discursive mobilisation of Webb as the reference point for the sport's boundaries of authenticity is a common strategy in attempts to distinguish the social world of 'Channel rules' marathon swimming from other forms of open water and long-distance swimming. US swimmer, blogger and co-founder of the MSF, Evan Morrison, made this case explicitly, positing 'the tradition' as the first of three traits that make marathon swimming unique:

> The tradition. The knowledge that when we enter the water to begin a long swim, we're using the same simple technology (textile suit, cap, goggles) as those who came before us, as far back as the 19th century. What other sports can boast as level a playing field over time? (Morrison 2011)[5]

Strauss argues that when sub-worlds split off from parent social worlds, the process often involves the rewriting of the prevailing social world history by discounting some aspects of the past or toppling the acknowledged 'founding fathers' in favour of 'real' alternatives that fit the sub-world's narrative and 'operational ideologies' (1984: 129). However, in the case of marathon swimming, the authentication of the sport is achieved not via an alternative history, but the retrenchment of a history that is perceived as under threat of being forgotten.

But it is also important to note that the origin story of Webb setting the technological boundaries of marathon swimming is a strategically partial one, representing an ideological rather than literal allegiance to the past. In particular, the Channel rules of 'textile suit, cap and goggles' are commonly cited as a direct inheritance from Webb's trail-blazing 1875 swim, when in fact, he wore neither cap nor goggles. Furthermore, even within the bounds of 'textile suit, cap and goggles' there have been significant permitted technological developments in materials and designs that have undoubtedly changed the experience of marathon no detrimental effect; and indeed, many land-locked marathon swimmers like myself have benefitted from the burgeoning triathlon industry, which has led to the opening up of new training locations in lakes and reservoirs across the country. Furthermore, many marathon swimmers also compete in wetsuit swims and triathlons, moving between social (sub-)worlds rather than holding a rigid allegiance to one. Instead, this is a clash of *social values* – a far more intractable form of contestation that cannot be resolved through negotiation over resource use or 'zoning' strategies (Carothers *et al.* 2001), and which is much harder to pin down through regulation.

Significantly, these fiercely contested debates around social values, while absolutely central to the social (sub-)world of marathon swimming are invisible to those outside of that social world. As such, those debates are internally definitional, but externally are largely irrelevant (Strauss 1982: 189; see also, Kiewa 2001). Consequently, while debates within marathon swimming, and particularly within dedicated discussion forums that have purposefully cohered around 'traditional' values, might focus on delineating between acceptable and unacceptable innovations and practices, debates between those inside and outside the social world of marathon swimming are more fundamentally about whether regulation is necessary at all.

The language of 'assistance' in marathon swimming opens up a further space for these conceptual miscommunications between insiders and outsiders, as well as providing discursive weaponry for insider debates about permissible technologies. In relation to Nyad's 2013 swim, for example, many marathon swimmers continued to insist that her claimed successful crossing was an assisted swim primarily because of her use of a stinger suit and face mask, in contrast to 'non-assisted' Channel rules swimming. Opponents to this view pounced on the rhetoric of non-assistance, highlighting the use by 'Channel rules' swimmers of obviously assistive technologies such as GPS navigational systems, technical nutritional products, modern suit fabrics that are a far cry from the waterlogged woollen suits of the early marathon swimmers, leak-proof, anti-fog goggles and so on. This highlights the inevitably arbitrary nature of the traditional rules in terms of which technologies require regulation, but also the very specific use of the term '(non-)assisted', which opens up a further gulf of (mis)understanding between insiders and outsiders in the debates.

The invisibility of the debates around technological innovations and wetsuits in marathon swimming to outsiders to those debates is evident in the public comments responding to the stories of both Brittany King and Diana Nyad, particularly in their clashes with marathon swimming insiders. For example, on the *Daily News of Open Water Swimming* blog about Brittany King, a reader left a lengthy comment attacking the blog's author, Steven Munatones, for summoning up wrongdoing where none existed:

> This appears to simply be an athlete entering the waters off the coast of England, swimming stroke after stroke for 13+ hours, to complete a fund-raising commitment. Now, perhaps the captain of the pilot boat will come forward and assert that the athlete water-skied behind the boat, or sat in a small dinghy tethered

to the pilot boat ... Absent a captain's assertion, it remains highly unlikely that any of the pets who may receive life-saving support from the charity will give a rat's ass if their salvation came gift-wrapped in a wetsuit. (Reader comment on Munatones 2013a)

The 'purist' position here is rendered the domain of an unrepresentative handful of miserly, pedantic killjoys who take themselves and their sport too seriously, although it is important to note here that the author of the comments also draws a line of acceptability, albeit hyperbolically; water-skiing behind the pilot boat or being towed behind it in a dinghy would be a step too far, signalling a fraudulent claim to have swum rather than a swim under disputed conditions. The debate around swimming authenticity, then, becomes one of who can and cannot call themselves a 'swimmer', as illustrated uncompromisingly (and purposefully provocatively) by Scott Zornig, in his role as president of the Santa Barbara Channel Swimming Association (SBCSA) and author of two newsletters on the theme of 'What's wrong with marathon swimming?'. Arguing emphatically against the equivalence of wetsuit and non-wetsuit swimming, he declared:

> My single, simple request is please do not label [a wetsuit swim] a 'marathon or endurance swim' because it falls into a completely different category which the word 'swim' has no part of. (Zornig 2011b)

Kiewa (2002: 156) found the same linguistic territorialism among traditional climbers. As one of her interviewees protested:

> If you –
> Brag of your climbs
> Publicize your climbs
> Prefer new routes over quality routes
> Prefer higher grades over quality routes
> Climb in poorer style than the first ascent
> Bring the climb down to your level
> Call the climbs by numbers
> Make any monetary gains via the cliffs
> You're not a climber!

In the face of the ambiguity posed by technological and practical innovations, both swimmers and climbers have to turn to ideology to demonstrate commitment (Bogardus 2011). In both cases, this is a reactive response to perceived threats from less traditionally defined modes of the sports.

There is nothing new about this process of retrenchment. For example, the formation of the CSA in 1927 was motivated in part by a similar desire to hold back a perceived tide of value erosion in the sport:

> Means are now being discussed by several men interested in swimming to prevent this fine achievement of swimming the Channel from being ruined by the artificial means and lack of investigation, and to ensure that the course from England to France shall be the accepted one. It has been decided to form an Association, namely the 'Channel Swimming Association' to draw up a code of rules governing Channel swimming. (CSA n.d.)

While the foundation of the CSA was prompted by the absence of standardising rules for the relatively nascent sport of English Channel swimming, the contemporary retrenchments are strongly oriented towards the relatively new sports of triathlon and mass participation open water swimming, both of which are common routes into more traditional marathon swimming (and to which many either return or continue to participate in alongside marathon swimming). In short, Zornig's case is for 'marathon swimming' to be the unmarked category – *the* social world – from which others are offshoots. These different iterations of open water swimming can never be moral equivalents for Zornig (and those taking a 'purist' position in these debates). The rules may be arbitrary, but avowed allegiance to them (and the values they have come to represent) are a central element of marathon swimming belonging.

It is also important to note, however, that social worlds are defined by change, and within marathon swimming, there are significant ongoing divisions and retrenchments regarding legitimacy and authority. Specifically within English Channel swimming, this has taken the form of an enduring dispute between the CSA and the CS&PF, which was formed following a break away from the CSA in 1999.[6] As a result of these disputes, the CSA refuses to recognise English Channel swims completed under the auspices of the CS&PF as authentic, insisting upon its historical status as the only legitimate arbiter of authentic Channel swimming. There is also some tension between the specifically English Channel swimming community and the community that identifies with marathon swimming more broadly. These tensions emerged particularly in relation to the Marathon Swimmers Federation global rules, which were perceived by some as a failure to recognise the sufficiency of traditional 'Channel rules' and their definitional and historically proven status and utility within the sport. These debates highlight not simply a hierarchy between tradition-oriented swimming and its contemporary, non-traditional counterparts, but also rumbling hierarchical disputes within marathon swimming, with authenticity constituting a key axis through which belonging and in-group expertise and authority are discursively produced, negotiated and contested.

Respect

Key to the processes of rationalisation within the social world of marathon swimming addressed in the previous section is the question of 'respect' – for the sea, for the enormity of the task and for those who have come before. This mirrors the world of traditional climbing – something which one of the ardent traditional climbers in Bogardus' study makes explicit in his rejection of sports climbers:

> It's like socialization of the crags; everybody wants to be able to climb every route. Well, unfortunately that's not the way humans are made. Some people are better at it than others. Now if I can risk my ass to go lead a route that may be poorly protected … and somebody else can't meet that standard, then … they shouldn't suddenly drag it down to their standards and insult the risk I put into it. It doesn't matter whether [they] damage the rock, insult the first ascent party, insult the

whole climbing tradition of the area, they don't care. There are people like that. They're immoral. (2011: 298)

The 'immorality' of those climbers who 'insult' the traditions and first ascenders is replicated in swimming through the discursive mobilisation of swimming 'heroes' (Hargreaves 2000) – the ideological (and idealised) counterpoints of the 'villains' who are seen as trying to diminish the challenge to fit their own (lesser) capacities. This fits the contemporary competitive ethos, where hierarchies of accomplishment are seen as essential spurs to action and advancement, rather than inequalities to be erased. As already discussed, Matthew Webb is a commonly cited figure in this context, but each year a cohort of contemporary swimmers fulfil this 'heroic' discursive role, acting as ideological touchstones for honourable swimming. This might include noble failures who stayed within Channel rules even if it meant not completing a swim; failures followed by hard-earned successes (showing patience and hard work); those achieving notable firsts; and those who have achieved record-breaking numbers of crossings, often over decades. To complete a swim in a lesser style is to disrespect the sport's heroes, and it is for this reason that Zornig provocatively proposes the terms 'swimming exhibitions' or 'adventures' for wetsuit and other assisted swims: 'This way, people can still receive some credit for their endeavours, yet it stops them from raining on the parade of true marathon swimming accomplishments' (2011b).

One of the key discursive strategies for establishing and maintaining the status of 'real' swimming is the invocation of Everest. One of the most commonly repeated 'facts' about swimming is that more people have climbed Everest than have swum the English Channel. The fact is an effective shorthand for emphasising the challenge of English Channel swimming in particular, and by extension, marathon swimming; in short, if Everest is the pinnacle of climbing achievement, then how much harder must the English Channel be for fewer people to have completed it over a much longer time period? In many ways, the comparison is illegitimate. The number of completed climbs/swims actually tells us very little about the popularity of particular endurance challenges at given points in time, the success or failure rates, or relative difficulty or risk. Indeed, while more people have climbed Everest than swum the Channel, significantly more have died trying to do so.

The mobilisation of Everest gains its discursive force symbolically rather than literally, particularly in relation to establishing what many see as the uniqueness of marathon swimming challenges. As US marathon swimmer, Phillip, argues:

> I think swimmers are somewhat unique because when we are swimming, we are in a whole different medium. Climbers are still on land. They may be on ice, but they are still climbing. They are still humans out there in the world. We immerse ourselves in an entirely different medium where we are not in control of anything except putting one arm in front of the other and breathing and taking feeds when we are told to.

Even while trying to demarcate a hierarchy between climbing and swimming, Phillip's description of the hard monotony of swimming echoes accounts of high mountain climbing, with its demands for determined, repetitive trudging and the climber's vulnerability to the elements (Mitchell 1983; Tullis 1986; Ortner 1999; Alvarez 2003; Tabor 2007; Davis 2012). Nevertheless, Everest is particularly useful here as a status-establishing comparison. Both Everest and the English Channel share a historically-established iconic status both within and outside of their own respective social worlds, even though they are not necessarily the most difficult or dangerous within their individual fields. As such, they have high levels of public recognition and are therefore discursively potent as an intelligible shorthand for narratives of challenge and overcoming; the hierarchical comparison with Everest makes an effective outward-facing claim.

However, Everest is also mobilised repeatedly within the marathon swimming social world as a cautionary tale – the example of what could happen to swimming if it is corrupted by consumerism and the erosion of traditional values in the interests of getting more people to the finish. As a leading figure in one of the governing organisations for English Channel swimming told me:

> The difference between Channel swimming and Everest is that they start you off at 17,000 feet and you've only got to do the last 10,000. Whereas in Channel swimming, they start you off on the very edge and we still require you to complete it with no water beyond and with no help. So you don't get a whole pile of sherpas taking your food with you.

The figure of the sherpas was also mobilised in the MSF discussions about Brittany King's swim. As one commentator remarked:

> 'Susie Smith climbs Everest!': they don't say that she paid $75,000 for a private climb and had 10 personal sherpas dragging her – literally – up the mountain. (MSF 2013a)

The Everest comparison here is particularly pertinent, given that King herself cites the 'fact' about more people having climbed Everest than swum the Channel in her own publicity before her swim and in the subsequent *Shape* article.

But if Everest is useful as an intelligible comparator for establishing the status of marathon swimming, the English Channel has an untouchable status as *the* swim – what one swimmer described in an interview as 'the most hallowed waterway'. In particular, nothing is more likely to raise the hackles of the marathon swimming community than to claim that a swim is equivalent to, or superior to, the English Channel without first having a successful Channel swim under your belt. For example, in 2009, US swimmer Kyle Taylor trained in Dover from the beginning of May. He struggled hard to cope with the cold, posting entertainingly graphic shivering videos and documenting his struggles on his blog. When the time came for his swim, he posted that poor conditions had made it impossible and that with his family having to return home and too short of funds to wait for a later slot, he had decided to abandon his Channel swim and set himself the alternative challenge of a twenty-five mile swim up and down Dover harbour instead. At the end of the report on his nine-hour swim, Taylor concluded: 'I think we may have invented a new swimming challenge – the Dover

Authentic swimming

Open-Water Marathon: Further than the Channel, 3000 times cheaper, just as cold' (2009). Other Channel swimmers and members of the volunteer beach training crew in Dover responded angrily at the comparison, highlighting the stark differences between conditions in the harbour and being out at sea, as well as the much longer distances covered during most Channel swims due to the movement of the tides. Attention also focused on his wetsuit-style 'shortie' swim suit, which would not be 'legal' under 'Channel rules'. Like King, his narrative was one of adapting to the conditions in order to achieve a higher fund-raising goal – in this case, raising a considerable amount of money for a young child who had lost his legs to meningitis:

> You must adjust to circumstances beyond your control.
> You can't live every day in fear of what others might think.
> There is more than one way to do something.

From the perspective of traditional Channel rules swimming's claims to authenticity, it is here that the faultlines open up – the clash between many ways and one way; from this view, equivalence with an 'authentic' English Channel swim cannot be achieved simply through matching single elements of the challenge. The same resentment was expressed towards Nyad in the claim posted online during her 2012 swim that she had already covered the distance of three English Channel swims; the discussion forums bristled with resentment, with many highlighting that Nyad has never swum the English Channel successfully (and therefore, was not entitled to make the comparison). The rhetoric of equivalence is only available to those who have successfully completed the swim; anything else is treated as disrespectful.

One further axis through which respectful adherence to the social values of 'real' marathon swimming is enacted, and which is also revisited in Chapter 5 in relation to charitable fund-raising, is through attitudes towards publicity-seeking, and especially that which is deemed to either overstate individual accomplishment or to misrepresent the sport to the outside world. This accusation was levelled at Nyad and King (and especially Nyad), both of whom enjoyed high levels of media exposure around their swims. In the case of King, one commentator observed:

> I can only speak for myself. It isn't the wetsuit and fins that make this so irritating, but rather the self-promotion with the skewing of facts where there were so many more deserving swimmers with amazing feats of courage who followed the rules. (MSF 2013a)

> So basically, she wanted the acclaim and publicity of someone who had swum the English Channel ... but in the end, was unwilling to put in the training and preparation necessary to, y'know, actually swim the English Channel. (Reader comment in Munatones 2013a)

The combination of non-traditional swimming and active publicity seeking is especially provocative for the marathon swimming community, since it effectively positions the assisted swim as superior – more newsworthy – than traditional swims that are lauded within the community but go largely unnoticed outside of it. This, in turn, raises accusations that they are in it for the 'wrong' reasons, seeking publicity and self-aggrandisement rather than the 'purer' innate satisfactions of the sport. As CS&PF president, Nick Adams, wrote in his 2014 annual report of the previous year's English Channel swimming season: 'Swim to swim. Don't swim to shine' (Adams 2014)– a warning against what the same report describes as the emergence of the 'ego swimmer'. A similar distinction emerged in Allen's (2011) study of young performing arts students' attitudes towards fame and celebrity, where fame and material rewards lacked the legitimacy of peer respect for hard work and talent. Indeed, one of the accusations fired at King (and other unrepentant wetsuit swimmers) is that she had been unwilling to put in the bodily work of becoming a marathon swimmer, particularly in relation to cold acclimatisation, while still wanting the status that a successful swim is understood to bestow. This reflects the privileging of work in the process of becoming a marathon swimmer, as discussed in Chapter 1.

The issue is never simply one of disrespect, but also of perceived active harm to the community through the dissemination of misleading information about what marathon swimming is. As Zornig argued: 'Once the media gets a hold of an erroneous story, the misinformation is on the Internet or in print forever, which takes away from the previous and future swimmers who legitimately complete the same swim' (2011a). The outward-facing representation of marathon swimming, then, takes on a pedagogical function – a means of teaching those outside of marathon swimming the authentic version of the sport, both by exposing inauthentic claims and by the promotion of the endeavours of the sport's heroes as a counter-narrative. This produces a disciplinary framework whereby wetsuit (and other non-traditional) swimmers can be accepted within the marathon swimming fold on the condition that they 'confess' the wetsuit use publicly and correct any media misunderstandings. In August 2013, for example, a female swimmer in the US completed a successful wetsuit crossing of Lake Tahoe – a challenging twenty-one mile, high altitude swim. One of her coaches posted a brief report about her swim on the MSF (2013c), noting approvingly that she had 'made [an] effort to explain to those following her and the media the difference in her wetsuit swim and a marathon swim'. Another member of the forum described her efforts at 'keeping the record straight' as 'exemplary'. Particularly since the furore around Nyad's Cuba–Florida swims, the overt performance of transparency itself, rather than simply practical allegiance to the rules, has become an increasingly important condition of belonging.

There is, however, a tension here between the identification of marathon swimming as distinct and beyond the comprehension of those outside of that social world, and as a mode of swimming about which the wider world needs to be educated. This compounds the paradox identified earlier in the chapter, whereby the social world of marathon swimming is positioned as an escape from rationalised modernity whilst being caught up in ever-decreasing circles of rationalisation within that social world. However, for all the irrationality of this rationality (Ritzer 2004; Monaghan 2007b), the circle is effectively squared by an appeal not to specific practices, but to the values that are deemed to underpin those practices. In this sense, the inevitable arbitrariness of the rules gives way to the more central convictions that there should be rules, that those rules should never be oriented towards lessening the challenge and that the overt performance of allegiance to those rules is central to social world belonging. As Kiewa argues in relation to traditional climbers: '[they] set themselves strict rules, which, although they appear arbitrary, afford them the opportunity to engage with an environment over which they deliberately exerted little control' (2001: 368). Consequently, while the purity that Scott Zornig aspires to in the chapter's epigraph is an impossibility and can never constitute self-evidently objective grounds for belonging that makes unmediated sense to those outside of that social world, the overt aspiration to purity continues to function as social capital for those seeking recognition within the community.

Conclusion

In Chapter 2, I described the value attributed to the inexpressible, but shared, pleasures of marathon swimming as one aspect of belonging within the social world of marathon swimming. This forms one element of the assemblage of pleasures, in interaction with suffering, that accounts for the compelling nature of marathon swimming to many of its practitioners. While this 'existential capital' is recognised but difficult to articulate, this chapter has focused on a different aspect of belonging – this time, one that demands articulation: the constitution of authentic marathon swimming. I have argued that the ongoing boundary work of defining and authorising marathon swimming is both an inward- and outward-facing task that attempts to shore up the boundaries of legitimate marathon swimming and distinguish it from related and intersecting (sub-)worlds.

Through this boundary work, marathon swimming is conceptualisd as a stripped-down encounter between the individual and 'nature', outside of the softening trappings of modernity. Following on from this, (some) technologies are positioned as assistive in ways that are deemed to be a threat to the 'purity' of the sport by lessening the challenge and blurring the boundaries between marathon swimming and other open water swimming sub-worlds. These boundaries, however, are inescapably arbitrary, and attempts to escape the rationalisations of modernity through marathon swimming simultaneously drive the increased rationalisation of marathon swimming itself in order to preserve its distinction. However, the precise drawing of these inevitably arbitrary boundaries emerges as much less important than overt allegiance to the values that provide the rationale for that boundary work. In particular, I have highlighted the central role of respect and hierarchies of accomplishment in the construction of authentic marathon swimming, alongside hard work and humility.

In making this case, I am aware that I have offered a rather polarised account of the boundary work of marathon swimming. This risks caricaturing the most strongly held positions for demonstrative effect whilst understating both the many expressions of ambivalence that also mark these discussions, and the high levels of volunteerism and community contribution that many of those holding 'purist' views demonstrate. By taking a discourse analytic approach to these debates, and by exploring how the different cases are made, I have shown that the work of becoming a marathon swimmer is never only about the embodied transformations discussed in the preceding chapters, or a completed swim, but also about the overt performance of a set of values.

But even while marathon swimming self-defines strongly via resistance towards modernity and its presumed softening comforts and technological shortcuts, as the next chapter goes on to discuss, some technologies remain in high demand, with marathon swimmers appearing as eager adopters (and adapters). This is particularly true of biosensor technologies that are able to track movement through time and aquatic spaces. Both these technological artefacts and the data they produce are consumed greedily within the marathon swimming social world, and are central to the production of 'marathon swimming' as an object of consumption in its own right, rendering the intangible act of swimming both materially and symbolically 'real'. These acts of consumption are the focus of this next chapter, adding a final dimension to the work of 'becoming' in marathon swimming.

Notes

1 Both swims were firmly within the public domain prior to the discussions that followed, and my goal is not to pass judgement but rather to use them as a springboard for considering the fervent discussions that followed online. It is in these discussions that we can see the production of the marathon swimming social world in process.
2 English Channel swimming has two governing bodies: the Channel Swimming Association (CSA) and the Channel Swimming and Piloting Federation (CS&PF).
3 Unfortunately, the reader comments are no longer available to view on the *Shape* website.
4 Unfortunately, the blog posts introducing these devices have since been deleted from Nyad's website and are no longer accessible. A small number of posts from this period were retrieved from web archives, but not the full record.
5 Morrison also identified the unpredictability of the elements and the possibility of failure, regardless of preparation, as the other two defining features.
6 There is nothing to be gained from revisiting these rather bitter disputes; indeed, several of the key players told me in interviews that they looked forward to a future, perhaps when themselves and others were no longer actively involved, when the two organisations could come together more productively. My point here, then, is not to arbitrate between the two or align myself with one or other, but rather to highlight the ongoing disputes over whose legitimising voice has authority within the social world.

4

Making it count

June 2013

It is 7 a.m. on a morning in early June; 'air temp twelve degrees, feels like ten', according to the Met Office app on my phone. I am standing on the lake's edge, skin prickling with the morning chill and finding it hard to make the move into the water. I don't know the water temperature and don't have a thermometer – a deliberate choice to circumvent the inevitable horse-trading I'll do with myself: 'if it's X degrees I'll do Y minutes, but if it's Z degrees, I'll do…'. But a wetsuited triathlete beside me kneels forwards and drops a digital thermometer into the shallow water; he pauses to let the device calibrate then looks at the small screen and huffs dejectedly before showing it to his friend, who responds with an emphatic, 'Fuck'. I can't help myself and ask: 'What is it?' 'Thirteen,' he says, before asking incredulously, 'You're not going in like that, are you?' I laugh and determined to avoid a display of reluctance in front of these athletic men, I kick off my rubber shoes and wade purposefully into the water, pausing when it's up to my knees to scroll my watch to its 'stopwatch' setting. I take several strides further in until I am up to my belly button. This is the threshold – past the belly button, and you are more in than out and you have to go; before then, there's still some possibility of withdrawal.

I take a couple of breaths and pull my goggles down off my forehead, giving the inside of the lenses a quick lick with my tongue to stop them fogging before settling them in place. I look up to sight for the first buoy to head for, and then reach round with my right hand to the back of my head, where a compact GPS unit sits, tethered to my head by my goggle straps. I wobble it slightly between forefinger and thumb to check it's secure and then push the button at the bottom with my thumb to start it. It doesn't buzz or bleep, so I have to trust that it has started the work of measuring my movement around the lake, connecting with satellites in orbit around the earth to plot my location. No time to waste; if I hesitate now, the first 100 m of the swim will be recorded as hopelessly slow – a galling blip in the bar charts I will download onto my computer when I get home. I lower my right hand and quickly push the start button on my watch with my left index finger. The watch chirps and I break the water in a dolphin dive, surfacing to take the first strokes and exhaling against the cold rush of immersion before sighting forward again to the buoy to check navigation.

Two hours later, I swim back into the shallows, reaching once again behind my head to stop the GPS unit; I hold the button down firmly with cold-clumsy fingers and then stop my watch, struggling to hit the smaller button with my uncooperative fingers. When I get home, I plug the GPS unit into my laptop and download the data before logging on to a website that invites me to upload my swim onto my 'dashboard'. The upload complete, I am offered a summary screen of total time, distance and average 100 m pace, as well as bar charts giving times for each kilometre covered, and then further broken down into 100 m intervals. There's also a satellite map with a white line marking my looping swim route around the lake. I scour the data, and note that I went out too quickly, dropping off the pace in the second hour; there's a huge kink in one of the circuits as I strayed wildly off route before veering sharply back in the right direction. I type a second note – that I am still drifting off to the right when I lose concentration. I take a screen shot of the satellite map and post it on the 'Did You Swim Today?' Facebook group. I look at my diary and plan a training session when I will use a swim metronome – a small device that beeps at regular, predetermined intervals – to work on keeping a steadier pace.

July 2014

In our new house, we have a room dedicated to reading – two large reclining armchairs, a sofa, a log burning stove, thick curtains and packed bookcases. It's my favourite room, replete with the peaceful promise of long winter evenings in front of the fire, book in hand. On one wall is a framed picture – a map of Jersey with a thick black hand-drawn line that runs around its circumference marking the track of my swim around the island in 2009. The island itself is loosely rectangular, pitted with knobbly outcrops and swooping bays; it looks like the island of treasure maps in children's books, as if you might see pirate ships and sea monsters if you looked carefully enough. There is an overlay of deep green around the chart, surrounded by a slim, burnished silver frame. It is a quiet, soft-coloured image that suits the calm of the reading room. It's aesthetically pleasing and a visible reminder of my first marathon swim; the finishing time of ten hours and thirty-seven minutes is written into a panel in the corner of the chart along with the date and the signatures of the boat pilot and the president of the Jersey Long Distance Swimming Club. I have since accumulated several other swim charts – Jersey to France, the English Channel, the Catalina Channel – but the Round Jersey chart remains one of my favourite possessions, taking pride of place in all three of the homes I've lived in since then. It is, at once, a conversation piece and a beautiful object, evoking the visceral recollection of everything that I love about marathon swimming and marking a significant moment in my swimming biography.

September 2014

It is the first day of my new job and I am nervous; full of the insecurities of new beginnings and desperate to impress. I slip a discreet pendant on a leather cord around my neck and fasten the silver clasp. It is a small chunky silver circle about the size of a one pence piece, with a cutout curling wave inside. I bought it in La Jolla in San Diego when I was doing fieldwork for the swimming project; it was my treat to myself for completing the Catalina Channel the week before, but it has come to stand for all swimming and its manifold pleasures. I wear it a lot, but especially when I feel under-confident, recalling the sensations of power and coordination, of rhythmic movement and the musicality of water. I find myself rubbing it lightly between finger and thumb when I'm nervous, feeling the curve of the wave and imagining the comforting pleasures of swimming.

Marathon swimming has a 'realness' problem. Unlike hunting for mushrooms (Fine 1998) or stitching a quilt (Stalp 2007), a swimmer has nothing tangible to show for the hard work of a long swim (or the many months of training leading up to it). Swims, like all sporting activities, are happenings, not objects. But this ephemerality is especially marked in a sport like marathon swimming because of the fact that almost no one witnesses it directly. In common with other nature-based endurance sports such as mountaineering (Ortner 1999; Bayers 2003; Davis 2012) and fell running (Askwith 2013), the long slow journey of the marathon swimmer takes place across inaccessible and sometimes hostile spaces that generally preclude incidental or leisurely spectatorship. Furthermore, outside of the question of access lies the inescapable reality that, even if marathon swimming were easily accessible to spectators, they probably wouldn't want to watch for more than a brief, curious interlude in any case. Aside from the start and the finish, which have some entertainment potential, very little of note happens for hours at a stretch; there really isn't very much to see. The lack of potential for spectacle is compounded by the relative invisibility of the swimming body itself, largely immersed and out of sight, with even the face barely visible under goggles and cap. More spatially and temporally contained sports offer the adrenalin rush of a closely fought race, as well as the direct encounter by spectators with bodies in action as muscles and sinews strain and faces reveal the agonies and joys of the tight finish or the grinding discomforts of fatigue. This opportunity for spectators to forge an affective connection with the athletes is lost in marathon swimming, which lacks the drama of visible speed or physical and emotional duress. In short, it is a terrible spectator sport.

This invisibility gives distinction to marathon swimming, since the challenge of stepping out of customary locational bounds and the unpredictable unboundedness of time during a long swim both constitute defining features of the sport. However, the lack of spectacle (and therefore, spectatorship) brings its own challenges in terms of making a long swim 'real', both to the self and others. I can tell you that I swam the English Channel, but the sea bears no mark of me having passed through it and the act itself was witnessed directly by only five people, three of whom were paid either directly (the pilot and co-pilot) or indirectly (the official observer) by me to be there, and two (my support crew, Sam and Peter) who were drawn into the adventure through the bonds of friendship and intimate partnership, respectively. Marathon swimming, then, has a 'realness' problem, and a life event such as an English Channel swim is at once of enormous personal significance to the swimmer and yet virtually traceless.

This invisibility has two key consequences in terms of the 'realness' of marathon swims. First, it opens up the possibility for doubt about whether a swim happened at all (and under what conditions); and second, it leaves the swimmer without a material outcome from months or even years of hard training, or a single long day of enduring effort. This chapter explores this tension between the simultaneous ephemerality of swimming and its embodied and symbolic 'realness' for the swimmer, and investigates the multiple ways in which material and virtual artefacts are produced and mobilised to make swimming count and render it consumable. The chapter highlights three key functions of these artefacts, around which the chapter is structured: (1) as material evidence for the ratification of swims; (2) as training tools; and (3) as 'evocative objects' (Turkle 2007a), which signal the affective and social realm of marathon swimming. These render the social object of marathon swimming tangible, highlighting and facilitating marathon swimming as a form of consumption through which the entrepreneurial self is produced and sustained. I argue that, in spite of the deep suspicions held within marathon swimming about the corrupting potential of technology in relation to the integrity and spirit of the sport, the everyday practice of marathon swimming is highly (if selectively) technologised, and in particular, that material technologies of measurement, quantification and tracking, and their outputs, are integral both to social world belonging and the consumption of marathon swimming. This technological ambivalence is negotiated via prescriptive and proscriptive social world norms of data gathering, processing and sharing, with users positioning themselves as discriminating and restrained users of technology, rather than its slavish consumers. This highlights marathon swimming as a tradition-oriented practice, but with a profoundly contemporary inflection.

Bearing witness

Perhaps the most obvious hazard that attaches to an endeavour such as a marathon swim that occurs largely out of easy sight is the possibility of fraudulent claims. There is a long history of either exposed frauds or fervently contested claims in the worlds of expedition and exploration. In his engaging account of expedition hoaxes, Roberts (2001) concludes with some tentative efforts to identify the defining characteristics of the accused hoaxers. Unsatisfied by overly psychologised explanations, he highlights instead the fact that, in all of the cases he examines, the perpetrators 'all wanted the genuine achievement very badly' (Roberts 2001: 213). He cites the case of Robert Peary, whose discredited claim to have reached the North Pole in 1909 was preceded by seven Arctic expeditions, including the loss of several toes due to frostbite (Roberts 2001: 212). These hoaxes, then, according to Roberts, are 'last-ditch improvisations in the face of failure' rather than cynical and premeditated frauds; 'only when the goal was recognized to be unattainable did these men scrounge about and patch together the illusory data to support their hoaxes' (Roberts 2001: 213). Nor are they extravagant conspiracies involving multiple players, but instead, rather desperate, solitary affairs (Roberts 2001: 214).

The world of sport, too, has a sturdy roster of cheats and frauds. In 1980, for example, Rosie Ruiz's victory in the Boston Marathon was famously denounced as fraudulent, having missed out large portions of the course; and in 1999, Sergio Motsoeneng's ninth place in the fifty-four mile Comrades Marathon in South Africa was discredited when it was revealed that he and his brother had shared the running by switching places during toilet breaks (Bryant 2005: Ch. 18). Unlike the expedition frauds discussed by Roberts, these have a different quality, demonstrating considerable pre-meditation in order to circumvent the race monitoring 'chip' systems, check-in points and photographic evidence that would otherwise expose the claim. But they also operate on a much smaller scale. While many of the explorers discussed by Roberts had their sights set on 'firsts' that would have brought national and international prestige, a place in the history books and, in many cases, personal wealth, a marathon imposter would, at best, gain a small prize and perhaps fifteen minutes of fame. While there are significant, if precarious, pecuniary gains to be made from organised frauds within professional sports (see, for example, Walsh 2013), the gains to be made from these fraudulent amateur performances are oriented towards enhancing identity and social status, shoring up the good citizenship of the individual through (apparent) displays of bodily discipline and entrepreneurial selfhood. It is only in a social context where overt performances of amateur sporting accomplishment are lauded as exemplary that fraudulent claims of this kind make sense.

Unsurprisingly, marathon swimming too has its own scattering of claims which are either exposed frauds or subject to question. Perhaps the most (in)famous of these is Dorothy Logan's 1927 English Channel swim. Recorded at a record-breaking time of thirteen hours and eighteen minutes, the swim earned her $5,000 from the *News of the World*, but she soon recanted, confessing that she had only swum for a total of four hours, travelling the remainder of the distance on the boat (*Miami News* 1927). She subsequently claimed that her deception had been carried out in order to demonstrate the lack of regulating oversight in Channel swimming and its vulnerability to fraud. Whatever her motives, Roberts had a point about the lack of independent observation; as discussed in the previous chapter, the formation of the Channel Swimming Association earlier that year was a response intended to 'prevent this fine achievement of swimming the channel from being ruined by the artificial means and lack of investigation' (CSA n.d.). Logan's swim also had a collateral impact on another pioneering female swimmer, Mercedes Gleitze, who on 7 October 1927, became the third woman, and first British woman, to swim the English Channel, collapsing at the end of a hard, cold, late season swim in a time of fifteen hours and fifteen minutes. Four days later, Logan 'completed' her record-breaking swim, with her subsequent confession casting suspicion on Gleitze's swim. Two weeks after her first swim, Gleitze embarked on what became known as her 'vindication swim', which was ultimately unsuccessful but which took place under such arduous conditions that, following the signing of declarations by both Gleitze and her trainer about the veracity of her original claims, the Channel Swimming Association eventually ratified her crossing (Davies 2015: 246–250).

Turning to the more recent past, outright frauds in sites such as the English Channel have become increasingly unlikely. The English Channel is a heavily policed international border that also incorporates two of the busiest shipping lanes in the world. Consequently, all boat traffic in the Channel is carefully monitored and swims under the auspices of both the CSA and the CS&PF have to be registered in advance and are subject to extensive coastguard and border controls. While this doesn't prevent someone from making an outward-facing claim to have swum the Channel without even setting sail or getting wet, the publically available records kept by both organisations provide an easy means of checking those presented back for review in bar charts and graphs, breaking the swim down into 1 km and then 100 m chunks. This generates a degree of granularity that a notebook and pencil can never achieve. This points to a further dimension of the newness of these self-quantification practices; that is, the software predetermines the data that will be collected (Whitson 2013). This means that all of the individual data uploaded to a given website can be aggregated to provide a collective picture that in turn can be used to inform future marketing strategies or sold on to health researchers and policy makers. This highlights the ways in which self-tracking data 'is digitized, quantified, accumulated and analysed in order to generate commercially valuable data on the population', whilst simultaneously categorising the user-production of that data as 'not work' and therefore not requiring payment (Till 2014: 458). These most individualistic-feeling projects of self-development, then, are inextricably linked to global businesses and communication networks, as well as macro-level policy making. My recently purchased GPS watch, for example, uploads to the Movescount website,[3] which offers me the option 'to make my Moves really count' by making each of my recorded exercise events ('Moves') available to health researchers. But this predetermined collection also performs a pedagogic function, generating new compulsions for particular pieces of information. It is only when I have automatic access to precise data about how many seconds it takes to cover each 100 m during a long swim that that becomes a necessary and intelligible measure of my success or progress in training. In short, GPS and other self-tracking technologies are domesticated in wearable form through the cultivation of the desire for what they can provide (Lupton 2013b; Till 2014).

Aside from the obvious goal of improvement through measurement, self-quantification in marathon swimming performs two key functions in relation to the 'realness' problem: first, it offers a sense of progress and control over a long training cycle; and second, it produces belonging via the ability to share data, both in real time and *post hoc*, although neither of these are guaranteed:

> Jason walked stiffly out of the lake at the end of his customary eight laps of the 750 m loop. He raised his goggles onto his forehead and looked immediately down at the chunky GPS watch on his right wrist, pushing the stop button and scanning the small screen for the summary data for the swim. 'Bollocks!' he cursed emphatically. The watch screen was blank; the device had clearly run out of power during the swim. His plan was to download the data on to the device's dedicated website, inching up his totals for the season. He was aiming for a million metres in the calendar year; a prelude to an English Channel swim the following year. 'Dammit,' he moaned, 'now it won't count.' (Fieldnotes, July 2013)

A long swim is unforgiving of insufficient training, while at the same time, there is no definitive judgement on how much is sufficient. In the absence of quantitative certainty, the ongoing measurement, recording and documenting of swims can function as a reassuring reminder of consistency or improvement. One female prospective English Channel swimmer told me that when she was feeling full of doubt, she would scroll through her uploaded swims to remind herself that she was training hard; the maps and graphs made the training retrospectively tangible. Conversely, undocumented swims, like Jason's watch failure, are literally uncountable in the website's metrics, marking a fundamental shift in what 'counts' as legitimate exercise within the rubrics of digital self-tracking and 'an epistemological change in how exercise is understood' (Till 2014: 458). Tracking, then, makes the intangible tangible, although always via particular (and exclusive) digitised algorithms and displays.

This process of tracking and recording has the potential to introduce a playful element into the training process, providing an additional incentive to train and a welcome distraction from the constant demands of a hard and sometimes monotonous training schedule. Whitson describes this as 'gamification', applying 'playful frames to non-play spaces, leveraging surveillance to evoke behaviour change' (2013: 164). Digital devices are perfectly suited to this introduction of playfulness, enabling goal-setting and offering up celebratory rewards when goals are reached in the form of announcements, digital trophies, medals and so on. Even without digitised inputs, swimmers engage in a wide range of playfully competitive interactions with each other around the quantification of swimming: the most metres swum in a year, the most laps of a particular swim course and so on. But as Whitson (2013) notes, what the digitisation of the games adds is the possibility of global play. With the 'rules' already determined by the devices and software through the standardisation of what data is collected and how it is presented, play can occur between unseen rivals or groups of rivals. For example, Jason, whose watch failure I described earlier, was not simply hoping to accumulate a million metres, but was also taking part in a competition between a globally dispersed group of male swimmers, most of whom had never met, to see who would meet the million metre mark first – that is, a million metres accumulated on the website for the device which they all shared. Those are the only metres that count. These technologies, then, can make training more playful and less like work (Lupton 2013a, 2013b; Whitson 2013; Till 2014), simultaneously shoring up allegiances to particular devices and platforms, demonstrating responsibility through self-management, and fulfilling the promise of projects of neoliberal governance 'to make daily practices more fulfilling and fun' (Whitson 2013: 171).

This points to the second key function of self-quantification in swimming: the production of social belonging through the sharing of data in ways that not only mark individual successes but also membership of a community of shared values and practices (Whitson 2013). The live GPS tracks of long swims illustrate this perfectly, highlighting the social and game-like potential of the technology. GPS navigational technology is now standard equipment for marine traffic, capable of giving detailed information on location, speed, trajectory and so on, and the locations of vessels can be visualised online via dedicated marine websites. The same technology has been domesticated in handheld devices such as Spot systems,[4] which receive signals from the GPS satellite system and communicate them via commercial satellites and ground antennas to communication networks. These tracks can then be visualised on smartphones, tablets and computers in real time, providing interested others with the opportunity to 'see' the swim as it happens.

Social media is a key element in this novel, digitally mediated collective spectatorship. Links are circulated prior to swims, and, like many swimmers, I store these in my devices so that I can check in periodically during the day to see how swims are progressing, snatching peeks during work or waking up in the night to check. As discussed in the previous section, the tracks on their own offer useful but limited information about the lived experience of the swim, so this information is commonly supplemented with a live Twitter feed (or similar). Platforms like Twitter, which can be updated quickly via SMS text updates, are well suited to this purpose, enabling short newsflashes that give context and texture to the two-dimensional icon inching across the tracking 'sea', enhancing the spectator experience. Remote supporters can also text and tweet messages to the crew that can be shouted to the swimmer at feeds or written on whiteboards, creating a communal encounter, however digitally mediated, which mitigates the 'realness' problem and fosters a sense of community and belonging as swimmers are willed to finish. When I asked swimmers about the GPS tracks during the research, it was always this social, community aspect of tracking that came to the fore, rather than the authenticating function of the data. Live tracking, then, is a mode of technologically mediated affective relation, with the tracks bringing together a collective of globally dispersed swimmers not through discourse or representation, but through what Wetherell (2012) calls 'the push of the body' – the compulsion to keep checking, the concern for their safety as the hours of swimming draw out, the rush of pleasure at a successful finish or the sinking disappointment of the interrupted track of a terminated swim.

But it's also important to note the limitations of these digital quantifications of the swimming body and these novel modes of collective spectatorship. The first of these is the illusory nature of the sense of control that these technologies and their data produce. This has been well-documented within the domain of health, for example, where uncertain choices unfold out of screening data that purports to provide answers and point to solutions (Rapp 1999; Dumit 2012). Similarly, while the data from the various training devices appears to offer reassurance and a sense of control over the lengthy training process, in reality, it can tell you very little about what is going to happen on the day, since neither the body nor the environment is predictable. As Mol notes in relation to blood sugar monitoring, 'however much you count, your body cannot be counted on' (2009: 1757). And technologies too are not infallible; they malfunction, run out of batteries and lose the satellite signals, or, more prosaically, are subject to user error as stiff, cold fingers fumble for delicate buttons or a swimmer forgets to start, stop or charge the device. As Mol observes, 'technology is never quite tamed' (Mol 2009). Consequently, although many swimmers (including myself) have invested both financially and affectively in a variety of biosensor and tracking devices to support my training, they can never quite deliver what we might hope from them.

An example of this can be found in a relatively novel technology that has just started to enter marathon swimming from other sporting domains such as American football, as well as from the space programme (where it originates), the military and fire fighting: the ingestible thermometer pill. This is a body monitoring system that incorporates a crystal sensor that vibrates at a frequency relative to the body's internal temperature. This generates a signal that can be detected by a data recorder passed close to the body. The pill passes through the digestive system over a period of twenty-four to thirty-six hours, and is a considerable advance on earlier telemetric devices such as rectally inserted 'pills' or, in the case of some of the earlier research on cold water swimming and as Cox (2006: Ch. 11) describes from her own experiences as a human research subject, rectal probes connected by wires to recording instruments. The primary orientation of the pill is safety, offering, potentially at least, a way of seeing what cannot otherwise be seen and known in situations where timely warnings of unsafe core body temperature can be a matter of life and death.[5]

Like many biosensors, the ingestible thermometer is a developing and migrating technology and many technical problems still remain, particularly involving the real-time transmission and reading of data (Byrne and Lim 2007). Furthermore, as discussed above, bodies cannot always be counted on, and the body's systems and idiosyncrasies don't always cooperate. For example, one female UK swimmer used an ingestible thermometer during a challenging swim around an island off the Scottish coast. The device was part of a scientific research project, but unfortunately, a rise in adrenalin before the start of the swim caused the device to pass too quickly through the body. She noted wryly afterwards, 'that was a very expensive pre-swim poo!' (personal communication).

But aside from technical and practical difficulties, even when the device successfully transmits precise and usable data, in the context of swimming, it is not clear what that data means. Swim observers and safety crews conventionally base their assessments of swimmers' well-being on their observable state via indicators of demeanour, consistency of stroke rate, body position in the water and cognitive awareness. However, these signs of cold are often indistinguishable from the inevitable and generally less precipitously dangerous fatigue that occurs towards the end of a long swim. Consequently, crews may make a premature decision to terminate a swim, or more seriously, make the fateful decision not to. In theory, an ingestible thermometer pill should circumvent the problem of subjective judgement, but the work of identifying reliable indicators is confounded by idiosyncratic embodied responses by swimmers to cold. The swim organisation Solo Swims of Ontario (SSO) has started to use ingestible thermometers with the goal of generating data that in the longer term will contribute to swimmer safety – for example, by establishing thresholds, or patterns of temperature decline,[6] which indicate the need to stop a swim because of dangerous levels of cold (personal communication). The SSO researchers experimenting with the thermometer pills found that, in some cases, swimmers report being excessively cold and exhibit signs of hypothermia whilst still retaining a relatively 'safe' core body temperature.[7] However, others were able to continue swimming with good cognitive performance through falling core temperatures all the way into a state of semi-consciousness. This reflects the profoundly idiosyncratic response to cold; for example, some very cold water swimmers such as Lewis Pugh (2010b) or Lynne Cox (2006) have extraordinary physiological responses to cold, enabling them to endure temperatures that would have dangerous consequences for others. Just as Body Mass Index (BMI), for example, tells us very little about individual health status (Gard and Wright 2005; Jutel 2006; Monaghan 2007a), core body temperature does not straightforwardly speak its own truth, but rather, constitutes one part of a constellation of indicators upon which termination decisions can be based.

A second important limitation is that, in spite of the techno-optimism that surrounds self-quantification and the significant expectations that have been placed on the shoulders of these technologies for the cultivation of self-discipline, health and well-being, there is also considerable resistance to their use. At the most basic level, for many – and particularly for women, who tend to have narrower wrists – the bulk necessary to accommodate the GPS receiver renders wrist-worn devices simply too large to be usable over long periods without injury. For others, the devices constitute an unwelcome distraction, and an unnecessary layer of complication. For example, one participant in the research described GPS watches as 'expensive gimmicks for people with too much money', and as I hovered on the shore of my local lake struggling to prepare my GPS device because the bright sunshine was obscuring the screen, another said laughingly, 'You could have swum a bloody lap while you've been faffing around with that.' But there are also more ideological objections at work in the resistance to these technologies. For example, for some, these devices push at the boundaries of authentic marathon swimming, constituting a dangerous de-skilling, leading swimmers to rely on digital outputs rather than hard-acquired personal knowledge about the emplaced body and its capacities.

The paradoxical embrace and repudiation of technology that is evident in relation to these devices reflects a tension between the positive associations of normative masculinity with technological aptitude and comfort, and the suspicion within marathon swimming (as a site defined by masculine norms) regarding the potentially polluting effects of technology. This tension is resolved through discourses of control and autonomy: the authentic marathon swimmer is able to make *judicious* and *appropriate* use of those technologies without succumbing to seductive consumerist compulsions that render the swimmer indiscriminately reliant on the technology. This underpins much of the derogation of the triathlete, whose high-tech, equipment-heavy sport is commonly caricatured as a form of feminised hyper-consumption. As one male marathon swimmer observed: 'They're too easily distracted by shiny things.'

But beyond the relative minority of what might be considered the 'refusers' of these technologies, and outside of concerns about authenticity, even the most loyal users and eager early adopters are selective about when they use the devices, drawing distinctions between swimming as training, and swimming that has a leisurely or strongly social orientation. Writing about a hospital-run walking scheme for older people, Copelton (2010) observed that, even though members of the group were given pedometers when they joined, they all resisted their use because they were unwilling to introduce competition and hierarchy to an activity that was valued primarily for its sociality. In this sense, we can say that the walkers resisted the 'gamification' that Whitson (2013) describes. In a similar vein, my fieldnotes are punctuated with days when I abandoned all quantification to enjoy a beautiful day,

Making it count

or allow myself a relaxing recovery swim outside of the training regimen. 'Today, I just swam. I don't know how far, how fast or for how long. It was glorious,' reads a note for July 2010 during the tense and exhausting run-up to my English Channel swim. Quantification does not simply expose or reveal 'facts' about the swimming body and its movements, but fundamentally changes the nature of the activity itself.

Significantly, while I encountered resistance to these tracking devices in relation to practicality, authenticity and their potential to distract or de-skill swimmers, there was little concern about the ways in which the data itself was used by the corporations onto whose servers it was uploaded. The voluntary nature of the engagement with those technologies is central to this disregard for their unpaid labour and the extraction by corporatations of commercial value from that data (Till 2014). As Whitson argues, 'the fact that these are tools of consumer monitoring devices run by corporations that create neoliberal, responsibilized subjectivities becomes less salient to the user because of this freedom to quit the game at any time' (2013: 173). Instead, in exchange for their participation, users receive the commodification of their activities through the maps, graphs and other visualisations of the data, as well as through virtual medals and awards; a sense of control over their bodies and training; the satisfaction of social belonging; and the playful pleasures of 'gamification'. In short, the commercial appropriation of the data is not achieved through coercive or domineering acquisition, or sinister surveillance mechanisms, but through the development of devices and software that make collecting and sharing that data make sense for the wider project of entrepreneurial selfhood in which a given group of users such as marathon swimmers are collectively engaged (Lupton 2013b).

'There's no marching band...'

This final section explores a third dimension to the management of the 'realness' problem of marathon swimming: the production of memorial objects that retrospectively invoke both particular swims and marathon swimming in general. This highlights the role of marathon swimming as a form of consumable experience that is materially rendered in order to say something meaningful about the self.

As I have already discussed in the introduction to this chapter, marathon swimming leaves few tangible signs of itself *post hoc*. Furthermore, the minority nature of the sport and its lack of spectator appeal mean that aside from celebrations with friends and family, and perhaps some local media coverage, the international news headlines and ticker tape parades that Matthew Webb and Gertrude Ederle experienced are a thing of the past. As David, an English Channel swimmer from San Francisco noted, this relative absence of material reward or recognition is a defining feature of the sport:

> There's nothing rewarding about swimming the Channel, *per se*, other than self satisfaction. You know.... I also had to be very comfortable with that going in to it – there's no marching band, there's nothing but a pat on the back and that little piece of paper.

Consequently, many swimmers choose to memorialise their swims via testimonial objects that implicitly or explicitly evoke a long swim. We can think of these as what Turkle describes as 'evocative objects' (2007a). In the introduction to her edited collection of accounts of 'things that matter', Turkle (2007b: 59) argues that we are accustomed to thinking about objects 'as useful or aesthetic, as necessities or vain indulgences'. But we are less familiar when considering 'objects as companions to our emotional lives or as provocations to thought' (Turkle 2007b). She encourages readers to make these connections across a diverse range of objects, focusing 'not on the object's instrumental power ... but on the object as a companion in life experience' (Turkle 2007b: 66). These objects, Turkle suggests in her conclusion to the collection, 'function to bring society within the self' (2007a: 2420), facilitating a traffic that crosses between the outside world and the inner self in a fluctuating series of border crossings – between human and non-human, born and created (Turkle 2007b: 2592). In living with these objects, she concludes, 'we will need to tell ourselves different stories' (Turkle 2007b).

Marathon swimming is replete with evocative objects, 'things we think with'. These objects take diverse forms: pebbles gathered from the final shore; clothing embroidered with swim times and locations; car number plates; tattoos; photos and videos; jewellery; and swim charts, framed and displayed. Particularly the swim charts intersect strongly with the quantification practices discussed in the previous sections. These charts can be hand-drawn onto marine charts, imposed onto digital satellite maps and charts or even snatched as screen grabs from the live feed. As with my treasured chart of my Round Jersey swim, these are often framed and displayed in homes and offices; digital screen shots of swim tracks appear as social media avatars and mobile device screen savers. These evocative objects serve as evidence of intangible experience and the qualities those experiences have come to represent. These testimonial artefacts, as emblematic of marathon swimming, function as 'lifestyle markers' that demonstrate 'one's ability to cut it in a dangerous and uncertain world' (Palmer 2004: 67).

These displays are far removed from the authentication and ratification functions of the tracks, evoking the affective dimensions of marathon swimming – pride, excitement, fear, relief. One female swimmer – a survivor of a violent relationship – told me that her English Channel swim chart represented the strength and independence that she had needed (long before her swim) to escape years of being undermined and abused. Another female swimmer told me proudly that her Catalina Channel swim chart was a constant reminder that it was okay to do something for herself sometimes amidst her onerous caring responsibilities. These are profoundly gendered stories, but ones that signal the boundary crossings that Turkle observes, bringing society into the self, but simultaneously learning to tell different stories.

Contributors to Turkle's (2007a) edited collection describe how some objects become inseparable from the body: a laptop computer, a blood sugar testing device. In the case of swimming, this is most apparent in the form of swim tattoos – a permanent embodiment of swimming accomplishments that is intended to outlive the always potentially transient physiological transformations of swimming. Tattoos, like all forms of body modification, are oriented towards saying something meaningful about the self (Atkinson 2002; Fisher 2002; Pitts 2003; Orend and Gagne 2009), each with their own narrative and biography (Davis 1995; Pitts 2003; Pitts-Taylor 2007). In the case of swim tattoos, the swims themselves offer the primary plot for these narratives, but often against a lengthy biographical backstory into which a long swim fits. For example, a female swimmer celebrated her breast cancer survival and subsequent arduous two-way English Channel swim in 2013 by having the digitised track of her swim – a beautifully symmetrical double-helix – tattooed onto her foot. When I asked her about the tattoo, she replied: 'When I see it, it reminds me of my grit and determination to succeed and just how tough but rewarding the journey was. It gives me hope and continues to make me believe in my dreams and trust me I still have lots to fulfil!' (personal communication). These evocative objects, then, make not just the fact of a swim 'real', but also affirm the values and qualities that are seen as necessary to make that swim possible.

Conclusion

In this chapter, I have argued that marathon swimming has a 'realness' problem, which is resolved through the mobilisation of material and virtual artefacts that make swimming 'count' and render it consumable. These mobilisations include the use of tracking and other documentary technologies to verify not only that swims took place, but also the style in which they were conducted; the use of biosensors and self-tracking devices to both enhance progress through training and facilitate social belonging through 'gamification' (Whitson 2013); and finally, the production of objects that are simultaneously testimonial to, and evocative of, the experience of marathon swimming. These technologies are mobilised both to shore up distinction (both within and outside of marathon swimming) and to produce social belonging – a strategic appropriation that highlights the ways in which marathon swimming, while tradition-oriented, has a strongly contemporary inflection.

The relationship within the marathon swimming social world to technology is paradoxically defined by both suspicion and embrace. In particular, the widely available GPS technologies for tracking the movement of the body through aquatic spaces have been appropriated enthusiastically for evidentiary, motivational and memorial purposes, while nascent technologies providing real-time navigational inputs or auditory feedback directly to the swimmer during swims are resisted. This paradox is negotiated via discourses of rationality and control, extracting useful value from those technologies within the bounds of allegiance to tradition-oriented rules, and without succumbing to the lure of 'shiny things'. Nevertheless, users are inextricably caught in a consumerist nexus, not only through the production of data from which surplus value is extracted by corporations, but also through the centrality of information and communication technologies to the construction of contemporary marathon swimming.

While (some) technologies can be understood as central to marathon swimming subjectivity, the analysis here also constitutes pause for thought for the study of self-tracking and quantification more generally. While this is undoubtedly a growing trend, it is neither ubiquitous nor unrelenting. Instead, this chapter demonstrates that, for all the belonging and collectivity that these technologies produce, and all the technological optimism that underlies the current rush of self-tracking and biosensor technologies both within and outside of sport, relations with those technologies remain ambivalent and episodic – even among a cohort such as this who have a prodigious appetite for data, the resources to acquire these devices and a practical comfort with technology. It is important, then, not to overstate either the ubiquity of these devices nor their disciplinary nature. Furthermore, those technologies are imbricated not only in the generation of positive, pleasurable and shared collective experiences of celebration and excitement, but are also inextricable from the shaming and exclusions that also constitute those same spaces and practices. These technologies and their data, then, do not simply need to be contextualised, but also need to be seen as part of that context, inextricable from the normative values and privileged positions that determine what makes counting count.

Notes

1 Roberts (2001: 218) also acknowledges the possibility of 'mirror image' cases: 'What hoaxes worked perfectly, fooled everybody?'
2 Following the uncertainty surrounding Diana Nyad's 2013 swim, the MSF has prioritised publicly available, comprehensive swim documentation. The website contains some excellent examples of this in practice (http://marathonswimmers.org/swims/).
3 http://www.movescount.com.
4 http://www.findmespot.eu/en/.
5 See, for example, the CorTemp® ingestible thermometer system, produced by HQInc. (http://www.hqinc.net/cortemp-sensor-2/).
6 For example, in Ice Mile swims, where participants aim to swim a mile in water at less than 5°C, the effect of cold on the body will follow different patterns from swimming for many hours in water at 15°C.
7 Hypothermia occurs when the body's core temperature falls below 35°C. If the temperature continues to fall, it will lead to heart failure and death. However, there are a small number of cases of individuals recovering, with extensive medical support, from very low body temperatures (including cardiac arrest) due to the potentially preservative effects of cold on the vital organs (see Fong 2010).

II
The good body

5

Who are you swimming for?

When I told people back in 2010 that I was swimming the English Channel that summer, one of the most common responses was to ask: 'Who are you swimming for?', or even just the declarative statement, 'I'll sponsor you'. When I said that I wasn't doing it for charity, responses ranged from surprise to disbelief to overt disappointment in me: 'You really should', 'You might as well'. Others simply handed me money anyway (which I returned with thanks, asking them to donate to a charity of their choosing). I had actively chosen not to 'swim for...' for a combination of reasons: I didn't want the extra pressure on the swim; it felt like an unnecessary complication for a swim that was already bound up in a research project; and I was uncomfortable with the trading of status-bearing displays of physicality for money. But my reasons are less significant in the context of this chapter than the fact that I have to have reasons; indeed, I have been back and forth about whether to even put forward my reasons in this chapter since to do so feels like a justification for something I'm not sure requires justification. This, then, provides the starting point for the chapter – not so much the act of swimming for charity, but rather, why it's so hard not to. How can we understand the normative congealing of the relationship between charitable fund-raising and marathon swimming? What social and identity processes and relationships are enacted (and resisted) through the practice of 'swimming for...', and to what effects?

The phenomenon of the 'charity challenge' is now a thoroughly ingrained part of contemporary neoliberal society. Perhaps the most high profile examples can be found in charity spectacles such as Live Aid or Comic Relief, where compassion is mobilised as entertainment (Tester 2001, cited in Moore 2008: 39). Mass-participation urban marathons are another popular site of charitable fund-raising, awash with charity-branded clothing and banners (Nettleton and Hardey 2006), and block-bought guaranteed entries sold on to runners by charities in exchange for four-figure fund-raising pledges (see also, Snelgrove and Wood 2010; Coghlan 2012). Another growing dimension to the 'charity challenge' is adventure philanthropy (Lyons and Willott 1999; Stanhope 2005), where individuals engage in adventurous activities such as trekking, sky-diving or long distance cycling in exchange for donations to a charitable cause. Coghlan and Filo describe this as an extension of the charity sporting event, with both 'requiring a registered participant to raise funds and complete physical activity, with proceeds benefitting a designated charity' (2013: 123). Volunteer tourism constitutes a further related dimension to these charitable practices, where individuals travel overseas to work as volunteers on charitable projects (Vrasti 2013; Mostafanezhad 2014; Snee 2014). The charity sporting 'thon' (Moore 2008), adventure philanthropy and volunteer tourism are most commonly orchestrated either via dedicated businesses, commercial organisations that have successfully aligned themselves with charitable fund-raising or by charities themselves, often in close concert with commercial sponsors (King 2001, 2006; Moore 2008). However, there is also a booming trend in independent charity challenges, often involving significant endurance endeavours such as cross-continent cycle or running challenges, or lengthy ocean crossings in kayaks or rowing boats. These frequently involve a significant investment of time and resources both before and during the challenge and a publicity strategy to raise funds to support the costs of the adventure as well as to raise charitable funds (Stanhope 2005).

As a charitable venture, marathon swimming falls somewhere between these different manifestations of the charity challenge. It is not a mass participation sport, and while the activity itself is externally organised and regulated, this is not done primarily with charitable fund-raising in mind. For example, neither the CS&PF nor CSA websites host fund-raising pages or offer fund-raising advice. Nor have charities themselves identified marathon swimming as a rich fund-raising source. This reflects the relatively small numbers of swimmers, the sport's low profile, the expense of undertaking a swim of that scale when weighed against the possible gains, and the lack of spectacle inherent to the sport (as discussed in the previous chapter).[1] But regardless of its lack of institutional connection with specific charities (as, for example, with Race for the Cure and Race for Life and their connection with breast cancer (Klawiter 1999; King 2001, 2006)), or with charity in general, in the popular imagination, marathon swimming and charitable fund-raising are intimately (and normatively) connected.

The main body of this chapter begins with a brief discussion of the social and cultural context within which charitable swimming has come to make normative sense, and then, drawing primarily on interview data, I explore the ways in which the marathon swimmers I met negotiated the concept of 'swimming for...'. The first section explores the ways in which, for some swimmers, not 'swimming for...' was simply unthinkable. The second section, following Titmuss' (1971) work on blood donation explores charitable swimming as an exchange, and the third section addresses the alliances of suffering that are constructed through fund-raising websites in order to connect the act of marathon swimming with particular charitable causes and interrogates their depoliticising effects. The final section explores the resistance that I encountered to 'swimming for...' in the course of the research. Through this analysis, I argue that the act of 'swimming for...' is a readily intelligible and sincerely intended means of constructing the good body/self, but that this simultaneously flattens out different forms of suffering and depoliticises social inequalities and ill health. Furthermore, the celebration of the endurance sporting body, and its reward through sponsorship, over-emphasises individual accomplishment whilst understating the privilege that facilitates those status-bearing acts. I argue that these elisions and exclusions are made possible by the inextricability of charitable swimming from the cultural logics of neoliberalism, by which we are not coerced, but to which we have become emotionally attached in ways that make 'swimming for...' make perfect sense (Vrasti 2013; Mostafanezhad 2014; Snee 2014).

In making this argument, I share Vrasti's concerns in her critical study of volunteer tourism that I will appear misanthropic and callous; in her book she recalls being chastised for writing a 'mean' thesis (2013: 4). My intention here is not to impugn the motives, sincerity or values of those who choose to swim for charity. Nor do I doubt that many recipient good causes have benefitted from charitable swimming, especially in the context of the retrenchment of welfare provision and the increased demands on charities to fill the subsequent gaps (Nettleton and Hardey 2006: 48). Nevertheless, as Vrasti argues, it is important to ask these questions *because* these practices are so hard to critique. The goal, then, is not to provide solutions, but to question received ideas of progress and justice 'together with the power relations that allow them to pass as normative truth' (2013: 4). This chapter aims to think critically about the ubiquity and normativity of 'swimming for...', and to interrogate what gets obscured by the win–win scenario of charitable swimming.

Charitable swimming

The sedimented relations between marathon swimming and charitable fund-raising arise out of a cluster of social factors that are very particular to the neoliberal present: first, the intensifying elision of health and fitness with good citizenship (Lupton 1995); and second, the rise of the body/self as an individualised, reflexive project (Shilling 1993). In 1994, Conrad coined the term 'healthicisation' to describe the normative cultural linking of health and morality (Conrad 1994). Significantly, for Conrad, it is not simply a state of health and wellness (however defined) that is virtuous, but rather, virtue lies in the act of working on the body (and in being seen to work on the body). Regardless of specific health outcomes, he argues, 'merely engaging in wellness activities is a virtuous activity' (Conrad 1994: 397). But over the subsequent two decades, the virtuous nature of wellness has increasingly taken the form of an obligation, with an intensifying emphasis on personal responsibility for health, particularly in relation to the proliferating roster of 'lifestyle' measures that are deemed to be within the remit of the individual (Fitzpatrick 2001; Hansen and Easthope 2007; Ayo 2012). For example, the contemporary 'war on obesity' is one of the most entrenched sites of 'lifestyle' moralising, with the nagging 'commonsense cure' (Ebbeling *et al.* 2002) of 'eat less, exercise more' dogging the visibly fat, regardless of the absence of a firm evidence base for its effectiveness as a weight management strategy (Gard and Wright 2005; Mann *et al.* 2007). Fatness is habitually presumed to be inevitably and expensively unhealthy, rendering those who are visibly fat failed citizens, regardless of specific health metrics (Aphramor 2005; Jutel 2005; Evans 2006; Murray 2008).

achieve something more for someone else.' Don's comment highlights the social precariousness of 'doing it for myself', averting the risk of appearing excessively self-regarding. This is a particularly potent risk in a resource-hungry activity like marathon swimming that demands significant time, money and physical effort over extended periods of time. The freedom to invest in the self is counterbalanced by charitable fund-raising, which inoculates swimmers against the charge of solipsism and self-indulgence, enabling them to walk the fine line between the socially endorsed investment in the self and deviant over-investment. A similar tension can be found in other technologies of the body such as cosmetic surgery (Pitts-Taylor 2007) or dieting (Bordo 1993), where working upon the body is simultaneously expected but also always potentially deviant, however uncertain the boundaries of excess. Walking this line in the context of marathon swimming is different from other body technologies, since although it is generally accepted that body management practices such as dietary management and exercise can (and indeed *should*) be done in consistent moderation, marathon swimming is already defined by its excesses. Consequently, the risk of excess cannot be mitigated by a reduction in the activity itself, but rather, has to be compensated for; in this case, by achieving 'something more for someone else' at the same time as for oneself.

But charitable swimming is never only a compensatory practice. Rather than a distinct counterbalance, charitable swimming also recasts the act of swimming itself and shores up the status of health and fitness as key markers of good citizenship under contemporary neoliberal governance (Nettleton and Hardey 2006; Ayo 2012). In this way, charitable swimming is not simply mobilised strategically in order to compensate, but directly intervenes in how the venture is viewed by others, aligning it with positive values (Anderson and Taylor 2010). The reflexive individual evaluates health information, assesses and understands risk and takes appropriate action, and public displays of athleticism and fitness in endurance sports affirm the successful management and production of the good embodied self who is contributing socially by maintaining a healthy, fit body. Charitable swimming solidifies this connection.

In contrast to Don's relaxed and relational approach to charity selection, Bill, who I introduced earlier as unable to imagine marathon swimming outside of a fund-raising framework, was much more strategic, settling on a small Lesotho-based water charity that built water pumps driven by children's playground roundabouts:

> My work has taken me on several occasions to countries where there is no water, or very little water, or dirty water, or diseased water, and I really thought that I had to use [the English Channel swim] to make a difference for these people. ... It is not for a country that I know; I don't know Lesotho. But the charity is doing great work. It is a very small charity that I knew would be of interest to people. If they read the story of how the charity was created, they would want to get involved.... I knew that nobody could fail to see interest in it.

Bill had an impressive charity challenge record and was a formidable and enthusiastic fund-raiser. His charity was selected for the quality of a cause that resonated rather indirectly with his personal experience, but also because of the marketable nature of its activities and message – something that he was able to mobilise extensively during an ambitious fund-raising campaign. At first glance, this thin, rather strategic, attachment to the particular cause could be interpreted as a compromising compassion; in the context of corporate compassion, for example, King argues that weak alignment between companies and causes risks the appearance of 'cashing in' (2001: 124). However, while corporate compassion is undoubtedly motivated, at least in part, by a desire for profits (Klawiter 1999; King 2001, 2006), Bill does not stand to make any personal pecuniary gains from charitable swimming and as such is buffered from such accusations. But more centrally, his calculated charity selection constitutes a display of entrepreneurialism that is completely in line with neoliberal selfhood. In a competitive market of 'good causes' and individual charity challenges, the reflexive individual surveys the market and identifies the best strategy to stand out among the crowd of people 'swimming/running/trekking for…'. By creating the optimal circumstances for the display of compassion, Bill both maximises the fund-raising potential and shores up the performance of compassion that makes the self visible and intelligible to others in socially endorsed ways (Moore 2008).

Marketability is a key aspect of the charity challenge; to successfully attract donations, sponsors must feel as though they are doing something to enact meaningful change by donating. However, marketability also places constraints on what can be taken as the focus of charitable fund-raising; the more controversial the cause, and the more complex the 'solution', the less secure the relationship between swimming and charity. This is evidenced by the causes that predominate. Health charities dominate the field, shoring up the connection between the healthy swimming body and its good citizenship. Other popular fields include development charities, emergency funds and environmental protection campaigns, especially for water-based issues such as water quality or wildlife conservation. I never witnessed anyone swimming for politically controversial issues such as abortion rights, and it is difficult to imagine someone swimming for charities that support groups socially abjected within neoliberalism such as immigrants or travellers (Tyler 2013). The beneficiaries of charitable swimming, therefore, are not simply disadvantaged, but have to be innocently so. Marketable charity needs both deserving recipients and socially palatable solutions – a combination that effectively silences resistance or alternative conceptualisations. As King notes in relation to the 1998 Stamp Out Breast Cancer Act in the US, the bill's passage relies 'to a large extent, on the assumption that no one can be *against* voluntarily raised funding for breast cancer research' (2006: 79, emphasis in original). She goes on to argue that to raise critical questions is to risk appearing 'misguided and mean-spirited', or worse still, to be positioned 'against finding a cure for breast cancer'. The effect of this is to create a 'mechanism for limiting how people think about, speak of, act upon, and constitute the disease' (King 2006).

This leads to an inevitable depoliticisation of ill health and social disadvantage in favour of fundable solutions. For example, in her analysis of the pink cultures of the breast cancer movement, King highlights the focus of charitable fund-raising on breast cancer as a scientific or medical problem that can be resolved through increased funding of research. This is as opposed to conceptualisations of breast cancer as an economic, social or environmental problem that requires interventions far less amenable to charity marketing and fund-raising than the search for 'the cure' (King 2006). Similarly, while 'awareness' is a stated goal for many of the swimming fund-raising websites, especially for causes that have been obscured by fund-raising behemoths such as breast cancer or heart disease charities, very few swimmers are actively engaged in the work of the charities themselves or politically active in agitating for a particular cause. Moore identified a similar trend in her study of ribbon culture; the ribbons, she argues, are more about *showing* awareness than *spreading* awareness (2008: 89).

This depoliticisation is not confined to 'swimming for...' but also characterises the wider community itself, which actively eschews controversial political debate in order to maintain harmony across a geographically and socially diverse group of individuals. The shared identity of 'marathon swimmer' is repeatedly mobilised to produce a narrative of sameness that rises above politics and cuts across internal differences (Wheaton 2013: 788). This is, however, to ignore the politics that run not only through the social world of marathon swimming, but also through many of those charitable causes that are habitually treated as outside of the political domain. For example, military charities that support wounded personnel are popular fund-raising targets for swimmers and yet still sit comfortably within the domain of non-political good causes. Fund-raising for breast cancer charities is an equally political non-political act, shoring up the emphasis on the search for a scientific and medical 'cure' over complex relations of inequality and perpetuating a young, white, middle-class model of cancer patienthood (Klawiter 1999). It is, then, perhaps incorrect to describe this as depoliticisation; rather, it is a reconfiguration of what counts as politics that is characterised by 'the emergence of an ethicopolitics of self-fulfillment and community action through volunteerism and philanthropy more generally' (King 2006: 45). This reflects a shift towards what Giddens describes as 'life politics' – a politics 'concerned with human self-actualisation' (1991: 9), as opposed to an 'emancipatory politics' whose primary focus is 'liberating individuals and groups from constraints which adversely affect their life chances' (Giddens 1991: 210). Life politics is, according to Giddens, a 'politics of life decisions' (Giddens 1991: 215); the exercise of choice, then, both to 'swim for...' and who to swim for, is part of the identity work of self-actualisation.

Win–win

The self-actualising role of 'swimming for...' highlights the fact that 'giving' is never purely altruistic but is also an expression of people's relationship to society. Titmuss famously argued in his study of blood donation that stranger donation should be understood as 'creative altruism' through which 'the self is realised with the help of anonymous others' (1971: 212). This approach offers an important reminder that, even though there are strongly self-oriented aspects to giving, those same acts 'may also be thought of as giving life, or prolonging life or enriching life for anonymous others' (Titmuss 1971). Giving is not a question of being altruistic or not, but rather, is always about *more than* altruism, performing a range of functions including self-actualisation. In arguing, then, that the demonstration of the self as compassionate is a core function of charitable swimming, I am not suggesting that those demonstrations are cynical and without meaning to that individual or to the recipients of that philanthropy. It is more appropriate to say that, in the current moment, charity challenges are a key repertoire for the exercise and demonstration of compassion, which in turn 'is not only a prized character trait, but has come to constitute a central aspect of identity in contemporary society' (Moore 2008: 26).

Instead of an act of 'pure' giving, then, charity challenges, including 'swimming for...' can be understood as an exchange that in its ideal form creates beneficial outcomes for all parties. The swimmer has an exciting adventure and a personal challenge; charities and the recipients of their service receive much-needed funds; and friends and family donating simultaneously support a loved one in their venture and a good cause. The act of 'swimming for...' ties individuals and organisations together in novel assemblages through a series of provisional exchanges and alliances. For some charity challenges, this assemblage is formed around narratives of pleasure and celebration. Klawiter describes the celebratory atmosphere – or what King describes as 'pink ribbon perkiness' (2006: 108) – of a San Francisco 'Race for the Cure' event where the buoyant mood was bolstered by freebies of cosmetics, snacks and drinks, a triumphant parade of survivors and the promise of prevention through early detection and treatment (Klawiter 1999). This positive aura is compounded by the acts of running or walking themselves –practices that are easily coded simultaneously as a celebration of and investment in individual and collective health.

But for a sport like marathon swimming, this celebratory and sometimes playful tone doesn't align easily with the solitary, out-of-sight, prolonged nature of the activity. This makes collective play and celebration an unsustainable tone to strike in the act of 'swimming for...'. Instead, the different actors in the 'swimming for...' assemblage are bound discursively not through explicit shared investments in, and experiences of, health and well-being, but rather through discursive alliances of suffering. Inevitably, all charity challenge fund-raising relies to some extent on the trading of suffering for donations; an entirely pleasurable experience or luxurious practice would not 'earn' sponsorship. But in the case of marathon swimming (and other ultra-endurance sports), the willingness and ability to suffer is taken as a defining feature, particularly in outward-facing representations of the sport, and it is this suffering, in turn, that is exchanged for donations. To use Atkinson's phrase, it is suffering, and the risks of even greater suffering, that gives marathon swimming its 'exciting significance' (2008).

Charity webpages bear this out, invoking cold water, rough conditions, physical pain and discomfort, fear, boredom, the presence of predatory or venomous aquatic wildlife and the prolonged demands of intensive training. These dramatic catalogues of suffering provide the context for the invitation to donate to the chosen charity; suffering is exchanged for donations. But the flow of benefits never

Running, he argues, has given him a sense of purpose: 'it has allowed me to think of something, someone other than myself, in what can often be a solitary and selfish sport' (Karnazes 2005). It is only through the normative equation of physical endeavor with compassionate action that this conclusion can even begin to make sense.

Karnazes is an extreme, and somewhat distasteful, example, displaying a striking lack of reflexivity about his own privilege and significantly overstating his own role in relation to the lives and treatment of these sick children. But it illustrates well my broader point about endurance sport itself constituting a mode of action that is easily aligned with positive accomplishment and morally sanctioned entrepreneurial selfhood. High profile swimmer, Lewis Pugh, mobilises swimming-as-action directly in his environmental campaigning. In a Ted Talk in September 2009, he described the retreat of the north polar sea ice as a symptom of global warming, and his subsequent decision to take symbolic action in the form of a 1 km swim at the North Pole:

> And I wanted to really shake the lapels of world leaders to get them to understand what is happening. So I decided to do this symbolic swim at the top of the world in a place which should be frozen over but which now is rapidly unfreezing. And the message was very clear: climate change is for real and we need to do something about it, and we need to do something about it right now.
> (Pugh 2009)

Pugh's symbolic swim is figured as an active response to the looming crisis of global warming. Unlike many examples of 'swimming for...', he draws a tangible connection with the cause he is advocating for by swimming where swimming should not otherwise be possible. But nevertheless, this is a campaigning act that aligns comfortably with neoliberal modes of compassionate action, particularly in relation to the entrepreneurial selfhood that emerges simultaneously. The swim is not an act of disruptive protest, but rather, one of awareness-raising through which new opportunities for selfhood simultaneously emerge. In parallel with his enthusiastic environmental campaigning work, for example, Pugh has also built up a significant motivational speaking and autobiographical publication business, branded under the tagline, 'Achieving the Impossible.'[2] Central to Pugh's brand is the highly individualised rhetorics of mind over matter; for example, in a second Ted Talk in July 2010, reflecting back on his North Pole swim, he argues that 'there is nothing more powerful than the made-up mind' (Pugh 2010a), and his Twitter feed regularly incorporates inspirational memes that trumpet the power of the mind over the body. My point here is not to cast doubt on Pugh's commitment to the environmentalism about which he speaks so eloquently and passionately. Instead, I want to highlight the ways in which entrepreneurial selfhood does not simply happily co-exist with compassionate, philanthropic or awareness-raising activities, but has also become synonymous with them.

This is exemplified by UK swimming entrepreneur, Adam Walker, who successfully completed the 'Ocean's Seven'[3] grouping of marathon swims in 2014,[4] whilst simultaneously building the successful Ocean Walker coaching business.[5]

In October 2014, Walker took part in a panel interview for the One Young World organisation, chaired by former tennis professional Boris Becker, and including Grenadian sprinter, Kirani James, and retired English footballer, Sol Cambell.[6] The all-male panel's focus was the power of sport to create social change, and Walker described his transformation into a marathon swimmer, arguing that he hadn't wanted his gravestone to read, 'there goes Adam. He was a salesman, just like everybody else'. He added: 'I didn't want to be like that. I wanted to make a difference.' Adam's story is one of injury, determined recovery, a complete stroke overhaul and an impressive roster of long, difficult swims, combined with a vigorous self-branding strategy. Like Pugh, Walker's business is informed by a commitment to environmental issues as well as to aquatic safety. In the interview with Boris Becker, we learn that he is an ambassador to both the Royal Life Saving Society and the wildlife charity, Whale and Dolphin Conservation, before he adds, 'and I no longer sell kettles and toasters'. The narratives of involvement with good causes and of self-improvement go hand in hand, and when Walker is asked what his message is, he replies with his branding tagline: 'Never give up on your dreams'. As with Pugh, this aligns easily with neoliberal celebrations of individual autonomy, efficacy and self-discipline, and effaces the social inequalities and structural barriers that constrain self-transformation. In short, it is simply not true that all obstacles can be overcome and that it's never too late; as Sanford notes in her account of her childhood experiences of achondroplasia:

> I no longer accepted the adage 'You can do anything if you put your mind to it', knowing full well that my chances of becoming an Olympic figure skater were not worth calculating, and that most people who used such a phrase were either gold-medal Olympians or individuals who had yet to face such words as *handicap* and *lifelong condition*. (2006: 30, emphasis in original)

US swimmer, Sarah, is another highly accomplished marathon swimmer and formidable fund-raiser, raising almost $30,000 for a breast cancer charity between 2007 and when I interviewed her in 2011. Hers is a story of serendipitous fund-raising, finding herself on the receiving end of unsolicited donations once she began blogging about her swimming, before moving on to actively soliciting donations with each year's swims. Like Pugh and Walker, she also delivers motivational speeches, although as an adjunct to her ongoing employment in IT rather than a replacement for it:

> I know there's other people out there who raise $29,000 in one year of swimming. But for me, that amount in the four years that I've been swimming is pretty good, because I have a full time job, so with training, fundraising, trying to get sponsorship. I do motivational speeches around, when people ask. So I've spoken to kids, I've spoken to teachers. And I've seen people come up to me afterwards, and for me, you just have to change one person's life, because they're going to go on and change somebody else's life. And I've had people come up to me and say, you know what, I don't know why I've been waiting to do X in my life. I'm going to go and do X, I'm going to figure out a way to do X, and for me, I think, it's six degrees of separation, and hopefully that ripple will cause a ripple for somebody

else, which will cause a ripple with somebody else. So that's why for me, not only I love it, but I do think that I can change something through it.

Sarah's story shares many elements with those of Lewis Pugh and Adam Walker, but her entrepreneurial selfhood is muted by a profoundly gendered concern about heavily investing in a higher profile, both for her swimming and her fund-raising efforts:

> When I say I want to swim professionally, I have this hard balance … how much do I want to be in … it's a hard question for me, because I don't want people to be like, she's a prick because she's got this big ego. … But I don't….Yeah. I don't want people to be like, well, she thinks that she's just the cat's miaow [laughs]. Because I'm definitely not like that…. I have a lot of problems; I'm just like everybody else.

Sarah's concerns are justified, since normative femininity does not sit comfortably with self-promotion; as discussed in Chapter 6, the role of sporting hero and leader does not attach so easily to women (Hargreaves 2000). Consequently, women pushing themselves into the spotlight are much more vulnerable to accusations of vanity, egotism and selfishness than men, and their path to entrepreneurial selfhood through sport is more precarious as a result.

Swimming to swim

For all the self-evident nature of 'swimming for…' and its status as compassionate action, I also encountered considerable cynicism and concern in relation to the pressure and expectation to incorporate charitable fund-raising into marathon swimming. This is reflected in the trapped disillusionment expressed by the swimmers for whom charitable swimming became such a burden, but was also expressed directly by several swimmers who either rejected charitable swimming or purposefully rendered the fund-raising component incidental to swimming itself.

San Francisco swimmer, David, for example, actively rejected the possibility in favour of a much more pleasure-oriented motivation:

> I was just swimming because I wanted to swim it [the Channel]. There are lots of causes that I want to raise money for and do, but I didn't want the pressure or the hassle or the detail … because I'd spend so much time and so much organisation doing it that I thought I'd just leave it.

David's decision to swim because he wanted to swim is a socially risky one in a context where 'swimming for…' is a presumed norm. As Moore observes in relation to a breast cancer charity: 'In a culture of compassion, those who choose not to be charitable are judged to be deviant, maladjusted human beings' (2008: 145). However, this is negotiated partly by signaling his charitable identity elsewhere, and partly by highlighting the importance of not doing a job – fund-raising, in this case – half-heartedly. He positions himself, then, as compassionate, disciplined and self-reflexive – all socially valued traits. This is not to suggest that he does not have those qualities, but rather, that the absence of charitable involvement in his English Channel swim has to be accounted for. This notion of 'swimming because I wanted to swim' also recalls what Nettleton and Hardey (2006) describe in their study of urban marathon runners as the 'purists', for whom running and fund-raising were mutually exclusive practices, placing a greater focus on the intrinsic pleasures and challenges of running (or swimming). This is a position that is more commonly taken up by, and available to, those for whom marathon swimming is an ongoing activity rather than an exciting one-off adventure.

UK English Channel swimmer, Greg, on the other hand, took a more directly critical approach and launched into a vociferous tirade against individuals who he felt overstated their charitable intentions whilst understating their personal stake in the venture:

> What I object to ... is when this kind of thing is trumpeted about and presented as someone doing something because they have a calling to do something to do with charity: 'I'm not swimming the Channel because I want to swim the Channel, or because I want a personal challenge; I'm swimming because I want to raise money for this cause or that cause.' And it really irritates me. There's this person [at my swimming club] who sends emails about three times a year saying 'I'm doing this now. The reason I'm doing it is for this cause.' And my response is: bollocks. The reason you're doing it is because you want to swim the Channel.

Greg's cynicism does not reflect a complete rejection of charitable swimming. Although he originally didn't intend to swim for charity, following a comment from his mother that 'people will think it's a bit weird if you don't do it for charity', he eventually decided that 'it's probably a big enough challenge that people may ... friends may actually want to support it'. Others reached a similar decision after people sent money unsolicited, and like Greg, many compromised by opening an online fund-raising account and directing inquiries about charity to it without actively promoting it.

Rather than denying the legitimacy of charitable swimming, Greg is insisting on the dual aspects of the practice and on the importance of recognising the personal benefits that accrue from a Channel swim. He resists those who he deems to be overplaying the 'compassion' card, and who he sees as attempting to position themselves as morally superior to those not swimming for charity. As Greg remarked: 'You don't want to be that person.' Instead, Greg insists on the self-transformative pleasures to be gained from the challenge of marathon swimming, laying claim to an authentic swimming selfhood that eschews the seeking of attention but instead is motivated by the pleasures of the activity itself. As discussed in Chapter 2, this marks an appeal to another alliance of suffering – that among the swimmers themselves for whom the encounter with suffering through swimming (as a complex assemblage of pleasure and excitement as well as pain and discomfort) is a defining aspect of social world belonging. Consequently, charity fund-raising activities are generally outward-facing, since within the social world of marathon swimming, the defining suffering of the sport is rendered relatively mundane, and except for swims of extraordinary length or duration, fails to qualify as a deserving exception that can be traded for sponsorship.

6

Gendering swimming

It is almost 9 a.m. on a cloudy morning in June 2009. My friend, Jenny, and I are standing on the pebble beach of Dover harbour, stripping down to the swimming costumes we put on under our clothes when we got dressed this morning. Another fifty or so swimmers are also there – both relays and solo swimmers – most training for English Channel crossings that season. A six-hour swim today for the solo swimmers. Jenny and I are a little late, and we can hear the shouts and laughs of swimmers already entering the water. We apply thick layers of suncream to the backs of our legs, the face and shoulders; we do each other's backs, careful to smear cream well underneath all of the costume edges to guard against a painful stripe of sunburn later. We each snap on a latex glove and stand, one at a time in practised choreography, arms up, while the other daubs Vaseline in the armpits, along the costume straps, to the back of the neck, to prevent painful chafing. Even though we're late and we are already receiving stern glances from the beach crew who oversee the training sessions, we haven't seen each other for several weeks and our preparatory regimen is punctuated with friendly laughter and urgent catching-up as we daub and smear. Eventually, we are ready, and shiny with Vaseline and suncream, we head down the stony beach to the water's edge. We throw our shoes onto the pile with the others, and hobble the last metre or so awkwardly, pebbles biting into our insteps, until the cold water is around our ankles. The tide is out, and the stones soon give way to sand, easier to walk on, oozing between our toes. By the time we are up to our hips in the cold, green-brown water, each wave rolling further up our torsos, we have started to do the belly-button hop – rising onto our toes with each wave, elbows held up and out to the sides, ribcage lifted. We huff and groan when each wave comes; lots of laughter; the occasional muttered expletive. We know that it will be fine once we're in, but the moment of immersion is cruel and we are prevaricating. A voice calls from the water: 'Come on, girls: man up and get in.' (See Figure 8.)

Sport is a domain where gender boundaries are carefully drawn and policed. In most sports, men and women compete either in separate events, or results and records are categorised separately, and formal mechanisms exist to reinforce gender binaries, including through genetic, hormonal and physiological testing (Wackwitz 2003; Sloop 2012). Gender remains a primary demarcation within

Figure 8 Swimmers enter the water in Dover harbour.

sport, and is rigorously maintained (Theberge 2000; Guerandel and Mennesson 2007; Anderson 2008). For example, in the run-up to the 2012 London Olympics, the Amateur International Boxing Association, when confronted with the inclusion of female boxers in the Olympics for the first time, engaged in lengthy debates about whether women should be required to wear skirts in the ring in order to enable audiences and judges to distinguish them from their male counterparts (BBC 2012). This adherence to gender binaries is underpinned by the firm conviction that women's bodies have different, and significantly, lesser, physical abilities compared to men, holding in place the male body (and especially the white male body) as the archetypal sporting body and as the standard against which other sporting performances can be measured (Kay and Laberge 2004). This determined insistence on the gender binary highlights the status of the athletic body as 'a site of anxiety' (Magdalinski 2009: 93), where deeply entrenched convictions about the 'naturalness' of gender relations and performances have to be defended against the disruptions of athletic female bodies (see Cahn 1994; Hargreaves 1994).

Within marathon swimming, the prevailing ideology is that it is open to anyone without regard for gender, race, age and so on, and that our identity as swimmers prevails over other forms of social difference. The focus on completion rather than competition facilitates this, reducing the need for gender-based categorisations of accomplishment, and there are repeated assurances that 'girls' (as women are habitually referred to throughout this and other sporting domains) can be just as good as men. However, this veneer of equality belies the inescapability of gender (Laurendeau and Sharara 2008). To be 'just as good as a man' betrays the expectation that it is men who set the standard of sporting accomplishment, and swim threatening weakness is intractably associated with the feminine through exhortations to 'stop crying like a girl' or 'stop being such a woman' (or homo, gay, puff, pussy) (Messner 1988). Conversely, more courageous or determined performance is aligned with masculinity, as in demands to 'man up' or 'grow a pair'. It is in this way that it is possible to describe Jenny and I as something that we are not (girls) and then to encourage us to become more like something else that we are not (men). There is no obvious lexicon or conceptual framework for female sporting accomplishment outside of this gendered hierarchy of feminine weakness and masculine capability. As Young argues: 'It follows that if there is a particular female person participating in sport, either she is not "really" a woman, or the sport she engages in is not "really" a sport' (2010: 14).

The chapter begins by exploring the construction of marathon swimming as a domain that transcends gender, race, class and other axes of social difference and inequality. I argue that the contemporary construction of swimming as a gender-appropriate sport for women alongside the relative invisibility of the marathon swimming body contribute to this perceived neutrality. The following section considers this assumption critically, identifying the ways in which intersecting axes of difference and inequality seep through the cracks of normative representations of the sport, particularly in relation to the enduring association of women with the body, the assumption of a (hegemonically) masculine standard against which others are measured, and the impact of factors such as the division of household labour and resources, and its associated entitlements, on the ability to participate freely in the sport. The final section explores some of the ways in which swimming emerged as a platform for gender-defiant experiences of embodiment, and the possibilities and limitations of these for a feminist politics of marathon swimming.

'We're all just swimmers'

Throughout the research process, and particularly when fellow swimmers discovered my gender studies background, I was repeatedly reassured that there was no gender dimension to swimming; that 'we're all just swimmers'. This is another dimension to the apolitical gloss observed in relation to charitable swimming in the previous chapter, and is a social strategy for giving coherence to a diverse group of geographically dispersed individuals, and sustaining the valued belief in the inclusivity of the community (see also, Wheaton 2013: 3819) – a conviction that is given substance by the generous hospitality conventionally shown to swimmers travelling away from home and in search of local swimming company, or support crew for events. However, this also risks obscuring those differences behind a veneer of common ground that is inevitably marked by axes of social difference. But while the discourse of 'we're all just swimmers' is a problematic assumption that ignores the many practical, ideological and social barriers to participation, it is also the case that, with the exception of the keeping of separate male and female records, there is very little of the overt gender segregation or directly sexist behaviour towards women that characterises more traditionally masculinised sporting domains such as rugby (Pringle and Markula 2005), boxing (Mennesson 2000), wrestling (Sisjord and Kristiansen 2009), ice hockey (Theberge 2000) or soccer (Cox and Thompson 2000; George 2005). There are, for example, no separate regulations to minimise contact or harm as with ice hockey's 'no body checking' rule for women (Theberge 2000); nor is there a parallel to climbing's decorative 'belay bunny' (Robinson 2008: 92) or ice-hockey's 'puck bunny' (Crawford and Gosling 2004). A similar slackening of gender divisions has also been noted in the context of windsurfing (Wheaton and Tomlinson 1998) and running (Smith 2000), with gender rendered a 'passive identity' (Wheaton and Tomlinson 1998: 265) in the everyday 'doing' of the sport. Within marathon swimming, there are a number of possible explanations for this.

First, swimming is conventionally viewed as an appropriate sport for women, facilitating belonging to that sporting community. This was not always so, and as discussed in the Introduction, historically, Western women have been constrained by the demands of modesty and decency (Love 2007a; Bier 2011; Ayriss 2012; Davies 2015). Dawson (2006) notes how West African women were not subject to the same restrictions within their own cultures until enforced under slavery, especially in the American South, highlighting the social and cultural specificity of these restrictions. In response to these constraints, Victorian women such as the actress Annette Kellerman campaigned against the dangerously heavy skirts and pantaloons that women were forced to wear for public bathing, leading to her arrest in 1907 for public indecency after appearing in public in what became her signature one-piece swimming costume (Davies 2015: 100).

Nevertheless, swimming was increasingly viewed as an appropriate activity for nineteenth-century women for reasons of health, safety and the benefits of the aquatic environment (Parker 2010). This positive association gained further momentum in light of the featuring of female swimmers in films and the success of touring diving and swimming exhibitions (Bier 2011; Davies 2015). As early as 1874, swim teacher Kate Bennett declared that 'the best swimmers always prove the best dancers and walkers' because 'the grace which they acquire in the water clings to them on the land' (Bier 2011: 33), and swimming remains a sport that is concordant with normatively feminine modes of movement, lending itself to gentle, impact-free motion that doesn't jar or jiggle the body. While these are very different motivations and modes of engagement with swimming than are evident within marathon swimming, the presumed comfortable fit between swimming and women means that women are not as obviously perceived as out of place as they might be in more relentlessly male-dominated sports.

The second explanation for the apparent loosening of gender divisions within marathon swimming is that the body, which is conventionally taken as the primary marker of gendered distinction, is largely invisible in the everyday practice of the sport. And even where it is visible, it is rarely so in a glamorous, spectacular or objectifiable manner. At the end of a swim, the body is bloated, the skin pale and blotchy, and the lips and tongue swollen. Most swimmers cover up quickly against the post-swim drop in core temperature, bundling up in robes, oversized sweatshirts, woolly hats and thick padded coats. And as discussed in Chapter 4, the marathon swimming body is rarely gazed upon in the way that a track athlete's or gymnast's is, and the opportunities for gendered performance are very limited. Bodily difference, then, is literally submerged, rendering gender less overt, and bringing a more ostensibly generic swimming body to the fore.

This is in contrast to non-competitive pool swimming, for example, where gendered aesthetics are granted a much greater role in the surveillance of swimming bodies. The confined, regulated spaces of the pool, the clarity of the water and the visibility of the body on the poolside create plentiful opportunities for the careful policing of female bodies (James 2000). The UK Amateur Swimming Association's (ASA) Swimfit website, for example, includes separate guides for men and women on choosing 'the right swimwear for your shape'. Women are invited to locate themselves on a list of eight flawed body types: short torso, long torso, pear shape, large bust, small bust, plus size, flabby stomach and boyish body. For example, the pear shape, we are told, 'has often been the plague of women' but with 'an eye-catching bikini or tankini top with subdued bottoms in a dark color', the attention of watching others will be drawn 'toward your more appealing characteristics'. Plus-sized women are also urged to seek out darker colours for their minimising effects, reassuring them that this doesn't mean purely black swimsuits, since 'deep reds and blues will have the same effect and are a bit more appropriate for summer fun' (ASA n.d.a). While the women are left to contemplate the heady possibilities for summer fun that lie in dark clothing and the relentless efforts to shrink, compress and minimise their bodies, male swimmers are divided into five body types: tall and athletic, short and athletic, tall and thin, tall and big, and big tummy (ASA n.d.b). While women's bodies are carved into flawed parts, with the exception of 'big tummy', which men are advised to manage by wearing solid colours and possibly a T-shirt, the remaining categories speak to whole body types, including the tall and athletic ideal, who is reassured that 'anything will do'. No ideal is available for women, whose bodies require closer and more rigorous surveillance and management, both in and out of the water. Unlike the changing rooms and deck of the public pool, where women are taught to anticipate the surveillance of others, the aquatic borderlands of beaches, river banks and lakesides where marathon swimmers gather, change, prepare and then re-change after swimming, are practice-defined zones that also facilitate the ostensibly generic swimming body. Although some swimming venues have changing facilities, many do not; in Dover, for example, everyone changes on the harbour's stony beach – a sometimes precarious affair, especially at the end of a swim when damp skin, cold-numbed hands and wind-blown towels and changing robes make the guarding of modesty a hit and miss affair. Changing, of course, remains a gendered practice in itself, since while it is acceptable for men to bare their chest in public, especially in the context of swimming, the exposure of naked breasts, except in particular sunbathing contexts, is socially unacceptable and readily coded in sexualised terms, leading women to cover up as much as possible (and however awkwardly). Nevertheless, the practical function of these spaces as staging posts creates a largely de-gendered and de-sexualised zone governed by what

Goffman (1963) calls 'civil inattention' – an unobtrusive means of making privacy in a shared space possible.

This civil inattention also extends to the use and experience of touch in these peripheral aquatic spaces. As Scott (2010) argues in relation to public pool swimming, touch, however accidental, is something to be avoided and apologised for. However, in the case of open water swimming, touch – even between relative strangers – is a common occurrence. The pre-swim rituals of suncream and Vaseline application require a degree of touch that is far outside of normal social boundaries, since products have to be applied well under the costume edges, which have to be lifted away from the body for access; they also have to be firmly rubbed in, not just on the relatively socially neutral space of the back, but also under the arms and the back of the thighs – bodily spaces where we are much less commonly touched by others outside of medical practitioners and other body workers (Wolkowitz 2006) or by intimate others. But this too is normalised and sanitised through a combination of civil inattention and light humour; swimmers laugh and joke as they snap on latex gloves, pass tubs of pastes and creams back and forth or line up ready to be daubed. Similarly, while changing, it is common to reach over to someone who has become tangled up in a top or sports bra and to pull the back of it down into place, or to help someone with fumbling hands to put their socks on. While gender can never be absent, it is pushed into the background in the embodied practices of public changing. These all contribute to the creation of marathon swimming as a de-gendered space that appears to escape the objectification, particularly of the female body, that characterises other sports. In this way, the claim that 'we are all just swimmers' constitutes an intelligible, if problematic, account of social relations in swimming.

Making gender matter

However gender neutral marathon swimming may appear, particularly in relation to sports that insist upon strictly gendered boundaries of participation, the gendering of the swimming body seeps through the veneer of generic swimming embodiment. Instead, we can understand the gendered swimming body as both present and absent in particular moments, and a more fruitful question is not *whether* the swimming body is overtly gendered, but rather, *when* and *how* the gendered body is pushed to the foreground and when it is rendered passive. This section explores two examples of this foregrounding of women's bodies: first, as explanations for female high performance; and second, in the context of menstruation.

As with other endurance and lifestyle sports, it is not uncommon for women to out-perform men (Hanold 2010). For example, in the Manhattan Island Marathon Swim (MIMS) over a thirty-year period, Knechtle *et al.* (2014) report that the best women were 12–14 per cent faster than the best men (although the top ten race times ever remained lower for women than men). More generally, the differences between men's and women's marathon swimming times remain narrow and unpredictable, particularly over longer distances. For example, an analysis of the best annual performances by men and women English Channel swimmers between

1900 and 2010 concluded that there was no significant difference between the two (Eichenberg et al. 2012). Eichenberg et al. conclude that this 'suggests that women ultra-swimmers are capable of similar performances to men during open-water ultra-swim events' (Eichenbarg et al.: 1300). It is unclear why this only 'suggests' this capability, but what is more striking here is the fact that female sporting accomplishment constitutes a reportable research finding at all. This is reproduced in other papers on the gendered distributions of performance in endurance sports. Rust et al. (2014a), for example, in their analysis of race times from the 36 km 'Maratona del Golfo Capi-Napoli', argue that, while both male and female times show steady improvements since the swim's inception in 1954, those of women have shown greater improvements. This leads them to suggest that 'women will be able to achieve men's performance or even to outperform men in the near future' (Rust et al.: 11). Conversely, in a similar analysis of ultra-triathlon performance between 1978 and 2013, Rust et al. conclude that, in this case, 'it seems very unlikely that women will ever outrun men in the ultra-distance triathlons' (2014b: 16).

This determined analysis of male and female performance in marathon swimming echoes the long-standing preoccupations of sex difference research to establish innate distinctions between men and women. Popular science books use the gloss of science to make the case for fundamental and biological differences between men and women, down to the level of brain structure and chemistry, hormonal profiles and genetic predispositions (see, for example, Moir and Jessel 1991; Baron-Cohen 2003). These arguments have been roundly denounced by feminist writers such as Fausto-Sterling (1992) and Fine (2010), who meticulously unpick claims to 'scientifically' established sex difference to highlight the socially constructed nature of such 'facts'. This echoes Butler's famous claim that 'gender is not to culture as sex is to nature; gender is also the discursive/cultural means by which 'sexed nature' or 'a natural sex' is produced and established as 'prediscursive', prior to culture, a politically neutral surface on which culture acts' (1990: 7). In short, to seek out sex difference is to already presume its existence and significance, and to (re)produce it as such.

The studies cited above that compare male and female performance draw on anthropometric data at the population level, citing biological advantages as possible explanations for female high performance. Eichenberg et al., for example, cite greater swimming economy among women than for men as a result of biomechanics, metabolic differences that preserve muscle glucose, and higher levels of body fat that provide both insulation against the cold and additional buoyancy, enabling the body to remain in a more streamlined position more easily (2012: 1300; see also, Rust et al. 2014a). But these studies are unable to consider the anthropometrics of the individual swimmers, primarily due to the lack of available data. Consequently, sex (gender) figures as an over-determined category through which bodies can be known, ranked and ordered. But what is striking about these studies, as with all sex difference research, is the social investment in difference, and by extension, in the hierarchical relationship that conventionally defines men and women in relation. It is only in this context that female high performance in marathon swimming constitutes a research finding of note.

This is reproduced in the everyday discourse and practice of marathon swimming, particularly in the context of high female performance, when the gendered body is pulled into the foreground, primarily through discourses of biological advantage. For example, women are commonly described as benefitting from higher levels of body fat, more favourably distributed around the body, than men. After a long sea swim during a training camp in Malta during which a high performing female swimmer had repeatedly lapped several other members of the 'fast' group, one male swimmer remarked: 'Well, you have fatter thighs.' Another commonly referenced advantage is of the higher tolerance for pain that women are presumed to enjoy as a result of their reproductive capacities, particularly in the context of childbirth (Dally 1991; Bendelow 2000). 'Women,' commented one male swimmer on the same camp, 'don't feel pain like men.' Whether these claims to biological advantage are 'true' is less significant here than *when* they are mobilised; that is, as a means of accounting for female high performance. In discursive terms, then, strategic biological reductionism functions as what Ford and Brown describe in the context of surfing culture as 'an implicit defence of patriarchy' (2006: 90).

This resort to the biological can also be seen in the suggestion, as discussed in the Introduction, that the paucity of non-white marathon swimmers reflects a 'natural' lack of buoyancy due to low body fat and high bone density' (Allen and Nickel 1969; Wheaton 2013) – an explanation that was recounted to me repeatedly in the course of the research, effectively naturalising the marathon swimming cohort's whiteness while sustaining the narrative of inclusivity. Writing of black basketball players, Shogan argues that they are caught in a 'double-bind', that 'white athletes are successful in sport because of their intelligence and hard work and black athletes succeed because of their natural athleticism' (1999: 66).[1] A similar case, then, can be made about female swimmers, whose accomplishments are more likely to be attributed to biological stereotypes than to the socially privileged traits of hard work or skill.

This is a reiteration of the gendered split between mind and body that is central to the normative disjuncture between femininity and sport. The conventional relegation of women's lives to the uncelebrated domain of the body in all its leaky unpredictability highlights women's presumed lack of reason and psychological and emotional fortitude – a conviction that is inextricably bound up with the depreciation and degradation of women (as well as other oppressed groups) (see also, Grosz 1994; Spelman 2010: 14). According to Young, this underpins the identity of women as Other, and as body-object as opposed to the male body-subject (2010: 13). This has particular salience in the context of sport, which, Young argues, 'exhibits the essential body-subject', calling upon 'the body's capacities and skills merely for the sake of determining what they can achieve' (14). It is in this sense that she argues that, as Other, women and sport are necessarily mutually exclusive (see also, Cahn 1994; Hargreaves 1994; Scott and Derry 2005; Magdalinski 2009).

Following the work of Spelman, this is not to argue that the mind–body dualism is inherently or intentionally sexist or oppressive (2010: 36). Indeed, as discussed in Chapter 1, I carelessly reproduced this mind–body split in my application and there is a 'kernel of truth' to it in the experience of the body that makes it make sense (Leder 1990: 107). Nevertheless, just as the body recedes from awareness in times of wellness, there is a similar recession of the gendered body in swimming when everything is in hierarchical order, and its rush to the foreground when that order is disrupted. Marathon swimming, then, is not without its female heroes, but they are much less easily coded as such than their male counterparts, and when they are, it is *as women* (Hargreaves 2000: 2).

This can be seen, for example, in the popular marathon swimming documentary, *Driven* (Pitterle and Hall 2014), which, according to the film's promotional description, follows the journeys of 'swimming veteran Evan Morrison, novice swimmer and single mom Cherie Edborg and 13-year-old Fiona Goh' as they prepare for Santa Barbara Channel swims (*Driven* 2014) – a nineteen-mile crossing for Morrison, and a twelve and a half-mile crossing for the two female swimmers. The film is also interspersed with commentary from four experienced swimmers – all male – who act as authoritative experts, interpreting and explaining events. It is an engaging and evocative film, which movingly captures many of the challenges and pleasures of marathon swimming, but the gendering of both the swimmers and the commentators demonstrates the ease with which the authoritative veteran swimmer is so easily imagined as masculine, while female swimmers emerge as novices, mothers and children. This reflects Hargreaves' observation that, while men 'easily transform into heroes', women are 'ambiguous heroines', caught between the demands of heroism to be exemplary and the construction of the feminine as inferior (2000: 2). She argues that, while 'sportsmen today are readily heroised when they break physical barriers, endure adverse conditions, overcome seemingly impossible obstacles, drive their bodies to the limit, risk death, and go further, higher and faster than any other living man' (Hargreaves 2000), heroines can only be defined by conventionally feminine attributes. While not necessarily constituting a purposeful exclusion, then, it is no coincidence that it is men who are chosen to represent authority, expertise and experience in the film, and that Edborg is the only member of the cast whose reproductive status is highlighted. The dualistic story, then, however benign and habitual in its everyday mobilisation, 'often ends up being a highly politicized one' (Spelman 2010: 36).

Menstruation offers a second example of the gendering of the swimming body, this time through its compulsory *in*visibility. As already mentioned earlier in the book, from 2009 to 2011, I took part in several iterations of a commercially-run long distance training camp on the island of Gozo in Malta, first as a swimmer and then briefly as a guide. The camps are very popular, especially among aspiring English Channel swimmers, combining an escalating series of sea swims culminating in the chance to complete a six-hour qualification swim, alongside a programme of informational seminars. I joined one of these camps in April 2010 as a swimmer as part of my preparations for my English Channel swim that season, and mid-week, it was time for the infamous 'Three Ps' seminar. The three Ps refer to 'piss, poo and puke', and the seminar is designed to address the management of these 'creature releases' (Goffman 1963). The seminar was conducted in a lighthearted tone, addressing a set of issues that can easily stop a swim but which people can be reluctant to raise. As the seminar came to a close, a female swimmer (one of only a handful in a room of men) asked: 'What about periods?' The jovial mood in the room melted away and the atmosphere thickened and tensed. Eyes fell to the floor; people squirmed uncomfortably. The male seminar leader eventually stepped in, inviting a female coach to offer advice; a joke from one of the male swimmers about sharks scenting blood lightened the mood.[2]

But the instant collective reaction in the room was striking – a mix of disgust and embarrassment at the unexpected airing of a topic that women are expected (and expect other women) to keep to themselves (Laws 1990; Moreno-Black 2005). And perhaps inevitably, even the subsequent rather reluctant discussion of menstruation in the seminar focused on strategies for keeping it hidden, either through the use of hormonal pharmaceuticals to prevent menstruation or through practical strategies of disguise and discretion. One particular tension for women in negotiating menstruation is that, while the use of 'feminine hygiene' products such as tampons meet the normative demands of menstrual invisibility, prolonged use of a single tampon not only has possible health risks, but would also inevitably lead to leaks and therefore potentially cease to perform its concealing function once out of the water. Consequently, while peripheral aquatic spaces operate as de-gendered spaces governed by an unspoken contract of civil inattention, the successful maintenance of that contract also requires women to be vigilant about concealment.

Women told of having friends or partners stand on the shore with a dark towel to wrap around their middle before walking up the beach, or of running quickly up the beach to cover up with a long changing robe under which a tampon could be discretely inserted or underwear pre-prepared with a sanitary towel slipped on. Others avoided swimming on 'heavy' days, or took hormonal medications that enabled them to 'skip' a period, both to relieve symptoms and to avoid the stress of concealment, especially in the intensive weeks leading up to a big swim when back-to-back multi-hour swims increased the risk of exposure. At the borders between the shore and the water where swimmers feed and change, spit, snot, belching and even vomiting are common and unremarkable creature releases that are either the subject of civil inattention or, alternatively, collective humour. But menstrual blood remains abjectly unspeakable in this morass of bodily fluids and seepages, except in the whispered conversations among women. Gender, it turns out, couldn't matter more in this social world of self-proclaimed gender neutrality.

Gendered lives, gendered leisure

The gendering of swimming lies not only in the fleshy realities (and imaginaries) of the body, but also in the ways in which social roles, structures and the division of labour are intractably both marked by and productive of gendered social relations. As Young reminds us, the lived body is 'a unified idea of a physical body acting and experiencing in a specific sociocultural context; it is body-in-situation' (2005: 16). If we see gender as an attribute of social structures rather than individually held, innate qualities, then the deconstruction of the apolitical gloss of being 'all just swimmers' demands the analysis of the social structures that underpin gendered (and other) inequalities and their embodied effects on the lives of women. Rather than marking out a separation between the individual, fleshy body and social structures, then, the phenomenological approach mobilised so powerfully by Young highlights the ways in which the 'body as lived is always enculturated: by the phonemes a body learns to pronounce at a very early age, by the clothes the person wears that mark her nation, her age, her occupational status, and in what is culturally expected or required of women' (2005: 17). In the context of marathon swimming, this is exemplified by the gendered division of domestic and reproductive labour, which constrains and delimits women's access to the sport and its pleasures.

Ideologies of femininity dictate, first, that domestic and reproductive labour are fundamentally the work of women; and second, that those responsibilities take precedence over self-directed desires and interests. These intertwine to produce the potent rhetorics of blame around the social perils of 'bad' motherhood (Ladd-Taylor and Umansky 1998) and the accusations of selfishness that attach so easily to women who choose to live without children (Faux 1984; Morell 1994; Campbell 1999; Morell 2000). These gendered expectations delimit access to leisure time and activities both materially and symbolically, impacting on the time and resources available to women to pursue self-oriented projects that compete with domestic and reproductive labour. The refusal to relinquish self-directed leisure activities renders women's normative feminine status in peril via the punitive discourses of the 'bad' mother/carer/woman; this means that sustained immersion in any leisure practice requires strategies of negotiation, impression management and, in some cases, outright defiance (Gillespie *et al.* 2002; Raisborough 2006, 2007; Dilley and Scraton 2010).

The majority of female marathon swimmers I encountered in my research either didn't have children (as in my case) or their children were older and moving towards greater independence. Indeed, throughout the research, I didn't meet any women actively training for a marathon swim who had pre-school aged children. In the course of my research, no one ever explicitly cited a commitment to swimming as a reason for living without children (see, for example, Wheaton and Tomlinson 1998: 261), but for several younger women, an ambitious swim, with its all-consuming training demands, was conceptualised as a precursor to reproduction; one swimmer described it as 'getting it out of my system' before 'settling down'. These women were excited about their hoped-for reproductive future, but it comes at a cost that was never articulated by male swimmers at similar life stages. Similarly, those women who were parents or had other caring responsibilities found it necessary to account for time spent on swimming in a way that wasn't necessary for the male swimmers. For example, Melissa – a single parent to a teenage boy – defended her decision to devote time and resources to marathon swimming by arguing:

> I've made many sacrifices, you know. As a mum, you know, in the course of [my son's] life, I have gone over and above, I believe, as a mother for him and have put everything in to him.

Male swimmers were undoubtedly taking parental responsibilities into account in organising training or making decisions about whether to sign up for a big swim, but for women, prior reproductive labour has to be *traded publicly* for the right to invest in the self, while for men, that right requires no public explanation. The pleasures of swimming, then, do not flow unproblematically to women (Smith 2000: 203), because they sit in tension with their 'unleisured lives' (Deem 1987).

This can be seen, for example, in the appropriation by female swimmers of the contemplative, restorative pleasures of swimming that were described in Chapter 2. Swimming can be an affectively transformative experience (see also, Straughan 2012). As one older female swimmer described it: 'If I go in a cranky sea lion, I come out like a smiling dolphin' (Rodgers 1999), while a male US swimmer and IT worker told me it was his daily 'hard reset'. But there is a gendered note to these contemplative pleasures, and for many women swimmers, there is an inescapably mundane and sometimes compensatory aspect to their recollection signalling their embeddedness within the material and social norms of gender. For one female swimmer, being in the water was 'like prozac'; for others, it was 'better than therapy', and a missed swim was like 'missing a meal'. Especially for those women coping with significant burdens of paid, domestic and caring labour, their regular swim emerged less as a route to transformative contemplation, and more as a piece of jealously guarded 'me-time' (see also, Little 2002). As one female swimmer with heavy caring responsibilities notes, '[it's] a chance to be something other than their cook and nurse'. This 'me-time' is protected against the endlessly encroaching demands of caring labour through narratives and performances of commitment. Signing up for a long swim was seen by many of the women in this study as a means of preserving the legitimacy of their claims to time, rendering regular training a non-negotiable commitment that had to be built into household plans (Raisborough 2006, 2007). As one female swimmer observed: 'They have to know that it's got to be done.' For others, swimming was a chance to recuperate from a loss of identity – for example, following divorce, bereavement or children leaving home. Swimming, then, is an opportunity to have a sense of identity detached from others (Young 2005: 42), but the fact that this has to be purposefully sought speaks volumes about the gendered constraints on identity formation (Wheaton and Tomlinson 1998: 262).

Resisting gender

But this is never simply a story of repression and constraint, or of time clawed away from domestic and reproductive labour (Little 2002). Instead, many female marathon swimmers were actively mobilising swimming as a means of carving out new modes of female embodiment that are quietly (and sometimes less quietly) resistant to the constraints of normative femininity. This can be seen across three related domains: the repudiation of domestic labour; the celebration of non-normative embodiment; and eating freely in public.

In her study of quilting, Stalp (2007) argues that the women she interviewed were able to combine their passion for quilting with their domestic responsibilities both by hiding their 'fabric stash' to avoid ostentatiously taking up space and by ensuring that familial responsibilities were met before devoting time to the activity. But while this is an effective strategy for leisure activities that take place within the home, this kind of 'doubling up' is less tenable because of the spatially and temporally distinct nature of the activities. Instead, and in common with other studies of women's committed leisure activities, many of the female swimmers publicly recounted their own failed domesticity, citing messy homes and a lack of attention to time-consuming domestic tasks such as baking or sewing as evidence of their commitment to swimming (see, for example, Raisborough 2006, 2007; Dilley and Scraton 2010). These tales of slovenliness were told as part of the homosocial talk among women, often accompanied by laughter and escalating stories of failed domestic femininity. They reminded me of the homophobic banter among men, whose humour relies on the shared understanding that the target of the banter is *not* gay; they serve to shore up a collective and valued identity rather than expose a 'truth', although always at the expense of the derogated Other.

In the case of housework, the derogated Other is the woman who prioritises domestic labour, in all its mundane, undervalued endlessness, over the self-directed projects of the discipline and efficacious subject. The privileging of swimming over housework is the triumph of the distinctive and celebrated over the trivial and demeaned. In a swimming clubhouse sauna in San Francisco one morning, the exhilarated post-swim chat moved to how lucky we all were, and how awful being 'just a housewife' would be. Also to be avoided was becoming a 'swimming widow' – a reference to those women who supported their male partner's swimming but who didn't swim themselves. Observing a similar trend among female windsurfers, Wheaton and Tomlinson argue that womanhood itself provides no useful grounds for bonding, and that being a windsurfer supercedes their identity as a woman (1998: 264). But the derisive rejection of the 'housewife' role exposes its own inability to dislocate women from those constraining normative expectations. For all their contempt for the status of 'housewife', their alternative, swimming-filled lives took the form of a 'lucky escape' rather than a social revolution, and their triumph is domestic labour's reprioritisation rather than its redistribution.

The second defiant mode of female embodiment that is opened up through swimming can be found in the body itself – its size, composition and state. Swimming builds muscle around the shoulders, neck and upper back in ways that potentially contravene normative gendered expectations of body size and composition (George 2005; Sisjord and Kristiansen 2009); it marks the body with eccentric suntan lines across the back and face; and, as discussed in the following chapter, it demands a level of body fat that is at odds with contemporary notions of lean, muscular sporting ideals. Regular pool swimming leaves the skin and hair with an inescapable chlorine odour, and affects hair and skin condition; sea swimming can leave chafe marks on shoulders and necks. Swimming, then, is literally written onto the body.

In a social context where women are expected to be contained, to not take up space and to be well kempt, these are defiant acts that mark a refusal to be objectified, shaped and contained – responses that are collectively endorsed by the social world of marathon swimming and its celebrations of body illegibility (see Chapter 4) but which also take on a specifically gendered dimension. Women spoke about the unexpected pleasures of strength and muscularity; of the fun in getting dirty and dishevelled; of not being what people expect (see also, Wheaton and Tomlinson 1998; Hanold 2010). In recognition of the easy disappearance of the post-menopausal body (Callahan 1993), an older swimmer noted that people were not often impressed with women her age and she relished the opportunity to make them rethink their expectations (see also, Tulle 2007). One told a journalist: 'You kind of disappear as you get older … this is my way of not quite disappearing just yet' (Rodgers 1999). Similarly, a female swimmer who identified as fat, and who recounted a long history of body dissatisfaction and restricted eating, choked back tears as she told me that after years of hating her body, she was amazed by how it felt in the water. She said that she felt angry that she and others had written off her body so easily because of her size. These are pleasures and small acts of defiance that are inseparable from the social ideologies and practices of gender that define their transgressive difference.

One final dimension to these transgressions, and one that will be dealt with in more detail in the following chapter, lies in the act of eating in public, and in particular, of foods conventionally coded as 'bad'. After long training swims, once everyone is changed and bundled up in their post-swim layers, hot drinks and energy-rich, easily digestible snacks circulate freely (see Figure 9). Food performs

Figure 9 Post-swim hot drink and snacks ready for swimmers.

a restorative function, replacing expended energy and soothing salt-sore mouths, but also operates socially, providing opportunities for mutual support and encouragement. But for women, eating in public, and its associated displays of appetite, can be a socially precarious activity (Lupton 1996). As one female swimmer with a long history of dieting and body anxiety told me: 'It felt so good to be able to eat.' In my fieldnotes, I record how liberating it is to see, and be among, women who are eating heartily and in public without the customary talk of necessary constraint – 'Oh really, I shouldn't' – or confessions of guilt and promises to 'be good tomorrow'. These pleasures in eating are sharply inflected through gendered ideologies of constrained appetites; even when all eating as swimmers together, gender may be passive, but it is always present. These public displays of appetite are never simply the act of 'manning up'.

A feminist politics of swimming?

In Chapter 2, I described a moment of sublime pleasure while swimming in Ireland; this was one of many experiences of extraordinary sensations of coordination, power and ownership while swimming (see also, Throsby 2013a). This is a profoundly gendered experience precisely because those sensations are so markedly at odds with conventional female embodiment – in particular, my own middle-aged, large body that is more likely to be overlooked or problematised (as overweight, as hormonally deficient) than celebrated. These novel feelings of whole-body engagement and belonging in a given space echo Young's proposition that, 'for many women as they move in sport, a space surrounds us in imagination that we are not free to move beyond; the space available to our movement is a constricted space' (2005: 333). These are enculturated ways of being in the world that are rooted not in physiology or essence, but in 'the particular situation of women as conditioned by their sexist oppression in society' (42). The exhilaration that I recorded in my fieldnotes, then, can be understood not only as a moment of personal pleasure, valued for its own sake, but also as a politically significant – although highly individualised – sensory experience; a chance to experience gendered embodiment differently. This matters because, as Young observes: 'If sport stands … as a symbol of freedom, then the exclusion of women from the idea of sport implies our exclusion from the idea of human freedom' (2010: 16). Indeed, the early female marathon swimmers recognised the political possibilities of swimming, linking it explicitly with the suffrage movement (Bier 2011; Davies 2015).

But my claims to a feminist politics of marathon swimming are cautious and tentative. First, marathon swimming, alongside many other lifestyle and endurance sports, is a privileged practice, and those who engage with it are, predominantly, already significantly advantaged by their white, middle-class identities and material realities (see also, Wheaton and Tomlinson 1998; Atkinson 2008). From this perspective, the privileges that enable access to marathon swimming facilitate those transformational embodied experiences; we may be all just marathon swimmers together, but not everyone can be a marathon swimmer. As Wheaton and Tomlinson note: 'Renegotiation of identity and the broadening of access to cultural and social space remain framed by the parameters of material and structural influences and constraints' (1998: 270). Furthermore, the act of swimming itself provides its own alibi for these contraventions of normative femininity; as a status-bearing activity, breaches of norms of body size and composition, grooming, consumption or dress are forgiveable in a way that those same 'deviances' among those abjected within neoliberalism are not (Tyler 2013). Indeed, as discussed in the next chapter in relation to fat, many of these embodied performances and pleasures can be understood as a form of privileged play whose 'fun' lies precisely in *not* possessing the socially derogated traits suggested by certain modes of embodiment.

This points to the second limitation to any claims to the feminist political potential of swimming: the empowerments and transformations that swimmers report and experience are highly individualistic in ways that work against group consciousness or collective action (see also, Hanold 2010; Thorpe 2011). Success in swimming is framed as enabling the individual to feel good about themselves, further driving both the desire to swim and the embrace of the 'swimmer' identity as empowering (Hanold 2010). This takes on a particularly gendered dimension in a social context whereby women are repeatedly valued for appearance over function, refused the right to take up space and warned about the instability and uncontrollability of their leaky, untamable bodies (Shildrick 1997; Birke 1999). These experiences then enhance the individual, deeply personal sense of an empowerment that seems to run against those constraining norms. These feelings of empowerment are deeply meaningful for many swimmers, including myself, and in many cases are in sharp contrast to learned experiences and habits of the body as unreliable and inadequate. But this individualised sense of empowerment comes at a price, particularly in relation to the strategies of distinction *between* women that it relies upon.

In the spring of 2009, my partner and I joined an early morning open water training session at a local lake. The two-hour session, organised by a triathlon club, was oriented primarily towards wetsuited triathletes, and I was one of just a handful of non-wetsuited swimmers using the sessions to grab some valuable open water time. At the end of the session, I paddled up to the boat slip and struggled awkwardly to my feet, peeling my goggles off my eyes and resting them on my forehead as I hobbled up the weed-slippery concrete. My face and hands were stiff with the early season cold, my skin was bright pink and my body was slightly swollen after two hours of immersion. A brown moustache of organic matter from the cloudy lake water clung to my upper lip and a few stray tendrils of weed draped over my shoulders. At the top of the slip, I saw a young woman, carefully made up and groomed, wearing a pretty, flowery dress and strappy sandals in the early morning sun. She, like many of the inhabitants of the park's campsite, had come down to the lake's edge to have breakfast at the café and to watch the unfamiliar spectacle of the swimmers, and she stared at me with an expression that can only be understood as disgust. 'It's like you were two different species,' commented my partner later. It was only later that I realised that I too had experienced disgust at her display of femininity, so alien to my own embodied selfhood and my prized identity as a marathon swimmer. Like the surfers mocking the housewives and widows (Wheaton and Tomlinson 1998) or the gap year students in Snee's study who derided fellow travellers who wouldn't relinquish their daily use of hair-straighteners (2014: 852), my own sense of empowerment relied upon a gendered hierarchy between my embodiment and that of the prettily dressed young woman at the lake, whose studied conformity I positioned myself against. Individualised narratives of empowerment are seductive, then, for the senses of pleasure and freedom that they induce, but always potentially false friends of a collective feminist political project.

Conclusion

In this chapter, I have argued that marathon swimming is governed by an apolitical gloss which flattens out social differences, including gender, under the prevailing claim to being 'all swimmers together'. This claim is endorsed by the perceived fit between women and swimming, the relative invisibility of the body as gendered while swimming, and the conventions of civil inattention that govern the peripheral aquatic spaces where swimmers gather and change. However, gender seeps out through the gaps in this de-gendered veneer, particularly via those moments when the gendered body is brought to the fore, either in order to account for high performance or through the refusal to embrace the fleshy realities of female embodiment. I also explored the ways in which wider social context, roles and expectations not only impacted on women's ability to participate in marathon swimming, but also have to be managed and negotiated publicly to account for their investment in the sport. This highlights the importance of placing sporting practice in its wider social and cultural context in order to capture not only structural factors influencing participation, but also the patterns of oppression that are embedded in everyday life (Raisborough 2007; Wheaton 2013).

This is not simply a narrative of oppression and constraint, and the research revealed multiple ways in which women resisted gender norms and carved out novel modes of embodiment that were experienced as empowering and pleasurable in their defiance of familiar constraints (see also, Little 2002). These included, for example, the repudiation, or at least re-prioritisation, of domestic labour, the celebration of non-normative modes of embodied distinction and the transgressive act of eating freely in public. This points to some potential openings for a feminist politics of marathon swimming, not least through the discovery of embodied pleasures and freedoms that are customarily denied to women in damaging and limiting ways. Undoubtedly, though, this is a constrained and privileged form of politics, since marathon swimming is a practice that relies upon already-existing privilege in order to accomplish these experiences of empowerment (Hanold 2010). Furthermore, marathon swimming exemplifies the treatment of the self as enterprise – of politics as self-actualisation rather than social transformation – and, therefore, aligns with the proliferation of difference through the celebration of self-management and individuality. Within this frame, the possibilities for collective critique and resistance are disarmed and absorbed: 'individual autonomy becomes not the opposite of, or limit to, neoliberal governance, rather it lies at the heart of its disciplinary control' (McNay 2009: 62).

With these caveats in mind, this is still not to argue that those individualised feelings of empowerment are not 'real', or that they are purposefully exclusive of less privileged others. Nor are the extraordinary pleasures and gender transgressions of marathon swimming entirely devoid of feminist political possibilities, however muted. Marathon swimming has been shown to offer up novel ways of experiencing the female body, and new ways of experiencing the world through the body, demonstrating the contingency of even the most entrenched ways of thinking about bodies and their possibilities. These transgressive pleasures, then, are not about becoming more like the idealised masculine heroes of endurance sport, but rather, reflect the embodiment of new modes of marathon swimming subjectivity that suggest an alternative vision of the sport itself, outside of the masculinised rhetorics of 'manning up' (Young 2010).

Notes

1 Cahn suggests that gender and race intersect here, arguing that the 'assertion that sport made women physically unattractive and sexually unappealing found its corollary in view of black women as less attractive and desirable than white women' (1994: 128).
2 Subsequent iterations of this seminar became the 'Four Ps' to incorporate the issue of menstruation.

7

Heroic fatness

Whenever marathon swimmers gather, usually along banks and shorelines of the aquatic spaces that we have temporarily claimed for our leisure, someone will usually remark, to knowing laughter, what a 'fine' set of specimens we are. Marathon swimmers constitute a diverse array of body types, sizes and compositions, none of which can be mapped cleanly onto expectations of performance, and many of whom have purposefully either gained or maintained weight that in other contexts might be defined as 'excess'. This places many swimmers at odds with the contemporary 'war on obesity' – the attack on fat as a pervasive social, economic and health threat against which action must be taken (WHO 2000; Foresight 2007). Within this framework, fat bodies are seen as the embodied consequence of negative traits such as laziness, greed and poor self-discipline (Murray 2005, 2008; Featherstone 2010; Hardy 2013). From this perspective, the fat body cannot be a sporting body, since socially privileged traits such as the reflexive self-disciplining of bodily boundaries and appetites are strongly associated with the production of contemporary sporting bodies but are conventionally treated as antithetical to fatness (Shogan 1999; Zanker and Gard 2008; Magdalinski 2009). This is, of course, to oversimplify, since ideal sporting body size and composition varies enormously with fields such as sumo, rugby, wrestling and field sports all demanding both fat and muscular bulk in ways that challenge conventional stereotypes of athleticism. Nevertheless, lean, taut embodiment remains most easily socially coded as 'sporting' and the morally privileged antithesis to the presumed moral failures of fatness (Markula 1995).

Within the dominant anti-fat framework, the relationship between sport and fatness is conceived primarily in terms of sport's presumed role in facilitating weight loss, usually via discourses of 'health' and to the exclusion of pleasure or other metrics of well-being (Brabazon 2006; Synne Groven *et al.* 2011). This represents the key exception to the normative mutual exclusivity of fit and fat, where fat bodies exercising explicitly for weight loss purposes can be celebrated in anticipation of the future alignment of the disciplined self and body. This positioning of sport and physical activity as one part of the 'solution' to the 'obesity epidemic' is evident in the legacy action plan for the London 2012 Olympics. Citing the 2007 Foresight report's pessimistic predictions for future obesity rates and their imagined costs, the plan concludes that the London Olympics are 'the best chance in a generation to encourage people to be more physically active' (Department for Culture, Media and Sport 2008: 22). The presumed relationship between increased physical activity and tackling the 'epidemic' is never directly stated in the action plan, but the contiguous location of the Foresight report's predictions and the physical activity goals invoke that relationship. Indeed, it could be argued that the connection is so ubiquitously asserted through anti-obesity policy and practice that a direct statement is no longer necessary (see, for example, Department of Health 2004).

So what does this mean, then, for the sport of marathon swimming, which actively *demands* the acquisition, or minimally, the maintenance of body fat as a performance advantage? How are legitimate endurance swimming identities constructed, contested and embodied in such a seemingly paradoxical context?

For most endurance sports, the normative mutual exclusivity of fitness and fatness is given 'common sense' reinforcement by the fact that leanness offers a performance advantage by maximising the power to weight ratio and increasing speed and agility.[1] The training process for those who want to improve their performance in endurance sporting competition, then, frequently involves the development and maintenance of a leaner body, often combined with sport-specific targeted muscularity (Chapman 1997; Abbas 2004; Robinson 2008). In marathon swimming, however, alongside swim-specific muscularity and appropriate technique, body fat itself, *qua fat*, is prized for its insulating properties, enabling swimmers to stay in the water for longer periods without succumbing to hypothermia. As already mentioned, marathon swimming is not the only sport that demands 'bigness' from its participants. Nevertheless, the purposeful acquisition or maintenance specifically of body fat renders the marathon swimming body a significant anomaly. This is firstly because, while there are certainly other sports that demand bulk, including fat, this is not the case for endurance sports; and, secondly, while other bulk-demanding sports value both fat and muscle for the added force and heft they provide, in the case of marathon swimming, fat is valued specifically for its insulating properties and is not interchangeable with muscle. This anomalous status is compounded by the prevailing normative opposition of 'fit' and 'fat' in the contemporary 'war on obesity' and the repeated coding of endurance sports such as distance running as both contributing to, and demanding, weight loss.

Fat acquisition is not the only strategy for coping with the cold in marathon swimming. As discussed in Chapter 1, the body's thermoregulatory systems can be prompted to adapt to exposure to cold in a variety of insulative, hypothermic and metabolic ways through regular immersion in cold water (Hong *et al.* 1987; Vybiral *et al.* 2000; Makinen 2010), although Makinen notes in the conclusion to her overview of the research on cold adaptation in humans that 'human physiological responses against the adverse effects of cold are rather limited' (2010: 1061). Furthermore, while the very limited research on marathon swimmers supports a positive relationship between body fat and resistance to swim-stopping levels of hypothermia (Keatinge *et al.* 2001; Branningan *et al.* 2009), they are too compromised by small sample sizes, problems of measurement and their inability to reflect the effect of changes in body size and composition to offer guidance on how much body fat is enough. Furthermore, as discussed in Chapter 4, individual responses to cold are highly idiosyncratic, making generalisations impossible. Nevertheless, the basic principle adheres and some weight gain, however arbitrary in degree, is a common part of the training process for many marathon swimmers leading up to a big, cold water swim. But as I argue in this chapter, the social potency of fat means that this weight gain can never only be experienced in instrumental terms, however reflexively framed via the body's vulnerabilities to cold, requiring extensive discursive work and negotiation in order to align the fat(tened) marathon swimming body with notions of 'good' sporting embodiment.

Like many marathon swimmers, my body is not one that is easily coded as 'athletic', especially outside of the social world of marathon swimming. In clinical terms, I have hovered for years around the medically-drawn boundaries of 'overweight' and 'obese'; I'm a comfortable UK size sixteen, with wide hips and thighs, a stomach which rounds over my belt when I sit or bend and small arcs of fat that squeeze round the edges of my bra straps. I have been lighter and leaner at various times in my life, mostly when I was much younger and usually as a result of the rigorous, punishing and ultimately unsustainable dieting and exercise regimes that make up most women's sporadic realities. But in the more recent past, and certainly into my forties, this mundanely 'overweight' body of mine has been my stable and increasingly contented reality. Like many swimmers, I purposefully gained some weight (approximately ten pounds) in the months leading up to my English Channel swim and I don't know whether this made a material difference to my ability to swim and tolerate the cold, although I certainly found reassurance in it.

When I first started reflecting on swimming fat, as a swimmer, a fat woman and via my allegiance to the broader critical field of Fat Studies (see, for example, Gard and Wright 2005; Rothblum and Solovay 2009; Tomrley and Kaloski Naylor 2009; Cooper 2010), I approached the topic in a mood of political optimism. I was excited by my discovery of a sporting site that appeared to directly repudiate the conventionally competing values of fitness and fatness that I found so problematic in other aspects of my academic and personal life. However, closer inspection revealed a much more complicated relationship with fat that simultaneously comprises a profound allegiance to the rhetorics of bodily discipline and control, antipathy towards fat *and* the (contingent) valuing and celebration of fat. This apparently contradictory embrace and repudiation of fat is held together for many of the swimmers, and especially those with a formerly lean, 'athletic' embodied identity, through what I have called 'heroic fatness', and it is this concept that is the focus of this chapter. Through heroic fatness, marathon swimming fat is framed as an undesirable but necessary act of bodily discipline and sacrifice in the service of the swimming endeavour. This renders purposeful swimming fat a transformative bodily sacrifice that aligns easily with a sport like marathon swimming, which is already strongly self-defined in terms of suffering, enduring and overcoming. Fat becomes another form of suffering, nobly borne. But my use of 'heroic' is ironic here, since the construction of purposeful fatness as courageously self-sacrificial obscures the necessary 'not-me-ness' of the fat that immunises the heroically fat swimmer against the negative stigma of 'real' fatness. In essence, like medical fat suits designed for training or health education (Hardy 2013), dramatic fat suits or fat gained by an actor for a specific role (LeBesco 2005; Mendoza 2009), heroic swimming fat is rendered safely inauthentic by its presumed provisionality and incongruity; in short, the fat is fake.

The 'not-me-ness' of heroic fatness, then, reveals little of the reflexive critique of the 'war on obesity' that I was naively hoping for, but it does still have much to say, however inadvertently, about the 'world of *constituent affective relations* with fat/ness' (Hardy 2013: 6, emphasis in original). Like the lump of fake fat that is at the centre of Hardy's analysis, heroic fatness is articulated through explicit narratives of neither health nor physiological function (Hardy 2013: 8), and nor is it constituted through straightforwardly form-as-function rationalisations in relation to cold tolerance. Instead, it operates in a primarily affective register; that is, through the 'non-verbal, non-conscious dimensions of experience' (Blackman and Venn 2010: 8). In this chapter, I argue that these affective dimensions of swimming fat elucidate both the profoundly entrenched and embodied nature of learned responses to fat *and* the uncontainability of fat within the narrow constraints of the prevailing rhetorics of the 'war on obesity' and its utilitarian appropriations of and by sport.

The main body of the chapter is divided into two sections. The first sets out the ideal-type of heroic fatness and the ways in which the constructed fakeness of the fat is used to distance the self from the negative character traits that fatness is commonly assumed to embody. The second section explores the much more ambivalent modes of fatness that occur alongside, and in response to, this heroic ideal, exposing the disjunctures and ambiguities that constitute the prevailing knowledges and lived experiences of both fatness and sport. These more ambivalent embodied relations reveal a less adversarial encounter with swimming fat, and the (always constrained) possibility of what Hardy describes as 'new tissues of affective experience' (2013: 21) that feel cautiously 'against the grain' (Hardy 2013: 19).

Heroic fatness

There are two key elements to the construction of ideal-type heroic fatness: first, its status as an undesirable necessity; and second, the presumed malleability of the body.

Amidst the uncertainties about how much body fat is enough, a singular certainty emerges within the dominant narrative of marathon swimming: that fat is both undesirable and necessary. This is encapsulated in the commonly circulating maxim, 'You can't be too vain to gain if you want to swim the Channel', which presumes the unattractiveness of the fat body. For many swimmers coming to the sport from other endurance sports, the concept of purposeful weight gain was an anathema to their sporting and social identities. US swimmer, Alice, for example, was in her early twenties when I interviewed her, with an accomplished history as a competitive pool swimmer. As she transitioned into marathon swimming, an experienced local swimmer mentored her:

> Well [he] told me I needed to gain weight when I first told him I wanted to do [a marathon swim], and he told me I needed to gain fifteen pounds. I mean I was thinner [than I am now] and I said no [laughs] and he said okay, how about half of that. And I said yes but in my mind half of that was five, rounded down, I was like, I could gain five pounds [laughs, gesturing ambivalence]. ... So I really was not going to do anything. But what I started to notice in the winter was that I almost ... it just changed the distribution of fat. I don't know if this is even true, or it is in my head, or I just naturally gained weight but it seemed like I carried more weight around my core. Erm ... it did not bother me too much because I knew that it was temporary....

Alice's internal bargaining over weight gain signals her discomfort with purposeful fat as part of her personal and sporting identities, and her account shifts responsibility for increased fat (or at least its redistribution) to the body itself, which is framed as seeking protection against the assault from the cold by laying down fat around its core. This partially neutralises the potential toxicity of body fat by positioning it as a 'natural' response rather than the failure to discipline the body. The final caveat is significant too, and constitutes a defining feature of heroic fatness: its provisionality.

UK swimmer, Simon, on the other hand, was an experienced and accomplished endurance athlete and climber whose relatively lean 'athletic' body made him vulnerable to the cold – a problem experienced during training and then in an initial, unsuccessful English Channel swim, forcing him to embrace an accelerated programme of weight gain:

> [The] thing is, I was fit enough to swim, but it just seemed so gloriously unfair that with swimming, it does not ... well, with channel swimming ... it is almost the opposite, isn't it, because in other sports, the fitter you are, the leaner you are, the more muscular you are, you know, equals improved performance. But of course, you learn in Channel swimming ... it is about getting your body in the right sort of shape in terms of being acclimatised, increased body fat and buoyancy and technique.... It just seemed so alien to me to be on the one hand just banging out as much swim time as possible, but on the other hand, you know, eating five doughnuts a day, getting up at 5 a.m. ... having a fry-up before you go to work, eating bars of chocolate....

Simon identifies body fat as one of a number of sport-specific bodily requirements, but it is the need for weight gain that is singled out as 'gloriously unfair' and at odds with other sports. He experiences this as a tension not only between his endurance sporting past and his swimming present, but also within swim training itself, experiencing disturbing dissonance between 'banging out' laps and gaining weight, and struggling to align a diet of doughnuts and fry-ups with an endurance sporting identity after years of the disciplined high protein regimens of those aiming for lean muscle gains.

Heroic fatness

For Claire – a UK swimmer and fitness professional – this dissonance was a driving force in her decision to relinquish her English Channel swimming ambitions:

> You know ... a lot of people mentioned to me ... probably around Christmas time when I had visibly lost some weight [from swim training] and a lot of the people that I swim with at the triathlon club said to me, 'Oh, you are going to have to put that back on though. You are going to get cold woman.' And I immediately kicked against it because I mean I saw, I was like ... but I didn't want to. I was feeling so good, I was feeling the fittest I have ever been, I was like you know ... and ultimately if it came down to it, if you asked me would getting across the Channel be more important or would being in good shape and feeling as good as I have been in the last few months be more important, I would go with the second one ... I love being fit and also I preach, I am spending my day trying to get kids and adults to eat in the right way and train in the right way ... and it is not about looking good but it is about treating your body the right way and I have always exercised because I ... I really have respect for my body and I want to treat it really well you know ... I really like it when I am feeling really fit. I feel a lot more energetic at work, you know it is the whole package in it and that is how I felt the last two months and I thought, oh this is ... I was loving the training so I was like, yes I am really feeling in great shape, and then at the back of my head I thought, no ... if I had to, you know I was really struggling ... I was thinking if I had to put on more weight to be able to achieve this, would I want ... And I thought, no, I would not.

The intensity of winter training for an English Channel swim had given Claire a sense of fitness and well-being that was easily intelligible to her as healthy, but the need to gain weight, and what she would need to eat in order to gain weight, was irretrievably incompatible with that sense of health and fitness. Her profession amplifies this discomfort, producing a disjuncture between what she 'preaches' and how she lives. For Claire, purposefully acquired swimming fat could never be heroic, however provisionally, and she found herself forced to choose between her personal and professional commitments to a particular conceptualisation of health and fitness and her desire to swim the English Channel.

In contrast to Claire, however, Simon's objections to his own weight gain were never articulated through the rhetorics of health, but rather, his dissatisfaction registered affectively as disgust and horror at both the fattening body, and the process of weight gain. As he was talking, he gestured an exaggeratedly rounded belly and blew out his cheeks to make a 'fat face', exclaiming: 'and I could see all the weight going on....' The suddenness of the exaggerated gestural transformation echoes the use of fat suits in films, where lean actors perform fatness 'for cheap laughs at the expense of fat people' while simultaneously affirming the inauthenticity of their own provisional fatness and distancing themselves from authentically fat others (LeBesco 2005: 237). Simon's 'fat face', therefore, simultaneously recognises the association between fatness and the failed self and repudiates it *in his own case*, but not in principle. This is the defining accomplishment of heroic fatness, and it relies upon two strategies of distinction: first, between purposeful fatness and having 'let yourself go'; and second, between the toughness of fat-facilitated marathon swimming and normatively 'athletic' leanness.

My fieldnotes are punctuated with commentaries from swimmers about the fat bodies of non-swimming others – as 'disgusting', 'just wrong', 'criminal'.[2] These commentaries were primarily inward-facing performances of disgust rather than direct attacks on the targets of their contempt, oriented towards cementing group belonging and the careful drawing of distinctions between acceptable and unacceptable fat. For example, during a training camp in Malta, a swimmer pointed to a male holidaymaker whose rounded stomach hung heavily over the waistband of his shorts, remarking laughingly: 'He'd make a good Channel swimmer.' This commonly repeated 'joke' finds its humour in a shared recognition that the body fat of the swimmers and that of the non-swimmers on the beach may be materially similar, but is symbolically different. The non-swimmers have 'let themselves go' while the swimmers have purposefully made fat happen. For all the monolithic anti-fat rhetoric of the 'war on obesity', then, not all fat is equal, and heroic fatness is dependent on the careful, but precarious, distinction between fatnesses.

The second strategy of distinction is the comparison of marathon swimmers with open water swimmers who use wetsuits. As discussed in Chapter 3, there is considerable contestation within the marathon swimming community about whether a wetsuit swim can legitimately be categorised as a 'marathon swim', regardless of duration, since neoprene provides both insulation and additional buoyancy. Among the non-wetsuit faction, the boundaries of authentic swimming are policed through the use of banter, contrasting 'wimpsuits' with the marathon swimmers' reliance on 'bioprene' alone – a neologism that encapsulates both the distinction between fatnesses and that between wetsuit and non-wetsuit swimming. This strategy of distinction also encompassed elite athletes who were repeatedly cited as unable to complete a marathon swim because of their unsuitably lean physique. As US swimmer, Phillip, noted: 'When I began to meet Channel swimmers I realised that most successful Channel swimmers were not svelte, petite, small hips. Michael Phelps could never swim the Channel.' Endurance cyclist and triathlete, Lance Armstrong (before his fall from grace for using performance-enhancing drugs (Walsh 2013)), was also repeatedly invoked as an example of an elite sporting body that would simply not be up to the task.

In these accounts, the purposefully fat swimming body is positioned as distinct from (and superior to) both the failed fat body *and* the lean body of even the most elite athletes. It is a strategic reproduction of a fat/lean binary that flattens out the complexity and variety of sporting embodiment in order to reinforce the exceptionalism of the marathon swimming body. This can be seen as both outward-looking in accounting for fat gain in a fat-phobic society, and inward-looking within the open water swimming field. As is also evident in other sporting subcultures – for example, snowboarding (Thorpe 2011), surfing (Booth 2004; Wheaton 2004b), skateboarding (Beal and Wilson 2004) and climbing (Lewis 2004) – distinctions between groups within those subcultures establish (contested) hierarchies, which in turn 'command different degrees of capital conversion' (Thorpe 2011: 120). For example, Wheaton (2013: 890–898) describes how, among windsurfers, the 'wave-sailors' garner the highest respect, and they look down on speed or slalom sailors as over-reliant on equipment. In turn, the surfing media derides windsurfers as 'wind-wankers', and body boarders as 'spongers' or 'shark biscuits'. In the struggle for status in the wider worlds of open water swimming, and of endurance sports more generally, swimming fat is mobilised here as evidence *par excellence* of a status-bearing willingness to suffer and endure – both in terms of exposure to the cold and in the willingness to risk the social stigma of fat. It is in this way that fatness is positioned as both enabling and causing suffering, which is heroically borne, although it is also important to note that swimmers are also warned against the moral hazards of over-relying on weight gain to the exclusion of acclimatisation practices – a perceived easy path that is counter to the prevailing social world ethic of training as work. This echoes the 'quick fix' accusations that attach so easily to those undergoing obesity surgery as a means of achieving weight loss, as opposed to the morally privileged 'lifestyle' interventions of diet and exercise (Throsby 2009, 2012).

The second key element in the construction of heroic fatness is its provisionality, and by extension, the presumed malleability of the body – the assumption that weight loss (or gain) is (and should be) within the remit of the disciplined individual. As one experienced male swimmer who was planning to retire from swimming at the end of the season told me: 'I'm going to hang up my trunks, get rid of the flab and go back to running.' The assumption of the body's susceptibility to purposeful transformation is entirely in line with the contemporary 'war on obesity' and its assumptions regarding the predictable malleability of bodies when subject to the appropriate degree of bodily discipline (Ogilvie and Hamlet 2005). The provisionality of the heroically fat swimming body, therefore, firmly locates the swimmer within positively valued traits of reflexive self-discipline and self-efficacy because it embodies both the acknowledgement of fatness as contingently necessary but fundamentally undesirable, *and* the presumed ability to lose weight once the swimming challenge has been completed. This once again invokes the fat-suited actor, or the actor who gains weight for a role – a greater degree of dangerous closeness to 'real' fat bringing 'career-making accolades' for those brave enough (LeBesco 2005: 235). LeBesco argues that, in both cases, we are reassured by seeing 'lean, conventionally attractive actors unencumbered by fatness *outside* of the film's frames' (236, emphasis in original). The inauthenticity of purposefully provisional (fake) fat offers the reassurance that the individual is 'in no danger of a slide into obesity' (238). As one male US swimmer noted: '[The fat] is okay because it's not who I am.'

The presumed malleability of the body, however, cannot always be relied upon, as several swimmers discovered to their disappointment. Don, for example, described a familiar weight trajectory of having been 'a little bit overweight to begin with' followed by weight loss and increased muscular definition as training intensified. He then realised that he needed to regain weight for insulation, 'so I did go out of my way to put about one and a half stone [twenty-one pounds] on':

> It was harder than I thought because when you are swimming that much, you are losing so many calories and you have got to eat your normal calories plus what you have lost and you have got to eat an extra on top of that. I ended up,

I was having bigger portions obviously, eating more often. I ended up just eating junk to be honest, chocolate, crisps, Magnums.[3] I had a thing for Magnums, you know a Magnum a night. It is just you know getting as much calories in me as I can. That is how I managed to put one and a half stone on. ... I did not like the thought that I was deliberately putting it on because it's unhealthy but I knew it was to achieve what I wanted to achieve.... What I was not happy about was that I could not lose it again after because obviously I'd stopped swimming. I have still kept it [swimming] up but nowhere near as much ... but I found it hard to cut down on the food.

Don's narrative contains many of the familiar elements of heroic fatness: the acknowledgement of the 'wrongness' of fat; and the privileging of the swimming endeavour itself as a justification for weight gain. Like Simon, the urgency of the pending swim led to eating patterns that fell well outside of conventional dietary advice, with the intensive physical demands of marathon swimming serving both compensatory and justificatory functions. However, for Don, the necessary provisionality of heroic fatness was elusive, and the pleasures of less-restrained eating were hard to relinquish. Over two years later, at a stable but intractable weight that he was unhappy with, it was increasingly difficult for Don's swimming fat to be rendered 'not me'; the inauthenticity of fat and its provisionality are inextricable. His struggle to lose the weight he had gained reflects what many of those engaging with weight loss interventions already know about the limited effectiveness of 'lifestyle'-based interventions (Mann et al. 2007), and this struggle signals a chink in the armour of heroic fatness; a first indication that, in spite of its clean simplicity, it both produces and relies on exclusions and contradictions that quickly unsettle its own narrative.

Unsettling heroic fatness

The previous section set out the ideal-type of heroic fatness in marathon swimming, which remains simultaneously in line with contemporary anti-obesity values even while (provisionally) embracing the fat body/body fat – a circle that is squared through the rendering of purposefully acquired swimming fat as inauthentic and as 'not me'. However, as the mundane example of Don illustrates, this ideal-type figuration is replete with contradictions between the prevailing norms and embodied experience. In particular, and following on from the previous chapter, the section explores, first, exclusions in relation to gender and, second, in relation to those who are already fat at the start of the training process. I then move on to highlight a more ambivalent framing of the fat swimming body that steps cautiously outside of the dichotomy of real/fake fat upon which heroic fatness relies.

Among (some) groups of men, increased body fat was a source of considerable humour and banter, and those who gained significant amounts of weight over relatively short periods of time were granted heroic status within the homosocial group. In a small number of cases, this even extended to a collective project of 'feeding up' one of the group. This was particularly evident in Dover, where there is a seasonal concentration of individuals training primarily for English Channel swims, creating a critical mass that is absent from year-round training sites that include marathon swimmers among a wider community of open water swimmers but which are not defined by them. This homosocial celebration recalls the Clydesdale runners described by Chase (2008) who compete in weight rather than age categories – an innovation designed to level the playing field for heavier runners. Chase notes that, at the pre-race weigh-in, male runners would applaud each other if they had gone up a weight category, while such public celebrations of fatness were not available to women (Chase 2008: 139). My fieldnotes also recall multiple incidences of men naming their stomachs – 'It's time to feed Norman' – or animating the fattened stomach by grasping it with both hands to make a fold, opening and closing it like a mouth to demand food: 'Feed me, feed me.' While the gesture is designed to invoke disgust at the exaggerated mobility of fat and skin, the men on the beach domesticated their fat stomachs, rendering the fat almost pet-like. It is in this way that their fat can be understood as fake; to all intents and purposes, they are playing at being fat, whilst being protected from its negative attributions by their cultural and physical capital as athletes, prospective Channel swimmers, and as men. This behaviour was particularly evident among relatively small groups of 'laddish' young men (see also, Wheaton 2004b: 146), and it relies upon a shared understanding of the inauthenticity of fat in much the same way that homophobic banter (also evident among these groups, along with sexism) affirms heterosexuality, and by extension, masculinity (Beal and Wilson 2004; Bridel and Rail 2007). As such, this fat play can be understood both as a celebration and a collective defence against the shaming possibilities of weight gain.

This is a profoundly classed form of play, since fatness itself is a mode of embodiment that is deemed antithetical to middle-class values of self-efficacy and bodily discipline (Herndon 2005; see also, Mansfield 2011). As Skeggs notes, middle-class people can 'play' at being working-class – for example, wearing grunge clothing or through allegiances to certain kinds of music – because they already possess considerable cultural capital that is not threatened by those performances (1997: Ch. 5). This 'play' was evident not only through performances around fat, but also in the relishing of mismatched casual clothing and hats that are piled on after swimming and in the extravagant consumption of fast food, both of which were commonly framed, especially in the UK context, as a playful 'letting go' of constraint that aped stereotypes of working classness. This recalls the experiences of unintelligibility described in Chapter 2, where misreadings of the shivering or oddly dressed body were easily dispelled and playfully recounted in ways not open to those for whom those misreadings have more serious and inescapable consequences. On the beach in Dover, this classed performance is intensified by the tangible tensions between the primarily middle-class swimmers and the predominantly working-class population of the town, particularly in leisure spaces such as pubs or on the beach in the height of summer. This was reflected in 'banter' about 'chavs' – an offensive and peculiarly British reference to a stereotyped, abject working-class embodiment (Tyler 2013) – which carefully cements the relationship between *playful* abjection and its very real counterpart. Indeed, the practice of marathon swimming itself can be seen as an extension of this tension, especially in locations such as the English Channel or the Straits of Gibraltar, which swimmers are able to take as spaces of leisure, but which for others are the sites of desperate, and sometimes fatal, attempts to cross closely policed international borders in search of a better life.

The classed performances of playful fat that were evident among these groups of men are also marked by gender, and while many of the women in the training communities gained weight in order to swim, I never saw this kind of physical comedy in relation to women's bodies or heard overt claims to heroic fatness. Furthermore, women were much more cautious about discussing it in the interviews, often locating their experiences of fatness within long histories of struggle with the diet industry, including exercise regimens oriented towards the gender normative management of weight and body composition (Markula 1995; Maguire and Mansfield 1998; Mansfield 2011). Female weight gain is not a route to homosocial status or belonging in the way that it can be for (some) men, and swimming weight gain, like muscularity, moves women further away from normative femininity, while moving men towards masculinity. This unspeakability renders the physical performances of fat out of reach for most women. As one female interviewee, Melissa, noted of her significant pre-Channel swim weight gain: 'I would say that while I've been training to swim the Channel I was probably quite … I probably thought of myself as quite an androgynous person. I was just a machine, that's all.' There is no readily available affirmative lexicon for female swimming fatness; there is nothing heroic about it, and it's not funny. Instead, for the female swimmers, swimming fat was expressed more commonly through the language of criminality, with a pending swim serving as an 'alibi' or a 'get out of jail free card' for fatness, rather than a heroic endeavour.

A second and related exclusion can be found in the fact that heroic fatness is the preserve of those who are not fat at the start of the training process. Instead, swimmers who already have sufficient (or more than sufficient) body fat to enable them to swim can never have heroically fat bodies, since *being* fat and *getting* fat (and then lean again) are symbolically distinct. This is another reason why heroic fatness is less available to women, since, as discussed in the previous chapter, their bodies are already seen as 'naturally' endowed with fat. For those who are categorised by their peers as already (authentically and therefore problematically) fat, the physical comedy and homosocial celebration of heroic swimming fatness functions not as a means of belonging, but instead as a form of symbolic violence; that is, in Bourdieu's terms, 'a gentle violence' (2001: 1) that naturalises the social order through apparently innocuous and mundane practices (Brown 2006: 167) – for example, through seemingly harmless physical comedy or through the reiteration of aphoristic wisdoms ('you can't be too vain to gain').

This is echoed in this extract from my fieldnotes:

> It was early morning on the beach in Dover on a bright summer morning in July, and swimmers were milling around changing, snatching last gulps of energy drink and smearing each other with Vaseline and suncream ready for the day's training.

> I was standing in line with Tim, waiting to have our armpits daubed by one of the beach volunteers. Tim was a tall, bulky man in his forties with a rounded stomach and double chin; he was a graceful, powerful, relentless swimmer, with wide shoulders and sporting a swimmer's tan from a season of hard training for an upcoming Channel swim. From our position in line, we watched as a small group of younger men noisily slapped and wobbled the recently acquired rounded belly of one of them – a young man whose dramatic weight gain over the last three months had granted him heroic status within the group. Tim leaned over to me and rubbing his hand across his own fat stomach, whispered: 'It makes you wonder what they must think of me.'

Citing Audre Lorde's realisation that 'it is *her body* that is disgusting to a white woman sitting next to her on the bus', Hemmings cautions that some people are 'so over associated with affect that they themselves are the object of affective transfer' (2005: 561, emphasis in original). My friend on the beach recognised his own status (and perhaps also mine, as a fat ally) as the potential object of the men's affective play; for them, it is his body (or at least bodies like his, or mine) that evokes the disgust that underpins the 'fun' of (fake) fatness. This also highlights the extent to which heroic fatness is the domain of hegemonic modes of masculinity (Connell 1995), rather than men *per se*, for whom the negotiation of the fat body in a fat-phobic society has its own complexities (Bell and McNaughton 2007; Monaghan 2007b, 2008).

Similarly, the ostentatious consumption of low quality food that marked many of the more dramatic and intensive efforts to gain weight can also be understood as symbolically violent towards those who are visibly fat, and especially those outside of the marathon swimming world and therefore without the protective gloss of overt athletic endeavour. The intensive consumption of fast food and other calorie-dense, nutritionally limited foods displayed by some swimmers constitutes a parody of how 'real' fat people are imagined to eat and how weight gain occurs; indeed, it is no accident that the abject fat bodies in the media images that routinely accompany 'obesity epidemic' stories are so commonly depicted clutching a burger in their hands or tucking into a carton of fries. This overlooks the complexity of most weight histories, which may be punctuated by periods of marked gain – for example, in relation to pregnancy or a debilitating injury – but are mostly elusively incremental and multi-factorial in ways that neither obesity science nor the individuals themselves can account for fully (Throsby 2007). Similarly, the presumed provisionality of the heroically fat body takes for granted the normative logics of the 'war on obesity' that body size and composition is, and should be, within the remit of the individual. This is an assumption that fails to account for the negative health effects of often decades of dieting and regain, the well-documented long-term ineffectiveness of 'lifestyle' interventions and intersecting factors such as poverty, ill health, distressing personal circumstances or other factors that may make weight loss either impossible or render it a low priority in the face of more pressing personal concerns (Herndon 2005; Mann et al. 2007). The celebratory playfulness that shores up heroic fatness, then, as with dramatic fat suits, is always at the expense of 'real' fat people, both male and female.

Particularly male swimmers can step outside of the heroic/unheroic fat binary and achieve social inclusion within the hegemonic group of heroically fat swimmers, primarily through alignment with other aspects of sporting identity which then discount the problem of 'real' fatness. For example, as has been observed among gay athletes seeking acceptance into male sporting communities (Bridel and Rail 2007), another route to inclusion is through high performance and competitive displays (see also, Jamieson *et al*. 2008). These hegemonic sporting performances neutralise the 'problem' of unheroic fatness by shifting the focus onto performance instead. Significantly, though, the fatness remains 'real'. As a male UK swimmer noted about a shared acquaintance: 'I don't think of him as fat. He's just a really great swimmer.' By implication, then, the fat can only be disregarded as long as he is still swimming so well. Even from my own position well outside the protective glow of high performance, I noted this same tension in my own fieldnotes as I struggled to manage my conflicted feelings about my own fat(tened) body. Two months after my English Channel swim, I recorded: 'The fat feels different now that I'm not swimming. The swimming body and the confidence I felt in it is produced by the action of long swimming; it's disappointingly hard to hold on to now I'm out of the water.' The swimming was more of a compensation for fatness than I had realised; for all the politicisation and raised consciousness that Fat Studies affords, it is never entirely possible to step outside of those anti-fat values into which we are all so determinedly inculcated (Throsby and Gimlin 2009). After my English Channel swim, a swimming acquaintance asked if I was planning to lose weight or do another swim; non-swimming fatness, it appears, is never an acceptable option.

LeBesco argues in relation to dramatic fat suits that the 'embrace of inauthenticity is revealing for what it tells us about the stability of fat-phobic anxieties' (2005: 238). However, in spite of the entrenched nature of the understandings of fat upon which heroic fatness relies, it is also clear that what Fat Studies scholar, Murray, calls the 'negative culture of collective "knowingness" about fatness' (2005: 154) cannot contain the embodied experience of fatness. Writing of the multiple masculinities in the surfing subculture that she studied, Wheaton (2004) suggests that, for all the displays of 'laddish' hegemonic masculinity that prevailed in the subculture, she also witnessed an 'ambivalent masculinity' that emphasised camaraderie and support. A similar ambivalence can be seen in relation to fatness among many of the marathon swimmers, where the dominant framing of swimming fatness as an undesirable necessity gave way to more ambivalent experiences of fat sporting embodiment that cannot be reduced to an authentic/inauthentic binary. This focus opens up what Lois McNay describes as a more 'differentiated or layered account of the entrenched dimension of embodied experiences that might escape processes of reflexive self-monitoring' (1999: 103). As one female swimmer who identified as overweight for large parts of her life noted: 'My heart rate is really good, my resting heart rate is phenomenal. My blood pressure is low. Well, you know, you swim and swim and swim.' 'I might be fat,' noted another female swimmer, 'but my body is amazing. Just amazing. Look what it can do.' While these stories were highly contingent and often opened with confessional statements – 'I know I'm fat, but...' – these experiences mark a changed awareness of what the fat sporting body could signify.

These assertions of wellness speak directly to the prevailing assumption that fat is synonymous with ill health, and particularly chronic conditions such as heart disease, high blood pressure and diabetes. This assumption was endorsed for many swimmers when they visited their GP for the medical that is a prerequisite of most marathon swims. In the course of the research, I was told multiple 'surprising body' tales of disbelieving doctors who refused to accept the evidence of their own instruments, such was their certainty that the fat body before them must be measurably unwell. As one male UK swimmer recalled, laughing: '[H]e just kept restarting the [blood pressure] machine again and again, and in the end, he went and got another one, but the reading was still the same.' These moments of disjuncture between medical expectation and measurement were a source of considerable pleasure to many swimmers, and especially to those whose bodies were disapprovingly 'known' in advance because of their size.

But this pleasure in the surprising body is never simply a reflexive re-evaluation of the 'facts' of anti-obesity campaigns, but also potentially reflects an affective transformation that in turn opens up a less adversarial relationship with the body, often after years of 'fighting fat' (see also, Hanold 2010). For example, a female UK swimmer told me that she had weighed herself every day throughout her adult life – a practice which she had stopped while gaining weight for a swim because she couldn't face seeing the rising numbers after years of close self-monitoring. Post-swim, however, she looked back on this habitual weighing as 'a bit psycho' and didn't return to her daily weigh-in. Another female swimmer spoke of the unexpected pleasure she found in the solidity of her heavier body, its occupation of space and the unanticipated freedom of no longer 'obsessing over food'. Melissa, who appeared earlier in this chapter describing her swimming body in very androgynous terms, observed:

> I've been this fat before ... unhappily so. You know, very unhappily so. You know, in a depressed state, hating my body. Whereas now, you know, I'm ambivalent about losing it.

This is a far cry from a wholehearted embrace of the fat body, and Melissa subsequently went on to lose a considerable amount of weight and to compete in Ironman triathlon events. But the transition from self-loathing fatness to a fatness that is at least thinkable marks a notable transformation in a social and cultural context where fat is so utterly repudiated.

There is a strong gender dimension to these transformations, since it is women who are the primary targets and consumers of the weight loss industry, and for whom the practices of close self-surveillance, guilt and obsession are a normalised aspect of femininity (Bordo 1993; Heyes 2006). They are also more likely to define themselves, and be defined by others, negatively in relation to fat (Mansfield 2011). Consequently, women were the primary tellers of 'surprising body' tales in the interviews – a trait that also aligns with the pleasures recounted in the previous chapter by older women who enjoyed confounding others' limited expectations of what their menopausal or ageing bodies would be able to do.

Even among those swimmers who were planning to lose weight after the swim season was over, the interviews and fieldnotes are full of examples of new-found pleasure in the freedom of being able to eat without guilt or recrimination, and of being *in* rather than *against* the (fat) body in ways that cannot simply be understood as playful transgression (see also, Maguire and Mansfield 1998; Sassatelli 1999; Maguire 2002). As discussed in the previous chapter, post-swim consumption of easily digestible, high calorie snacks is a key element in the sociality of swimming and novel source of pleasure, especially among those for whom guilt-free consumption was an anathema. This pleasure in eating is undoubtedly facilitated by a trade-off with gruelling training (see also, Gill *et al.* 2005); as one male UK swimmer joked at the end of a swim that had to be cut short by an hour, 'I won't be able to eat all my cake now'. This also mirrors the broader trade-off between marathon swimming and fatness that exchanges one as an 'alibi' for the other. But nevertheless, it signals a more ambivalent, and less instrumental, relationship with the fattening swimming body that is distinct from both the determined inauthenticity of heroic fatness and the (ostensibly) health-oriented anti-obesity rhetorics.

Conclusion

In this chapter, I have argued that the demand on marathon swimmers to acquire body fat as insulation against the cold is in tension with conventional understandings of what constitutes the 'good' sporting body. This tension arises because, in the contemporary context of a 'war on obesity', fatness is normatively associated with the failure to discipline the body and to exercise the self-efficacy demanded by entrepreneurial selfhood. This is resolved for some marathon swimmers through the mobilisation of 'heroic fatness', which positions fat both as an undesirable necessity and as provisional. I argue that this renders purposefully acquired marathon swimming fat as 'fake', freeing it from the negative associations of 'real' fat. This distinction holds in place the wrongness of (real) fatness, thereby securing the social distinction of marathon swimming embodiment without the stigmatising taint that otherwise attaches so easily to fat bodies. However, the discourse of 'heroic fatness' is not accessible for everyone, and both women and those who are already fat before training are excluded. In spite of the prevailing and unifying certainties of the 'war on obesity' that 'fat kills', then, not all fat is equal. This is not simply to suggest a hierarchy of more or less forgivable fatness, but rather, that there are different *kinds* of fatness. The experience of fatness has been shown here to be uneven and unpredictable, produced in interaction with, and always in relation to, dominant values, but not determined by them. This endorses the insistence within Fat Studies that, rather than simply debating 'truths' about the relationship between fat and health, the moral dimensions of the 'war on obesity' need to be kept clearly in sight (Gard and Wright 2005).

Throughout the course of my research within the marathon swimming community, I never encountered the overt resistance and politically oriented renderings of swimming fat of the kind you might find within Fat Studies. However, even though I failed to find the reflexive critique of the 'war on obesity' that I had naively hoped was embedded in this site of fat sporting embodiment, the research both exposed the stark limitations to the 'fat kills' rhetoric of the contemporary attack on fat, and unsettled those same values. When fat bodies are habitually made the 'object of affective transfer' rather than its subjects, the unexpected freedoms of guilt-free consumption, the pleasures of bodily solidity, and the liberation from shame-filled daily encounters with scales all signal a re-orientation, however ambivalent, towards fat. In short, the materiality of the fat body that is experienced as 'amazing' is very differently constituted to both the playfully wobbled body of the heroically (fake) fat swimmer and the abjectly (real) fat body that is the target of the 'war on obesity'.

The analysis offered in this chapter highlights the moral and ideological assumptions about fatness that seep out in the emerging spaces between the entrenched certainties of the contemporary hatred of fat. This has implications not only for the ways in which we have learned to think about fat, but also for the mobilisations of those conceptualisations within sport. This is an opportunity to look beyond impoverished, utilitarian visions of sport as a tool for weight management, and to access its manifold possibilities for pleasure and for unfolding new ways of thinking about and experiencing sporting embodiment. As argued in the previous chapter, this constitutes an opportunity not only to open up sport to more people, but also to rethink the nature of sport and physical activity itself (Young 2010). Marathon swimming is a minority sport, but the normative values that constitute the sport are inflections of those of the wider social and cultural context within which it is practised. Furthermore, those same values are intensified and made visible by the anomalous sporting embodiment demanded by the sport itself. As such, even while seeming to disregard norms of body size, composition and practice, marathon swimming speaks directly to those values in ways that challenge how we think about whose bodies count, and in what ways.

Notes

1 This is categorically not to argue that those with higher levels of body fat cannot practise those sports to a high standard; nor is it to deny the many other positive reasons why people of all shapes and sizes engage in sports and physical activities.
2 One of the most challenging aspects of managing my dual role as researcher and swimmer was knowing if, when or how to intervene in behaviour that I found offensive or troubling, and in which silence produces complicity (Throsby and Evans 2013).
3 A Magnum is a chocolate-coated ice-cream on a stick.

8

Failing bodies

24 August 2013: the 'Quiet' Manhattan Island Marathon Swim (MIMS)[1]

I knew that I had hurt myself. In spite of my determined denial, in the weeks running up to the swim, there had been a niggling bite to my left shoulder the morning after long training swims; nothing serious, but a sense of not-rightness that I was guarding cautiously. It would be fine, I had told myself; just the lingering effects of a hard season of training. But somewhere around the top of the Harlem River, my shoulder started to grumble. It was easy to ignore at first, but swelled in imperceptible increments into something sharper and deeper than the previous warning nips. I tried to focus on holding my stroke, keeping my hand below my elbow and my elbow below my shoulder at the front of the stroke before the catch. I suspected that the problem lay in the pernicious stroke defect into which I habitually fold as fatigue sets in – a sinking left elbow followed by the slightest sweep outwards with my left hand before the catch and pull. Holding my stroke as it is supposed to be helped, boosted by a couple of ibuprofen to take the sharp edges off the pain. By hour seven, flying down the Hudson on the back of a generous current, the pain was becoming hard to ignore, but the water was flat and calm, making it easier to maintain a pain-minimising stroke. I focused on keeping my head in line with my body, rotating only along the long axis, a single goggle-lens and a popeye-mouthed breath out of the water; this helped me to avoid my bad habit of levering myself up slightly on my left arm when I breathe to the right, cocking my head up out of the water and placing strain on the left shoulder. The subtle flaws in my stroke, repeated tens of thousands of times, were being sharply illuminated by the unfolding injury; I let the pain correct me. It felt manageable still, and I was buoyed by the growing certainty that I was going to finish the swim.

We hit rougher water half way down, the wind blowing against the tide and churning the river. The kayak danced in the waves and I heard my kayaker whoop with delight at the ride. After the predictable comforts of flat-water swimming, I struggled for balance, my whole body now actively in play to stabilise me in the water. The work of getting hold of the water in the mobile environment sent grinding pain down my arm. Relax. Don't fight the water. At some point, my recovering left hand clipped the top of a wave and was smacked backwards, pulling my arm with it; my shoulder flashed with white, hollow pain. It had a different quality now – bigger, hotter; every stroke a hot breath of ache from shoulder to elbow. More drugs ... only two hours since the last pills, but I didn't care. I visualised them killing the pain.

I tried to focus on my stroke, on the kayak, on the piers of Manhattan flying past as the swift tide carried me down towards the finish.

But I knew that this time I'd really 'done' something, and that to carry on swimming was to entrench the injury. It is always a choice: to stop and prevent further damage, or to carry on swimming and pay the consequences later. But with only an hour to go and the towers of lower Manhattan clearly in sight, sharp and shining in the late summer sunshine, there was no decision to make. I knew that I had a year without long swimming ahead of me – I would fix it then. For now, I would swim, happily trading the pain and the inevitable rehab for the longed-for completion of this swim on the most beautiful of blue-skied days.

Early October 2013

It is six weeks post-MIMS, and I still can't swim. I am beached both by my physiotherapist's proscription against it for the foreseeable future, and more definitively, by the inability to swim without pain. My shoulder still bites when I raise my arm above my head, swing on a jacket or make a forgetful lateral movement outwards to reach for something. It's no longer the hot, fiery breath of pain that I felt during the swim, but a sharp bite; a warning. On my first physiotherapy visit, I explain how the injury happened and how I'd kept swimming on it, and he responds with a weary laugh. He tests my range of motion in a variety of postures, poking and pressing. He says that if he could put a camera inside my shoulder joint, it would probably be very red and angry; when I go home, I look up arthroscopic images online and visualise my irritated tendons, repeatedly snagging between bones. I have a diagnosis now: a shoulder impingement ... or swimmer's shoulder as it is also tellingly called. And I have a comfortingly mechanical account of my injury to work with: the rotator cuff tendon is being trapped and compressed in the subacromial space between the acronium and the top of the humerus. The cure: rest, anti-inflammatories, and a programme of exercises so subtle that it's hard to believe they can be helping. I lie on the floor, lifting my shoulder up and back, holding for a count of ten. Ten repeats, twice a day; a ritualistic act of faith. Each day, I think of my exercises as another step towards recovery; it's training like any other, but nowhere near as much fun. I recall a friend – a runner benched by injury – observing that when you feel fit and well, you think it's going to last forever, and when you are injured, you think it will never end. Indeed.

My incapacity makes me feel broken and old, and I start to feel an unexpected encroaching discomfort with my body – a bit fat, greying, peri-menopausal – that is ordinarily pushed out of sight by swimming. In the water, swimming for hours, my body feels absolutely perfect; beached, it's so much harder to hold on to that feeling and I feel ashamed at the shallowness of my appreciation of this body of mine, and the precariousness of my détente with it. But being laid up is not all bad, I remind myself; I've reclaimed two to three hours a day that I used to spend swimming, and my neglected book (this book) has leapt to life, the unexpected beneficiary of my injury.

But God ... how I miss swimming. I crave swimming. I long for it. When I think of swimming, I can feel my body reaching quietly for the movements; it imagines itself stroking cleanly through the water. Without the comforts of swimming and full of anxiety about starting a new job, I'm unsure how to relax and can't quite tire myself out physically. My sleep has lost the sumptuousness that long swimming delivers, and the stock of nuts and muesli bars that I keep in my desk drawer goes untouched, my appetite dulled by the sudden drop from over 30 km a week in the water to nothing. I join the gym at my new workplace and go every morning. I can (could) swim for hours, but my lower body fitness has been neglected over the long summer of swimming; after just a few minutes on the treadmill or cross-trainer, my legs are burning and my face scarlet. But I persist; it is a new body project to occupy me, inching the duration up weekly in minute increments. I always choose one of the treadmills with a partial view over the swimming pool and I follow the swimmers travelling up and down the lanes with envious longing. I can't stop watching, like constantly finding a mouth ulcer with my tongue. I find myself compiling an uninvited critique of the swimmers below me: he's crossing the centre line with his right hand; she's scissoring her legs; that person's over-reaching at the front of the stroke. I imagine myself swimming in a fantasy of liquid smoothness and technical perfection as I trudge away gracelessly on the treadmill.

December 2013

It is just over fifteen weeks post-MIMS. Last week, I was able to take my first pain-free freestyle stroke. I only did a very tentative 100 m, but still ... progress at last.

Things began to change about six weeks ago, when I went to see the physiotherapist who tends to the university's sports scholars as well as to stray university-based lame ducks like me. On our first meeting, she gave an appalled gasp at the extent to which my shoulders are pulled forwards – a consequence of hours of front crawl swimming – although she also noted that my shoulder and back muscles are strong and in good shape, with 'nothing sticking out'. I felt oddly, unjustifiably proud at this assessment.

She uses deep tissue massage, using thumbs, the balls of her hands, her elbows to work on the muscles and tendons. The pain of the process is exquisitely intense. In my mind, it is a kind of mustard green – not sharp or hot, but unpleasant, nauseating. I have to be reminded not to hold my breath while she works on me; to breathe through it. The successful location of a particularly painful spot, signalled by a gasp or my tensing against her touch, is a prompt to dig deeper, to chase the pain along the particular muscle or tendon, breaking down the knots and stretching it out. She pauses from time to time and asks if I'm still okay with the level of pain and I tell her to carry on; I want her to do as much as she can, as much as I can bear. In the days that follow each session, I develop green-brown bruises, my skin sore to the touch, healing just in time for the next round. To complement the thumbs, I am given a new regime of daily exercises – simple, gentle stretches at first, then more pronounced ones to build on my increasing shoulder mobility, and now strengthening exercises to build the muscles at the back of the shoulder to better support the joint. I do them every day, twice a day, inching with excruciating slowness towards recovery.

Injury stories are often long stories. There is an anecdotal quality to them that fixes the focus of the narrative onto the causative moment of injury: a tumble down the stairs, a terrifying collision with a carelessly driven car while out cycling, an over-ambitious tackle in a rugby match. These are the stories that are recounted to shared horror, or perhaps sympathetic laughter, in response to the question, 'What happened?' In the case of marathon swimming (and other endurance sports), however, the moment of injury itself may be unclear. While swimmers may recall, as in my case, a time period over which a niggle transitions into an inescapably painful experience, the genesis of the injury may lie several days, weeks or even months in the past as an irritating gripe, studiously ignored. And behind the moment of any injury, either chronic or acute, and however spectacular or banal, lies a much longer, more mundane tale of debility and (attempted) recovery, sometimes stretching over months and even years. This is intensified in the case of the sporting body, which may have recovered to the point of everyday function but still be unequal to the movements demanded by the sport itself, or to the intensity of movement that characterises an individual's engagement with the sport. My narrative here, for example, stops four months after the injury, but I was only able to return to training a year later after months of work with physiotherapists, a sports massage therapist and a stroke correction coach. Even now, ostensibly recovered and restored, I perform religiously my daily regimen of strengthening and flexibility exercises, and nervously surveille my shoulder for nascent signs of instability. Recovery never takes you right back to where you were before it happened; bodies change and adapt, but never quite forget.

Injury, then, can be seen as a form of biographical disruption (Bury 1982): a disturbance to habitual exercise practices and goals, as well as to the sense of self that for many athletes is inextricable from their investment in those activities (Hockey 2005a; Nettleton 2013). Most sporting injuries, and particularly the predominantly chronic injuries of endurance sport, do not fit Bury's model exactly, particularly in the ways in which chronic illnesses necessitate fundamental and permanent revisions to expectations, biography and the everyday mobilisation of resources, disrupting relations within families and support networks through increasing dependence on others (1982: 169–170). While some catastrophic and acute injuries – for example, a spinal cord injury (Smith and Sparkes 2008) – have these effects, most sporting injuries are both provisional (or at least episodic (Sparkes 1996)) and do not impact chronically on the individual's everyday ability to move through the world. This is particularly true of a sport like marathon swimming, whose signature shoulder injuries are acquired through the wear and tear of repetitive movements that are often painful while swimming but rarely debilitating in everyday life. Furthermore, while injury may ultimately cost a professional athlete their livelihood (Roderick *et al.* 2000; Howe 2001), it is unlikely that a chronic shoulder injury will impact so catastrophically on the non-sporting career of the amateur marathon swimmer, most of whom are embedded in middle-class professions that lack the physical demands of traditional working-class employment (Smith 2000).

Nevertheless, the concept of biographical disruption is still helpful here because it captures the disruption to the sense of self that an injured athlete can experience (Nixon 1992; Aalten 1995; Allen-Collinson 2005; Hockey 2005a; McEwen and Young 2011; Nettleton 2013). For many marathon swimmers, as with other amateur athletes, swimming is a structuring feature of everyday life, impacting upon the scheduling of the day, dietary needs and sleep habits, as well as the way the body feels and looks. My identity as a marathon swimmer is etched into all aspects of my life and sense of self – not always at the forefront, but rarely absent. To not be able to swim, then, is to lose not only the immediate pleasures of swimming itself, but also this mundane presence, as well as the necessary revision, however provisionally, of my swimming goals and plans. It is in this sense that we can understand injury as a biographical disruption, however governed by a narrative of restoration (Frank 1995).

But even while injury is an unwelcome biographical disruption, paradoxically, it is also an anticipated and integral element of any sustained sporting practice, including marathon swimming (Roderick *et al.* 2000; Theberge 2000; Howe 2001; Turner and Wainwright 2003; Pike 2005; Smith 2008; McEwen and Young 2011; Markula 2013; Nettleton 2013). The repetitive strain of tens of thousands of strokes, both in training and during a long swim, places muscles and tendons under duress, always potentially magnifying even the smallest weakness or stroke defect into injury. This is compounded by the fact that the refusal of pain and discomfort and the celebration of resilience are already defining elements of the sport itself, impeding the early acquiescence to injury (Kortaba 1983; Roderick *et al.* 2000; Howe 2001; Pike 2005; Aalten 2007; Smith 2008; Hanold 2010; McEwen and Young 2011). Furthermore, as with my painful MIMS swim, the investment of time and money in a landmark event that is not easily repeatable mitigates against the common sense logics of stopping because of injury. Injury, then, becomes evidence of 'doing it right'; of pushing the body up to, and beyond, its limits. This also extends to unsuccessful swims, which equally serve to maintain the currency of marathon swimming through their confirmation of its status as 'edgework' at the limits of capacity (Lyng 2005). In marathon swimming, then, both injury and swim failure serve both as evidence of the toughness of the sport and the commitment to it, however unwelcome to the individual. In this sense, the failing body is simultaneously marked as the 'good body'.

This chapter explores the ways in which pain, injury and failure to complete a long swim are experienced and accounted for in marathon swimming, and asks what this means for our understandings of what counts as the healthy body. While sport is conventionally coded as 'healthy', and athletes are celebrated as role models of embodied citizenship, those same practices also have the inescapable potential for harm. This provides a productive site for interrogating the complex relationship between the 'good body' and 'health' – concepts that are conventionally treated as synonymous, but whose intersections are both tenuous and contingent. The 'culture of risk' (Nixon 1992) that contributes to injury, and both the stigmatising and lionising effects of injury, are core dimensions of this complex reconfiguring of 'health', and this is the focus of the first part of this chapter. The second section explores the alternative ways in which marathon swimming intersects with health narratives, particularly in relation to illnesses and injuries that are not caused by marathon swimming, functioning variously as evidence of recovery, the means of recovery and as a pedagogic device. And the final section discusses the experience of the DNF (Did Not Finish), highlighting the subtle hierarchies of failure and success that define good marathon swimming embodiment. I conclude by arguing that, rather than constituting mutually exclusive, zero-sum categories, health and injury, and bodily success and failure, are determined by the extent to which they can be aligned with normative social world values of autonomy, bodily discipline and self-reflexivity rather than demonstrable levels of sporting accomplishment. Furthermore, I argue that rather than marathon swimming *in order to become* healthy, or sacrificing health through exposure to injury, marathon swimmers possess sufficient physical capital (including that which is easily coded as 'health') to be able to convert that, through the risk and reality of injury, into other forms of capital. This highlights the provisionality of the normative linking of health and physical activity, and the failure of utilitarian notions of health to account for the sustained engagement with marathon swimming.

Injured bodies

As in many sports, as well as embodied performance practices such as dance (Aalten 1995; Turner and Wainwright 2003; Wainwright and Turner 2004; Wainwright *et al.* 2005; Aalten 2007; McEwen and Young 2011; Markula 2013) or music (Alford and Szanto 1996), pain is a normalised element of marathon swimming. This is not simply to argue that pain is incidental or collateral to the sport, but rather, to suggest that it is integral to it. In short, if it doesn't hurt to some degree, you're probably not doing it right. In a sport that self-defines through the pushing of the body's limits, the failure to experience some form of duress is the failure to test those limits. But at the same time, as discussed in Chapter 2, not all pain is the same, and swimmers have to learn to distinguish between different qualities and intensities of pain in the process of becoming a marathon swimmer, and to attribute meanings to those sensations. For example, sensations such as the lactic acid burn of a hard training session or the grinding fatigue of a long training swim are recalibrated through experience as evidence of a good workout or improved endurance. These are examples of what Howe (2004) calls 'Zatopekian pain', after elite athlete Emil Zatopek, whose gruelling training regimen was legendary. As in Aalten's work on ballet dancers (1995, 2007), Hanold's (2010) ultramarathon runners or Atkinson's (2008) triathletes, these sensations are actively sought as indicators of progress, belonging and social distinction, and marathon swimmers learn to relish them, even though they involve sensations that in other contexts might demand a day off sick or a trip to the doctor. Conversely, what Hanold (2010) describes as 'bad pain' signifies a potential swim-stopping injury. This is distinguished from 'good pain' both by the quality and intensity of the pain and the resulting restriction of movement or function that results from a breakdown in the structure of the body (Howe 2004: 2). This injurious pain is an insult not simply to the body, but to the sense of self, preventing the individual from pursuing their chosen activity for an uncertain period of time.

There is an extensive literature on the impacts of injury on athletes, and on the phenomenon of 'playing hurt', focusing primarily on the domain of professional sports. For professional athletes and performers such as rugby players (Howe 2001), footballers (Roderick *et al.* 2000), wrestlers (Smith 2008) and dancers (Aalten 1995; Turner and Wainwright 2003; Wainwright and Turner 2004; Wainwright *et al.* 2005), injuries can have materially tangible consequences in terms of loss of income and professional prestige, as well as the disruption of selfhood that comes from the potential loss of a way of life passionately pursued. Nixon (1992) argues that players and performers become immersed in 'cultures of risk' that are sustained by 'sportsnets' – the complex networks of structural constraints and inducements, institutional norms, rationalisations and socialisation processes that normalise injury and encourage athletes to continue to play while hurt. In the case of professional football, for example, Roderick *et al.* (2000: 176) describe the case of a player who was not told the serious nature of an ankle injury by his club doctor because of pressure from managers not to risk his value on the transfer market; another player undertook a series of painkilling injections for a broken toe in order to reach a contractual target of playing in thirty-five matches, for which he would receive a bonus (Roderick *et al.* 2000: 172).

To some extent, the logics of playing while injured unravel in the context of amateur sport, particularly in the non-elite domain, where institutional and economic incentives have less relevance. However, the amateur context can also constitute a site where pain and injury are normalised and the motivations to persist in the face of injury are strong. Allegiances to fellow players, fear of losing a treasured spot on a team (Pike 2005), the intimate entanglements of the activity with sense of self (Allen-Collinson 2005) and the learned, embodied pleasures of the activity (Wacquant 2004; Hanold 2010) all conspire to form what Adler and Adler (1991) call 'role engulfment' whereby individuals become enmeshed in the values and practices of a sporting subculture in ways that potentially normalise pain and injury not simply as unwelcome interruptions to an imagined sporting future, but also as evidence of effort and commitment.

In the case of marathon swimming, the highly individualised, amateur nature of the sport mitigates against the institutional, structural pressures of the 'sportsnet' described by Nixon (1992), but nevertheless there are potent motivations to normalise, and even valorise, pain and injury. First, as already discussed, in a sport that self-defines by the pushing of limits, pain, and the willingness and capacity to endure it, becomes a marker of authentic participation (Kortaba 1983). Like the pro-wrestlers in Smith's (2008) study, who treasured their catalogue of chronic injuries as evidence of the authenticity of a sport known to be theatrically choreographed, authentic swimming is in part defined by pain and the possibility of injury, and displays of endurance, even to the point of harm, are celebrated as exemplary (Curry 1993). After my successful, but painful, MIMS swim, I received nothing but praise from within the marathon swimming community for sticking it out, even though I had chosen to exacerbate a subsequently swim-stopping injury.

This positive reinforcement of a 'culture of risk' (Nixon 1992) generates its own incentives to keep swimming, not least because of its corollary: the suggestion of weakness and a lack of fortitude that attaches easily to the athlete who acquiesces (Curry 1993). As with Howe's (2004) elite runners, retreat through injury, particularly when physical harm is not overtly visible to others, draws the suspicion of weakness and malingering, or at least the fear of this perception on the part of others (McEwen and Young 2011). 'Weakness' is a powerful slur within the marathon swimming social world, and is encapsulated in the cries of 'wuss', 'sissy', 'pansy', 'puff' and 'girl' that are showered upon those deemed not to be sufficiently robust in the face of physical suffering. These sexualised, feminising insults reiterate the normative relationship between masculinity and suffering, where pain and injury are status-bearing for men, and particularly for those who are good at sport (Messner 1988; Pringle and Markula 2005). The relative invisibility of marathon swimming injuries compounds this problem, since there are none of the visible markers of spectacular injury such as blood, cuts or bruising to verify. The subjectivity of pain, then, opens the door for suspicions about its severity (Howe 2004: 77).

In the case of professional sport, this is policed through practices such as purposefully inconveniencing injured players (for example, through the imposition of longer training days) (Roderick *et al.* 2000) or making injured players exercise on rowing machines and stationary bikes in full view of the team during practice sessions (Curry 1993). But in amateur sport, even without these purposefully shaming measures, the desire to maintain the appearance of commitment reproduces the logics of persisting while injured (Pike and Maguire 2003; Pike 2005). UK swimmer, Cecily, told me how, following increasing 'niggles' with her shoulder while training for an English Channel swim, she had taken to heart her coach's warnings that 'No one ever died of a sore shoulder'; 'I couldn't bear her thinking that I wasn't in it 100 per cent,' she confessed. As with obligations to sponsors of charitable fund-raising swims, the fear of 'letting people down' creates powerful relations of obligation that can mitigate against acquiescence to injury.

Second, the telic nature of the sport provides its own logics for continuing in the face of pain and injury. Marathon swims happen over a long cycle of planning, training and swimming, and scheduled swims are not necessarily easily rescheduled or postponed; the greater the investment into a swim in time, effort and money, the harder it becomes to give in to injury. These pressures are magnified during a long swim, with the final goal tangibly in sight. Struggling painfully down the Hudson River in 2013, I chose to swim on my shoulder injury, even to the point of exacerbating it, because I wanted to finish. And Cecily, who I discussed above, successfully swam the Channel (with the support of heavy doses of anti-inflammatory painkillers) but was still unable to swim a year later and was waiting for surgery. It was, she insisted, 'completely worth it to get across'.

This points to a third factor in the normalisation of pain and injury in marathon swimming: pleasure. While pain and injury are defining features of marathon swimming, this is never all there is to the sport; as discussed in Chapter 2, the work of becoming a marathon swimmer involves the development of the capacity to find pleasure in a practice not self-evidently pleasurable on the first encounter, but which comes to constitute a compulsively desirable facet of the swimmer's everyday life (Atkinson 2008). 'I need to get my scales wet every day or I go mad,' joked one very experienced UK marathon swimmer; a US swimmer told me, 'When it gets to day three without swimming, I *have* to get wet.' Swimmers repeatedly spoke of not 'feeling right' and 'not feeling myself' without swimming. As

Pike and Maguire conclude in relation to the amateur rowers they studied, 'it has become apparent that athletes may risk their bodies because it is meaningful to do so, within their sense of what it takes to identify, and to be identified by others, as a "rower"' (2003: 246). The same can be said of marathon swimmers, for whom there are multiple incentives to normalise and minimise injury outside of the more obvious coercions of professional structures.

But even where injuries were accepted as 'real', this does not guarantee legitimation. In their study of elite women athletes, Young and White (1995) couldn't find any significant differences between men and women in the meanings of violence, pain and injury, except by degree, with both demonstrating conformity to the 'no-pain, no-gain' ethos and mobilising similar coping strategies. The same is true of the marathon swimming social world, where even divergence in the acceptable degree of injury for men and women was not evident. But while there is no obviously gendered hierarchy of acceptable injury, experience emerged as a key determinant of legitimacy, with novice swimmers often deemed insufficiently experienced to be trusted to distinguish between 'good' and 'bad' pain. Consequently, and in the absence of obvious indications of injury such as swelling or immobility or outwardly manifest signs of dangerous cold, their complaints are often disregarded, at least in the first instance. This was particularly evident on long distance training camps and in dedicated marathon swimming training locations, where a key goal is to enable novices to learn in a safe and watchful environment what it feels like to swim a long way and to recalibrate their sensory knowledges accordingly. In addition, even where novices' injuries were acknowledged, their status as legitimate could be undermined if the swimmer was felt by experienced others to have 'rushed into it' without completing the necessary apprenticeship. A UK coach described one such swimmer as 'wanting all the glory and none of the work'; another experienced marathon swimmer described such 'zero-to-hero' ambition as 'disrespectful' to the 'real swimmers' who had gone before. Conversely, experienced marathon swimmers whose commitment to the social world of marathon swimming is already established can legitimately claim injury more easily. This grants them entitlement to sympathy and support while they endure the frustrations of not being able to swim or have to modify training (Nettleton 2013). This not only exempts them from the suspicion of weakness or fraud that attaches easily to novices, but also enables them to draw upon the status-bearing possibilities of pain and injury as evidence of commitment to the sport. This highlights the ways in which the positive possibilities of pain and injury in marathon swimming do not attach uniformly, but rather, their legitimacy is inflected through moral values of commitment and hard work.

The 'work' of marathon swimming also extends to the management of injury, and while injury may (or may not) invoke collective sympathy, it remains framed as a question of individual bodily management, leaving the social world values that facilitated the injury intact. As discussed in Chapter 2, marathon swimmers (as with dancers and other athletes) have to defy the demands of the body to be listened and attended to, rendering pain 'actively absent' (Aalten 2007) in order to enable continued participation, blurring the boundaries between 'good' and 'bad' pain. For Leder, when the body seizes awareness in times of disturbance, it can appear opposed to the self, 'buttressing Cartesian dualism' (1990: 70), and this separation is compounded by the desire in the case of athletic injury to separate the sense of sporting selfhood from the failure of the body. Injury, then, once acknowledged, becomes a problem to be solved, distinct from the self (Allen-Collinson 2005).

In the case of my painful shoulder, poring over arthroscopic images online, I sought out medicalised and mechanical accounts of my injury as a means of rendering it simultaneously manageable and not-me. Without the easy access to the sports medicine specialists on hand for professional athletes, like many amateur athletes, I sought advice outside of the mainstream medical system, turning instead to physiotherapists, sports masseurs and stroke correction coaches in the private sector (Pike 2005; Markula 2013). I purposefully avoided consulting my GP about the injury, fearing that he would simply tell me to rest it, or that referral to a specialist within the UK's National Health Service (NHS) would mean a long wait. Instead, I was impatient to push forward with treatment from someone I trusted to wholeheartedly share my goal of returning to training (Allen-Collinson 2005; Markula 2013). This strategy reflects both the privilege of having the resources to fund these interventions, and the seductive appeal of narratives of self-efficacy and discipline (Atkinson 2008). Like the amateur athletes in Pike's (2005) study, the alternative therapeutic domain offered a sense of control over the injury that I was reluctant to relinquish to the role of patient in the medical domain; the daily exercise regimen, however frustrating, could still be framed as 'training', keeping my identity as a swimmer at least partially intact (Allen-Collinson 2005; Hockey 2005a). As Howe notes, rest may be good advice, but it overlooks the 'cultural importance of activity' (2004: 98). The body's dys-appearance through injury, therefore, is a disruption, however temporary, to a swimmer's sporting biography, but one that, once it can no longer be rendered actively absent, constitutes a problem to be solved by the individual through the seeking of appropriate care, the physical labour of rehabilitation and the defence of sporting selfhood through the objectification of injury and the application of work-like methods to its management. Like the dieter who instigates intensified regimens of documentation and self-monitoring to rectify a lapse (Heyes 2006), the acknowledgement of injury performs a confessional function through which the marathon swimmer examines the self and revises their practice and behaviours through the intensification of self-discipline (Foucault 1976).

'After all, you're doing your bit to stay healthy'

In the spring of 2013, before my MIMS attempt, I had to undergo a medical, including a chest X-ray and an ECG. My GP[2] referred me to a private hospital for the X-ray. It was my first ever encounter with private healthcare, for which I paid £200 and revelled in a thick, fluffy robe and a supply of hot drinks during my short wait for the procedure. I later received a cursory, if reassuring, final report that declared my heart and lungs to be the right size and in the correct position. The GP's practice nurse performed the ECG, and when I asked how much I would need to pay, she said that it was already included in the £80 cost of the GP medical: 'After all,' she said, sticking sensors to my chest, 'you're doing your bit to stay healthy.' During the same visit, I also received a Hepatitis A vaccination, again without further charge, to protect me against bacteria in the sewerage that occasionally spills into the rivers around Manhattan. She ran through my medical record, noting that I have a standing prescription for antibiotic eardrops that I can request without seeing the doctor – treatment for repeated bouts of the ear infection, *otitis externa*, or 'swimmer's ear'. She also noted that I take antihistamines most days to tackle the constant sneezing and runny nose from long sessions in chlorinated pools. It is hard to know what 'doing my bit to stay healthy' means in these moments. The medical form asks not if I am healthy, but if I am fit to swim; a significant distinction.

Sport and physical activity are so deeply interpolated with narratives of health that it is difficult to conceptualise them outside of the rubrics of 'good' embodiment. Sport's positive aura means that morally privileged attributes of discipline and self-efficacy attach easily to the sporting body. Framed by narratives of good citizenship, this in turn aligns easily with neoliberal rhetorics of health as a 'meaningful social practice' that is determined by individual choices and effective self-management (Crawford 2006). However, the complicated relationship between sport and health has been well-documented (Waddington 2000; Theberge 2008), highlighting the potentially health-damaging nature of many sporting practices, particularly when pursued to a degree far beyond the modest activity recommendations for healthy living. Just as the mobilisation of 'heroic fatness' exposes the moral foundations of the contemporary 'war on obesity' and its rampant inconsistencies, the same can be seen in a closer examination of 'health' in marathon swimming.

Physical activity is widely credited with improved weight management, stress relief and improved sleep patterns, as well as reduced risk of depression, Alzheimer's, osteoarthritis, type II diabetes and many forms of cancer, alongside many other possible benefits. As the NHS website assures us: 'Exercise is the miracle cure we've always had but for too long we've neglected to take our recommended dose' (2013). But a sport like marathon swimming does not fit comfortably into this model because of its commitment to excess and extremity, and however unsure policy makers and health professionals might be about what constitutes the 'recommended dose', we can be confident that marathon swimming represents an overdose. Consequently, while many would argue that marathon swimming offers distinct health benefits across some parameters such as cardiovascular fitness, it also presents a potential threat to health both in terms of the extraordinary duress of long, landmark swims and as a result of the 'mundane extremity' (Robinson 2008) of the everyday demands of sustained training. Some of these impacts are provisional – for example, intense fatigue, intestinal distress, vomiting, chafing, muscle soreness, metabolic disruption – while others are more enduring and less reversible. These include wear and tear on muscles, tendons and joints, repetitive stress, skin damage from prolonged exposure to the sun and tooth enamel erosion from the consumption of acidic, sugary energy drinks. It is unclear, then, what it would mean to claim marathon swimming as a 'healthy' practice or marathon swimmers as role models of healthy living. And yet, the positive aura of sport clings to the marathon swimming body, and landmark swims are heralded as status-bearing, notable accomplishments. Indeed, as discussed in Chapter 5, it is this positive aura, in tandem with the culture of risk, which makes the act of swimming for charity possible.

Although this positive aura of health attaches easily to the marathon swimming body through its displays of athleticism, this was rarely a frame used by the swimmers themselves to account for their practice. Indeed, most acknowledged that it was 'probably not very good for me', or, as one UK male swimmer observed, 'it's probably all a bit much, really' (see also, Theberge 2008). But 'health' was mobilised discursively in two key contexts: first, to mark a return to health after illness or trauma; and second, and less commonly, to challenge the culture of risk itself.

For several of the marathon swimmers in this project, landmark marathon swims were used to mark the restoration of health after serious illness: for example, the female swimmer mentioned in Chapter 4 in relation to her tattoo of the swim track from her post-breast cancer two-way English Channel swim. For UK swimmer, Mark Sheridan, a routine swim medical revealed a large, benign tumour requiring extensive surgery that left him without quadriceps use in his left leg. In a lengthy blog recounting this series of events, he noted that swimming (or at least the need for a swim medical) had probably saved his life, but also that swimming had enabled him to stay 'fit and healthy', as confirmed in the pre-operative checks and serving as a buffer against the rigours of surgery (Sheridan 2012). Mark went on to complete a number of long swims, including the English Channel in 2014; looking back on the first of these – a gruelling twenty-four-hour swim challenge – he noted in his blog that 'I felt I had given myself confirmation in this swim that I can put that [hospital] episode behind me' (Sheridan 2012). Marathon swimming, then, ratifies a return to health after illness, constituting an emphatic declaration of restoration (Frank 1995).

Marathon swimming not only marks recovery, but was also framed as aiding recovery after illness or other traumatic events. In the course of the research, I was told several 'surprising body' stories by older male swimmers who had experienced heart attacks and whose subsequent treatment – for example, the prescription of beta-blockers or the setting of a pacemaker – had been premised on assumptions of poor heart condition that were at odds with their low resting heart rates. One UK heart attack victim described his heart as 'strong', arguing that 'it was the tubes that were the problem' – a mechanical account of the body that leaves the positive effects of a lifetime of marathon swimming intact as foundational health against the potentially stigmatising debility of illness. This effectively separates the injured or failing body part from the self, and from notions of healthy embodiment.

Marathon swimming also performs a symbolic function in narratives of recovery, particularly in relation to the need for fortitude. The most explicit example of this is the case of Roger Allsopp, who swam the English Channel in 2011 at the age of seventy, breaking the record at that time for the oldest successful swimmer. In 2014, he was seriously injured in a car accident, and in an article in *H₂Open Magazine*, he described how he had used his experience of English Channel swimming to structure his recovery:

> It was going to be a long haul. I needed to break it up into manageable chunks … Instead of swimming from one feed to the next it was going to be surviving one day to the next. I had endured pain in the Channel and this was no different.
>
> …
>
> Whilst in intensive care I was surrounded by equipment with alarms going off all the time. I had, at one time or another, a tube in every orifice. This, I decided, was like being in the shipping lane and it was to be two weeks before I got to the transition zone. As with Channel swimming, I had to put total trust in my support team who worked day and night to help me recover. (Allsopp 2014: 37)

The article concludes with the observation that the lessons and experiences of marathon swimming 'stand us in good stead when it comes to facing other life challenges' (Allsopp 2014). Marathon swimming, therefore, is never only a potential source of risk and harm; rather, the culture of risk is also seen as providing a reservoir of physical, emotional and symbolic resources through which to manage illness, trauma and distress outside of swimming.

It is also important not to overstate the constraining effects of the culture of risk within marathon swimming, which does not go unchallenged. The most marked example of this from the research is Claire, whose resistance to purposeful weight gain was described in Chapter 7. Similar to her inability to resolve the dissonance between weight gain and narratives of health, Claire was also unable to reconcile the pain of marathon swimming with her own understandings of healthy activity. After a difficult struggle through a long-distance training camp in Malta, she had pulled out during the final day's six-hour qualification swim, and she subsequently cancelled her planned English Channel swim. She described her difficulties in coming to terms with the pain of long swimming, and in particular, the common practice of using anti-inflammatory painkillers in order to manage pain:

> I think [the six-hour swim] was the beginning of the end [of the Channel swim]. I mean basically, the first hour I was alright but I was not maybe comfortable and I was not … physically, I was fine, my shoulders and stuff were hurting but it was not really like unbearable. Erm … and also, I do not like taking painkillers. So, I would not take painkillers unless I was in a real … you see, this is another thing that did not sit right with me. If you are in pain then it is because you are causing damage to yourself, you know, your body is telling you that you are doing something you should not be. Taking painkillers to cover that up so you can keep going for hours does not sit right with me because you are just doing more damage and you are covering it up.

Presuming a good pain/bad pain distinction, I asked her whether she was referring to pain from injury or the generalised pain from long swimming, but she refused to accept the distinction:

> But I think that [generalised] pain will induce injury pain. You are developing an injury there and then and the longer you go … do you know what I mean? There

is fatigue, that is different, isn't it, like when your muscles are really tired and you cannot move your arms any more because your muscles do not work, and there is sort of stiffness and aching. But then there is that pain when you know there is over-use around there, which I guess, you know … I kind of believe that you are covering up the pain to keep going but you may end up with a problem. I didn't really like that.

Claire draws a distinction between fatigue and pain, rather than different qualities of pain, which she sees as always leading to injury. By refusing the concept of 'good pain', she also rejects the use of painkillers, which some swimmers see as enabling, but she can only experience as dangerously masking the body's dys-appearance (Leder 1990). Significantly, Claire was also one of the few participants for whom injury posed a significant threat to her ability to do her job as a strength and conditioning coach, for which she needed full use of her hands and arms to perform the arduous labour of sports massage. As well as being at odds with her professional role in injury prevention, therefore, injury also threatened her ability to earn her living. However, unlike the professional athletes and performers who mask injury in order to protect their professional identities, Claire's commitment to her professional role made the masking of injury untenable. Consequently, while the culture of risk forces the separation of injury from health, by resisting it, Claire forces them back together.

Claire's refusal of the culture of risk still leaves it intact since this effectively precluded her active participation in the social world of marathon swimming. However, even among those who identified as marathon swimmers, there was significant variation in the commitment to the culture of risk. For some, the one to two years of concerted training leading up to a target marathon swim was conceptualised as what one swimmer described as a 'health holiday': a provisional break from healthy practices to which they would then return. For these swimmers, a marathon swim figured as a temporary period of physically and emotionally stressful, potentially harmful, but pleasurably challenging, excess (see also, McKibben 2010). US swimmer, David, for example, trained hard for a successful Catalina Channel swim, but subsequently returned to his life-long routines – which he described as 'healthier' – of a mile a day in the pool after work as well as some cycling and running, with no plans to do another long swim. Long-standing habits of moderation and practices easily coded as healthy living figure here as providing a buffer against the potential harms and excesses of marathon swimming, enabling a hiatus in everyday routines in exchange for the 'exciting significance' (Atkinson 2008) of a marathon swim.

Others remained firmly within the marathon swimming social world, but set careful boundaries around what they were prepared to endure and what risks they were prepared to take. This included strategies such as refusing to push through injurious pain; aborting swims while they were still able to leave the water unaided; engaging meticulously in injury prevention regimens such as stroke correction and strengthening and flexibility exercises; and carefully spacing out long swims, including fallow years, in order to allow the body to recover. These qualifications to the 'no-pain, no-gain' ethos of the sport often arose, as in my case, out of experiences of injury and were particularly evident among more experienced swimmers for whom the acknowledgement of injury bore less social threat. In this sense, injury can be seen to have a pedagogic function, inviting reflexive assessment and modified, preventative practice in the interests of sustained engagement (Pringle and Markula 2005; Theberge 2008). This highlights the ways in which cultures of risk are never monolithically experienced, however definitional they are to the practice of the sport. Consequently, even though the amateur domain shares many aspects of professional sport's cultures of risk, a key difference lies in its greater potential for adaptation and preventative interventions than the tightly bound 'sportsnets' of the professional domain. Nevertheless, responsibility for these adaptations remains with the individual, reflecting broader trends of the individualisation of health and the management of risk.

DNF

Pain and injury are one form of risk in marathon swimming, but these are inextricable from the sport's prevailing risk: the failure to complete a swim. In a goal-oriented endurance sport where the primary aim for most is to finish (rather than to win, for example), an aborted swim is difficult to categorise as anything other than a failure, and the risk of a DNF (Did Not Finish) is a major preoccupation among marathon swimmers. It is a much more tangible and imaginable risk than that of injury, and is also a defining feature of 'authentic' marathon swimming: as in the case of injury, if the sport is defined by the pushing of limits, then the possibility of failure is inevitable and even necessary. But also as with injury, however necessary to the sport's self-definitions, when it happens, it can constitute an upsetting disruption to sporting selfhood.

My first DNF experience came in April 2013, when I attempted to swim the Cabrera Channel – a 25 km crossing from the island of Cabrera to Mallorca (Spain). It had been an unseasonably cold spring and the sea temperature was lower than I had been hoping for when I booked the swim; I was also nowhere near as well prepared as I had wished after a disrupted winter of training but I decided to go for it anyway – a gamble which didn't pay off:

> It was a beautiful, but misty, day, and I felt confident and strong at the start, but even by the third hour, I knew that all was not well. I was cold ... really cold. Unlike the usual chill of swimming, where cold nibbles away at the peripheries, I felt like I was being eaten by cold from the inside. I tried picking up the pace, and drank warm feeds every thirty minutes, but the gnawing of cold was miserable and relentless. I told the crew I was cold, and Peter started to ask me questions to test my cognitive state. I answered them quickly and confidently, knowing what he was doing, trying to buoy myself up with the knowledge that I must be okay, that I wasn't too cold to be able to answer. Over the next couple of hours, the white powerboat and I started to drift apart and I began to feel angry with them for not going straight, unable to understand that I was deviating wildly; I became convinced that they were taunting me by moving away, knowing I wouldn't be able to catch them. 'Are we half way yet?' I asked Peter; 'Keep swimming,' he

shouted back, looking concerned. In all our other swims together, I'd never asked for a progress update, happy to swim for as long as it took. And then I start to lose track of what happened. Miserable and confused with cold, I stopped to feed, and Peter asked, 'What's the name of our cat?' I remember looking at him, and slowly being carried away from the boat by the currents as I fumed with paranoid rage: why would he bother me with silly questions when I was so busy? How could he not know the name of our cat? It's… It's… I remember seeing Peter cross his forearms in an X in front of his body to signal the termination of the swim, then beckon me towards the boat, but I don't remember much very clearly after that – hands reaching down and lifting me out of the water, towels and blankets, socks and hats, a bumpy ride through the waves sandwiched tightly between two bodies for warmth. Shivering. Crying. Apologising.

Back on land, I recovered quickly, dressed and bundled up, sipping hot chocolate in a café with Peter and the crew. I felt embarrassed and riddled through with fatigue. I just wanted to take it all back, to have it end differently. Everyone was safe and well and it's only swimming, I told myself. But my first DNF left a sharp bruise.

There are many reasons why DNFs occur, including environmental conditions, insufficient training, injury or illness, hypothermia or simply overwhelming fatigue, but not all failures are treated equally. This reflects the moral dimensions of 'authentic' swimming, which privilege hard work, bodily discipline, individual responsibility and commitment to the 'authentic' practice of the sport as the markers of belonging. As with injuries, failures, then, are more or less forgiveable, depending on the extent to which the swimmer can align themselves with those values. Consequently, while marathon swimming has the superficial appearance of a zero-sum game, a closer inspection reveals subtle hierarchies of both failure and success. For example, those leaving the water after just a couple of hours without any other intervening factors such as illness, injury or deteriorating weather are held up as the archetypal inauthentic swimmers; they are deemed to have done insufficient training, and as having wasted a scarce swim slot that a 'real' swimmer could have used. But although these constitute a tiny minority of cases, they cast a long shadow, and like the imagined malingerer from whom injured swimmers need to distance themselves, they constitute the derided Other against which DNFs are measured and from which individual failures have to be distinguished.

As with the management of injury and the process of becoming a marathon swimmer more generally, the key discourse around which accounts of swim failure circulate is that of hard work, which is mobilised in a number of different, often complementary, ways to shore up a positive self-identity as a marathon swimmer in spite of the DNF. The first and most obvious usage of the 'hard work' discourse is to demonstrate that the individual swimmer had done all the expected work of training and preparation but had been thwarted on the day by adverse conditions or alternatively, by unanticipated and debilitating illness or injury. Elly, for example, experienced severe vomiting as a result of breathing in diesel fumes from the boat during an English Channel attempt, eventually rendering her unable to continue. In our interview, she described the carefulness of her preparation and her purposeful weight gain to resist hypothermia, as well as her experienced crew and the good conditions on the day, but the sickness proved unstoppable. 'I can do this, but not today,' she had rationalised as she left the water, positioning the sickness as an uncontrollable external factor that bore no reflection on her commitment to the training process.

Elly then mobilised a second inflection of the 'hard work' discourse, which is to take failure as a pedagogic opportunity. In future swims, she always took anti-emetic medication beforehand to forestall the destructive cycle of vomiting and exhaustion that is hard to stop once it starts: 'I look at it as a lesson from that one. I mean I will always take something before I swim just in case.' Similarly, Simon, who I discussed in Chapter 7 in relation to his determined weight gain after an unsuccessful English Channel swim, completely revised not only his diet, but also his training schedule following his failed swim, gathering intensity and committing to a succession of weekends of long, back-to-back training swims:

> I think actually, that period between the swims was really where I really felt like I understood Channel swimming and what it takes and … you know … and properly became like a proper sea swimmer. And I think … and you know up until that point I think I had been quite naive about it and … yes, I really felt like I earned it by going back and doing that.

There is a confessional note to Simon's account (Foucault 1976), admitting to his earlier naivety about what was required, while at the same time demonstrating his willingness to correct the perceived failing – a process through which he becomes 'a proper sea swimmer'. Through the discourse of hard work, he constructs himself as a reflexive practitioner who is able to take responsibility for the negative outcome and who earns his subsequent success.

Nevertheless, swim failure can be hard to deal with, and even several years after the event, several swimmers found themselves crying with frustration, regret and sometimes shame as they recounted their unsuccessful swims in the interviews. In some cases, this included potent relations of obligation towards known and unknown others, particularly in relation to charitable swimming, but also towards family and friends. UK swimmer, Rachel, for example, had engaged in a sustained programme of hard training, involving extensive fund-raising publicity and the support and involvement of her husband as crew. Her swim was curtailed by difficult sea conditions, and she cried as she described the moment of terminating the swim:

> It was just hideous. I think … I remember getting on the boat and just apologising to everybody [crying] … I was really upset but I did not want to show it and I just apologised to everybody and so I said that I was sorry, and I'm sorry for letting everyone down.

The knowledge of having worked hard at training provides some reassurance here, but it also highlights a frustrating disconnect between preparation and outcomes. In a sport where there are too many variables to control, the simple equation of hard work and self-discipline with positive outcomes cannot stand up to the vagaries of marathon swimming. This is compounded in those cases where swimmers reached a point of exhaustion or were experiencing the cognitive deficits of hypothermia, when they couldn't fully recall the events leading up to, or immediately after, the termination of the swim – another example of the divergence of the practice of swimming from conventional narratives of exercise as health. For example, Jen Schumacher, an accomplished US marathon swimmer with an extensive competitive pool-swimming background, was pulled out of an English Channel swim in 2012, but had little memory of the final hour of a swim that had otherwise been proceeding well. She was subsequently hospitalised for several days with breathing difficulties. In a moving blog about the experience (Schumacher 2012), she described waking up on the boat out of a confused dream state and startling her partner by asking, 'Am I turning into an armadillo?' Unable to remember the final moments of the swim, her account reflects her concern that she may have conceded too easily:

> Aside from a measly 'Are you sure?', I don't know what I said. I don't know if I fought for it. I don't know if I caved or made a case for myself and my training. I'm left with a fog.

She later met with her pilot and published a second blog detailing a list of 'a few things I could improve on', but her uncertainty about how readily she had left the water reveals the potent normativity of having endured in accounting for (un)successful swims. One means of managing this uncertainty is through the witnessing of knowledgeable others who can authorise the legitimacy of the unsuccessful attempt. Jen, for example, notes how her pilot confirmed that he thinks she can get across and that he would be willing to take her again; and Simon described how the pilot of his unsuccessful Channel swim described him afterwards as 'one hell of a swimmer'. These affirmations have strong currency in the production of legitimate swim failure.

But an unsuccessful swim does not always linger as 'unfinished business' or a source of shame, however disappointing at the time. For some, it served as a full stop to an exciting adventure that had run its course; as one female UK swimmer told me, proudly: 'Even though I didn't make it, I'll never regret it. It was a wonderful experience.' Others spoke of their pride at having done their best and pushed themselves beyond what they had ever imagined; indeed, in these cases, failure serves as confirmation of having pushed beyond individual limits – a valued accomplishment within the sport. Consequently, while marathon swimming appears to be a zero-sum game where you either make it or you don't, not all failures are experienced equally, and unsuccessful swims can also be remembered as successes.[3]

In the same vein, not all successes are experienced as such. For many swimmers, a completed marathon swim is a defining life moment, but for others, it was rather anti-climactic. For example, Ben, a male UK swimmer who successfully swam the English Channel in ideal swim conditions, spoke with slight regret about not having been fully tested; he was also concerned that people within the marathon swimming community 'might think that I only made it because of the weather'. Conversely, several of those who recorded slower times than expected expressed dissatisfaction about their performance. For example, Richard experienced challenging conditions, finishing in eighteen hours – a time well above the twelve-hour crossing he was privately hoping for. While appreciating a sense of achievement at having finished the swim, and acknowledging the unpredictability of finishing times, he confessed to feeling 'a bit defensive' about it: 'I always think, "Oh, I took eighteen bloody hours"'. It was, he argued, 'outside the area of respectability, and you have to account for it, and anyone that is in the business of Channel swimming would know [that it was a relatively slow time].'

Success and failure in marathon swimming, then, are not mutually exclusive, and like injury, a DNF can function variously as confirmation of (in)authenticity; as proof of socially endorsed levels of training and commitment; as a pedagogic prompt to better practice; as a full stop to an exciting adventure; or as a gnawing reminder of unfinished business. Significantly, the meaning of the bodily failures of a DNF do not speak for themselves, but like injuries, have to be explained, contextualised and accounted for in order to become aligned with the values of authentic marathon swimming and social world belonging.

Conclusion

In this chapter, I have argued that pain, injury and swim failure are inescapable, integral elements of marathon swimming – variously operating as markers of progress and 'exciting significance'; as providing social distinction and social world belonging; as pedagogic opportunities; or as material evidence of a body that has failed, both morally and materially. This discussion highlights, first, that health and illness are neither mutually exclusive nor zero-sum categories. Theberge argues that health is a 'robust concept' that needs to be conceptualised in ways that are 'attendant to concrete social and material experiences' (2008: 219). For marathon swimmers, as with many other athletes, the category of 'health' is defined by the capacity to participate, and is distinct from specific histories of injury, which are segmented off from the self as problems to be managed – both materially in terms of restoring the ability to participate, and symbolically, through the negotiation of the stigmas that attach easily and unevenly to failing bodies. This raises important questions both within swimming and in the wider social and cultural context about what 'counts' as a legitimate injury (or illness) and who bears responsibility for its cause and management. In particular, it is clear that legitimate injuries are not determined by the nature or location of the injuries themselves, but rather by the circumstances of acquisition and the values governing injury management. For example, physiologically similar shoulder injuries can be framed as the outcome of a heroic feat of endurance, a pedagogic prompt to engage in preventative work or a marker of the moral failure to serve the necessary apprenticeship. Just as not all fat is equal, neither are all injuries or failures, and the 'good' body is not necessarily either uninjured or successful in its athletic endeavours. This highlights the moral nature of 'health' and its symbolic role in determining legitimate citizenship – a process of social distinction within marathon swimming that is only possible because it already makes sense outside of that domain.

Second, in spite of the relentless linking of health and sport in the policy and medical domains, as well as in the popular imagination, health is not an organising motivation within marathon swimming. In general, participants do not do marathon swims in order to become healthy; indeed, many recognise the health-threatening elements inherent to the excessive nature of the practice. This disconnection from instrumental narratives of exercise for health opens up a space for thinking about the manifold other ways that marathon swimming is meaningful to those who engage in it. This includes, for example, the multiple pleasures of marathon swimming, including those elements of pain and suffering that mark its 'exciting significance', as well as the pleasures of social world belonging, social distinction and the easy alignment with privileged traits of bodily discipline, self-efficacy and autonomy. These diverse, interwoven pleasures reflect the values of middle classness that define the sport and its participants (Atkinson 2008; Hanold 2010) and that make marathon swimming meaningful to its practitioners.

This, in turn, highlights the nature of marathon swimming injuries as fundamentally privileged injuries: that is, injuries that both enjoy a privileged moral status and which are the result of privilege. In short, rather than swimming in order to *become* healthy, marathon swimmers are able to swim because they are *already* healthy (even when injured). More precisely, marathon swimmers already possess sufficient capital that can be coded as healthy to be able not only to experience injury without suffering a significant deficit in that capital, but also to *increase* capital through injury and swim failure – for example, through the symbolic capital that accrues to those who are deemed to have pushed up to and beyond their limits; through the social capital of social world belonging that the willingness to suffer generates; and, in some cases, through the generation of economic capital via coaching and event organisation business ventures. Consequently, while for some, injury can mark the end of a career and a loss of income, not only within professional sport but also across work requiring hard physical labour (Dolan 2011), within an amateur, recreational sport like marathon swimming, the possibilities offered by pain and injury far outweigh the constraints. No one wants to be injured, but the relative freedom to absorb an injury, and even to accrue capital as a result of injury (under some circumstances), marks out the mundane injuries of marathon swimming's excesses as privileged. This observation raises questions about the attribution of 'heroic' and role-model status to athletic performance, particularly in relation to health, but also in other domains. Injury is always more affordable to some than others, and the ability to capitalise on injury is highly contingent. In short, the playing field is never level, and the 'good bodies' of the world of sport are never simply made through sport, but also reflect values and privileges they bring to it (Atkinson 2008).

Notes

1 This was my second attempt at the Manhattan Island Marathon Swim – an anti-clockwise twenty-eight-mile circumnavigation of the island of Manhattan. On my first attempt, in June of that year, logistical problems and poor conditions led to a late start, causing a large proportion of the field of forty swimmers to be pulled out of the East River when they were caught by the turning tide. Most of the swimmers were then taken the short distance by boat to the mouth of the Harlem River, out of the pull of the tide, to continue the swim. However, the mid-swim exit from the water, even for a short time, means that this cannot qualify as a completed, unassisted swim. The organisers offered a second attempt – a 'quiet' swim without the fanfare of the June event – and nine swimmers returned for the rematch, all completing it successfully.
2 Within the UK's NHS, most GPs will perform medicals for sporting events and such like for a small fee. This would usually only include routine examinations that can be carried out in the GP's surgery.
3 In my own case, I continue to understand my unsuccessful Cabrera Channel swim as a failure, although I received nothing but support after the swim both for my endurance and my acknowledgement of my disrupted preparation. This regret is not so much because of the failure to finish the swim, but rather, because I pushed myself to the point where I was no longer safe to be in the water. For me, this involved a level of risk that was not concordant with my understanding of marathon swimming as leisure, as well as placing an unacceptable burden of worry and responsibility on my partner. This has led me to redraw the boundaries of acceptable personal risk much more conservatively.

Conclusion

Marathon swimming is a niche minority sport with a strong sense of its own history and traditions, but with a low public profile and limited recognition of its rules and practices beyond the marathon swimming social world. Yet for those within that social world, it is a deeply meaningful social practice that for many of its practitioners has become a fundamental source of embodied identity and pleasure, and which involves the extensive investment of time, money and energy. This book has explored the embodied and social processes involved in becoming (and being) a marathon swimmer, as well as the wider social relations within which those processes of becoming come to make sense as a site of bodily investment and transformation. The analysis, then, has explored the social phenomenon of marathon swimming, and used it as a lens for interrogating the wider social context. In particular, the key findings of the book centre around five divergences between marathon swimming's prevailing self-representations and its lived realities. These tensions do not reflect purposeful or cynical misrepresentations; rather, the dominant narratives of the sport should be understood as attempts to make marathon swimming make sense through the discursive resources available as the most readily comprehensible and intelligible means.

The first of these is the understanding of contemporary marathon swimming as historically rooted and resistant to the corrupting temptations of modernity. For many, marathon swimming can be understood as an 'escape attempt' – the desire to break out from the constraining comforts and predictabilities of everyday (middle-class) life, commonly expressed as a stripped down confrontation with Nature, devoid of the softening protections of modernity. This is exemplified by the vociferous defence of the tradition-oriented rules that govern the sport, and resistance to the introduction of assistive technologies that are feared to threaten the 'purity' of the encounter with the aquatic environment. Nevertheless, in spite of these suspicions, the social world of marathon swimming is also highly (if selectively) technologised in ways that have improved safety and enhanced both training and the success rates for completed long swims. Furthermore, in spite of the search for distinction through escape, contemporary marathon swimming also resonates with the prevailing cultural logics of neoliberalism, which privilege the autonomous, risk-managing (and risk-taking) individual whose entrepreneurial selfhood marks the triumph of good choices over poor ones and a readiness and capacity to thrive in the market. These two competing motivations – to escape and to meet the demands of institutional structures – reflect the fundamental paradox that Lyng describes in relation to 'edgework', representing 'two dimensions of the same social order in the late modern period' (2005: 10) whereby individuals are both pushed and pulled towards voluntary risk taking and the 'uncertainties of the edge' (4). It is in this way that marathon swimmers can be understood as simultaneously 'standing out while fitting in' (Anderson and Taylor 2010), pursuing a leisure activity that affords social distinction while meeting the conditions of the market. Marathon swimming, then, is a tradition-oriented practice, but one with a profoundly contemporary inflection.

The second tension emerges between the prevailing representations of marathon swimming as the triumph of mind over matter and the unsustainability of a mind–body split in accounting for the experience of the sport. A key element of the contemporary inflection of marathon swimming is the role of the body in late modernity as a site for the construction of the self. In line with other sites of bodily transformation such as weight loss (Heyes 2006; Throsby 2008) and cosmetic surgery (Davis 1995), not only is the body understood as saying something meaningful about the self, but the act of working on the body in itself is socially valued (although always within normative bounds) (Shilling 1993). The sporting body exemplifies this, with the entrenched associations of sport, health and good citizenship casting a positive aura over the process of athletic becoming. This process is comprised of the ongoing acquisition of a catalogue of mundane embodied skills and practices, which both facilitate the act of long swimming and demonstrate belonging through this shared specialist repertoire. These acquired practices produce not only changes in bodily capacity, but also in the materiality of the body (Reischer 2001) and in the ways in which the (aquatic) world is experienced through the body. The process of becoming a marathon swimmer, then, is an iterative one in which embodied technique and skill acquisition, a 'shifted sensorium' (Potter 2008) and the material transformations of the body work in concert with the aquatic environment. The marathon swimming body, therefore, is not simply the result of a body being purposefully acted upon, but also of the body acting and changing (and sometimes resisting or failing) in response to the demands and possibilities of the environment in which it is emplaced and the practices of training. Consequently, in spite of the persistent rhetorics of mind-over-matter in accounting for marathon swimming, like the Möbius strip described by Grosz (1994), the mind and body emerge as inseparable inflections of each other.

This understanding of the embodied process of becoming a marathon swimmer opens up a space for thinking about the sport not simply as an act of overcoming (of the body, of Nature), but also as a site of autotelic, embodied pleasure. This reveals a third divergence between the representation and the lived realities of the sport. Marathon swimming's self-definitions, and particularly its outward-facing representations, focus heavily on suffering and overcoming through the exercise of mind over matter. This can be seen, for example, in fund-raising pages that catalogue the sufferings that await the swimmer in exchange for promises of

Conclusion

sponsorship. There is some truth to these representations, since marathon swimming inevitably involves many possibilities for suffering, but the emplacement of the body, and its acquired kinaesthetic sensibilities to the aquatic environment also offer new ways of experiencing the body beyond that frame. These pleasures constitute the 'existential capital' of marathon swimming (Nettleton 2013), serving not only as a strong motivation to continue in the sport outside of the more obvious pleasures of completion, but also as a shared, inexpressible pleasure that constitutes a source of social belonging.

The cultivation of social belonging constitutes a fourth tension between representation and lived reality. The telic nature of the sport places the focus on swim completion; as I wrote in this book's introduction, in documentary terms, I became an English Channel swimmer when I stood on the French shore and heard the second honk of the horn. But belonging is never secured simply through the demonstrable ability to complete long swims; indeed, in a sport that self-defines as pushing at the edges of capacity, unsuccessful swims are essential to maintaining the currency of completion. Instead, and in addition to the shared inexpressible pleasures of swimming, belonging is produced, first, through displays of allegiance to tradition-oriented rules that nod, however arbitrarily, to the sport's origins; second, through a visible commitment to the work of becoming a marathon swimmer; and third, through the performance of respect – for the sport's 'heroes', for hierarchies of accomplishment and for the challenge itself. This echoes the willingness to manage (and take) risks, and the privileging of self-efficacy, bodily discipline and individual responsibility that characterise entrepreneurial selfhood, as well as highlighting belonging as based not simply on swimming performance, but also on the demonstrable allegiance to a set of values. These are policed within local swimming sites and in online communities, and are a key pedagogical site for novices.

This points to the final tension that emerges in the course of the book, between the sport's claims for itself as inclusive and open to all and the multiple privileges that facilitate participation and belonging. The body is not a blank slate in the process of becoming, but rather, individuals bring to it capacities, dispositions and values that both precede entry into the sport and make it possible and imaginable (Atkinson 2008). In this way, as with Atkinson's triathletes, marathon swimmers are neither drawn into the sport by accident 'nor systematically re-socialised by esoteric sport ideologies therein' (Atkinson 2008: 266), but rather, their backgrounds and biographies prepare them to enter the sporting social world. This is significant because it challenges the democratic self-representation of marathon swimming.

The prevailing narrative of marathon swimming is one of social inclusion – that 'we're all just swimmers' and given the appropriate level of work and commitment, marathon swimming is open to anyone. The simplicity of the sport's equipment gives sense to this claim, and the apolitical gloss that privileges the swimming identity over all other aspects of social identity facilitates coherence across a globally diverse cohort. This is not a cynical conviction, but rather, is endorsed by the ability to find common conversational ground in marathon swimming, the generous hospitality that welcomes travelling swimmers and the global flows of support and encouragement as people attempt challenging swims. However, this obscures the ways in which gender, race, class and sexuality are written in to the everyday practice and understandings of the sport, both delimiting belonging and structuring internal hierarchies. The work of becoming a marathon swimmer, then, is predicated on a cluster of capacities, resources, dispositions and expectations that are not within the remit of individual will or control, but are socially produced and constraining. In short, I was able to swim the English Channel (among others) in part because I trained hard and am a reasonable swimmer, but also because I have the financial resources, the freedom and flexibility over time and the physical capacities to train and swim. Furthermore, my middle class-habitus renders endurance sport a coherent means for self-actualisation, and my British passport enables me to travel freely, rendering aquatic spaces into sites of leisure.

This observation is particularly pertinent in relation to those stretches of water that are taken as the sites for marathon swimming endeavours, but which also serve as international borders and which are closely guarded and patrolled against the illicit passage of migrants trying to flee the dangers of home for a better, safer life – perilous journeys by unseaworthy, over-crowded boats, or even occasionally by swimming, which often end catastrophically (Andersson 2014). My freedom to travel across international borders and to be able to take those closely policed aquatic spaces for leisure signals the privilege of my own 'escape attempts' against the migrants' own literal attempts to escape. Ingold (2000) uses the concept of the 'taskscape' to capture the embeddedness of human practices in both the environment and the current of sociality, highlighting the mutual interlocking of practices and their inescapably social nature. Using this perspective, my swim across the Channel – an act of status-bearing physicality grounded in existing privileges of time, resources and wellness – interlocks with the plight of the desperate migrants attempting illicit and dangerous crossings. When the pilot boats that accompany English Channel swimmers are stopped by French customs officials to check that they haven't picked up illegal immigrants from the beach, our passports prove our legitimacy, and therefore affirm the illegitimacy of others. This is not an argument against marathon swimming, but rather, serves as a reminder that the appropriation of those aquatic spaces for leisure, or even simply for passage, is not open to all – an acknowledgement that tempers the lionisation of voluntary feats of physicality and endurance that attaches so easily to a practice like marathon swimming.

These disjunctures are not the outcomes of cynical misrepresentations or purposeful exclusions; rather, I understand them as faithful attempts to articulate a meaningful practice in ways that have become intelligible. As such, they represent a process of meaning-making in a particular social and cultural context, and as such, offer a productive path into thinking critically about the wider context within which those explanations make sense. Consequently, while I am cautious about offering commentary about the wider sporting field based on a minority practice, the continuity of discursive resources across contexts provides a tentative platform for doing so. In particular, the rhetorics of mind-over-matter, the depoliticising of sport and the moral status attributed to the sporting body are by no means confined to marathon swimming. For example, in January 2015, Sport England launched the 'This Girl Can' campaign,[1] which aimed to encourage women (as 'girls') to overcome the fear of being judged by others and to participate in sport. Through a series of posters and short videos featuring 'real' women, women were urged to recode the exertion and bodily disorder of exercise as sexy ('sweating like a pig, feeling like a fox') and as affirming femininity rather than defying it. There are many problematic aspects to the campaign from a feminist perspective (Throsby 2015b), but one of the posters in particular captures my point about the cross-over between the discursive justifications of marathon swimming and of sport more generally.

The poster is a picture of a woman on a bicycle, bent over her handlebars with the effort of getting up a hill that overlooks a cityscape. She is wearing casual clothes and is riding a city-style bike, distancing her symbolically from the lycra-clad sleekness of the experienced or competitive road racer. The text across the image reads: 'I'm slow but I'm lapping everyone on the couch'. This message is intended to encourage women to engage in sport regardless of ability, but its effect is to create a moral hierarchy between those who exercise and those who do not. However, while the 'couch' here symbolises laziness (as in the derogatory label, 'couch potato'), there are lots of reasons to be on the couch – for example, illness or disability, poverty, caring responsibilities or exhaustion from work.[2] Or perhaps the person on the couch was never taught to ride a bike (Nettleton and Green 2014). A focus on the disjunctures between the dominant representations of marathon swimming and its lived realities, then, opens up a space to reconsider the lionisation of sporting 'heroes', refusing the privileging of the sporting body as the 'good' body of contemporary society without accounting for the social and embodied privileges that enable those sporting practices.

Following on from this, a second contribution that a focus on marathon swimming can make to understandings of the social role of sport more generally is in relation to health. The moral privilege that attaches to those who engage in sport passes easily through the lens of health, and in particular weight management, rendering the exercising body the 'good' body, in contrast to the failed citizenship of the fat and those who are deemed expensively unhealthy through lack of personal responsibility (Ayo 2012). Marathon swimming benefits from the entrenched interpolation of sport and health; the 'good' bodies of marathon swimmers earn sponsorship for good causes, and are understood as exemplifying the prescribed investment in the self (although always potentially to excess). However, health does not emerge as a core motivation for engaging in the sport, and indeed, it is perceived by many as a practice precariously related to health because of the risk of injury and other enduring bodily impacts. Consequently, while marathon swimming can never entirely remove itself from the normative linking of sport and health, its detachment from instrumental accounts of sport for health exposes the ideological nature of 'health' as a moral category of 'good' embodiment.

It is important, then, not to overstate the embeddedness of the marathon swimming social world within the cultural logics of neoliberalism, and the disciplinary nexus of the 'conduct of conduct' (McNay 1999). Throughout *Immersion*, multiple moments of uncontainability emerge, seeping through the cracks in what appear at first glance to be solidly congealed exclusions and conceptual frameworks. This can be seen, for example, in the spaces between the playful fakeness of the heroically fat(tened) body and the cruel abjection of 'real' fat, or in the gendered pleasures of guilt-free eating, bodily solidity or demands for time to oneself. These do not translate into political solidarities and remain largely individualised experiences of empowerment and liberation; as McNay observes, 'the organization of society around a multiplicity of individual enterprises profoundly depoliticises social and political relations by fragmenting collective values of care, duty and obligation and displacing them back on to the managed autonomy of the individual' (McNay 1999: 65). But nevertheless, I am reluctant to relinquish entirely the possibility of social transformation that also lies within these novel experiences of embodiment, which also offer their own critique and prise open the spaces between the congealed normative frameworks available to us to make sense of our embodied social lives. In this, I share Wheaton's cautious optimism, expressed in relation to lifestyle sports, that even while those practices 'have become willing and perfectly moulded agents to further neoliberal discourses of individualism, self-reliance and health', they can also become spaces in which to develop a critical consciousness around questions of identity and inequalities (2013: 4581). In particular, this requires looking beyond the prevailing symbols and representations of the practice to the embodied experiences of those engaging in the sport (Wheaton 2013) – an approach that I have brought to marathon swimming through the (auto)ethnographic study of its representations, values and embodied practices.

In making this case, my analysis may be perceived by some marathon swimmers as overly critical – an affront to a much-loved practice that is closely held and personally meaningful. As highlighted earlier in the book, my aim here has never been to debunk or discredit; indeed, this would be a profoundly hypocritical act given my own deep personal investment. Instead, my goal has been to ask critical questions, particularly of those things that appear self-evident or irrefutable. It is only by asking these questions, and by placing marathon swimming in its wider social and cultural context, that we can begin to understand how the very particular activity of swimming a long way slowly comes to make sense as a meaningful, pleasurable and socially sanctioned practice.

Notes

1 www.thisgirlcan.co.uk/.
2 I am grateful to Stacy Bias for this observation.

References

Aalten, A. (1995). 'In the presence of the body: theorizing training, injuries and pain in ballet.' *Dance Research Journal* 37(2): 55–72.
Aalten, A. (2007). 'Listening to the dancer's body.' *Sociological Review* 55(S1): 109–125.
Abbas, A. (2004). 'The embodiment of class, gender and age through leisure: a realist analysis of long distance running.' *Leisure Studies* 23(2): 159–175.
Abu-Lughod, L. (1990). 'The romance of resistance: tracing transformations of power through Bedouin women.' *American Ethnologist* 17(1): 41–55.
Adams, N. (2014). President's Report (CS&PF Annual Report for the Year 2013). http://cspf.co.uk/article/76/2013-cspf-annual-report-pdf.
Adler, P. and P. Adler (1991). *Backboards and Blackboards: College Athletes and Role Engulfment*. New York, Columbia University Press.
Alford, R. and A. Szanto (1996). 'Orpheus wounded: the experience of pain in the professional worlds of the piano.' *Theory and Society* 25: 1–44.
Allen, K. (2011). 'Girls imagining careers in the limelight: social class, gender and fantasies of "success".' In D. Negra and S. Holmes (eds) *In the Limelight and Under the Microscope: Forms and Functions of Female Celebrity*. London, Continuum: 249–287.
Allen, R.L. and D. Nickel (1969). 'The negro and learning to swim: the buoyancy problem related to reported biological differences.' *Journal of Negro Education* 38(4): 401–411.
Allen-Collinson, J. (2005). 'Emotions, interaction and the injured sporting body.' *International Review for the Sociology of Sport* 40(2): 221–240.
Allen-Collinson, J. (2011). 'Running embodiment, power and vulnerability: notes toward a feminist phenomenology of female running.' In E. Kennedy and P. Markula (eds) *Women and Exercise: The Body, Health and Consumerism*. London, Routledge: 280–298.
Allsopp, R. (2014). 'A bad way to end a perfect day.' *H₂Open Magazine,* December 2014/January 2015: 36–37.
Alvarez, A. (2003). *Feeding the Rat: Profile of a Climber*. London, Bloomsbury.
Alvarez, L. (2011). 'Ready to swim 103 miles with the sharks.' www.nytimes.com/2011/07/19/health/nutrition/19swim.html?_r=4&ref=health%7C&.
Anderson, E. (2008). '"I used to think women were weak": orthodox masculinity, gender segregation, and sport.' *Sociological Forum* 23(2): 257–280.
Anderson, L. (2006). 'Analytic autoethnography.' *Journal of Contemporary Ethnography* 35: 373–395.
Anderson, L. and J. Taylor (2010). 'Standing out while fitting in: serious leisure identities and aligning actions among skydivers and gun collectors.' *Journal of Contemporary Ethnography* 39(1): 34–59.

Andersson, R. (2014) *Illegality Inc.: Clandestine Migration and the Business of Bordering Europe*. Oakland, University of California Press.

Aphramor, L. (2005). 'Is a weight-centred health framework salutogenic? Some thoughts on unhinging certain dietary ideologies.' *Social Theory and Health* 3: 315–340.

Arnot, C. (2010). 'Swimming the Channel in the name of research.' http://www.theguardian.com/education/2010/jul/19/research-extreme-sports.

ASA (2014). 'School Swimming Census 2014 findings revealed today.' www.swimming.org/schoolswimming/school-swimming-census-findings-revealed-today/.

ASA (2015). 'ASA launches manifesto for aquatics.' www.swimming.org/asa/news/general-news/asa-launches-manifesto-for-aquatics/23532.

ASA (n.d.a). 'Choosing swimwear for women.' www.swimming.org/swimfit/womens-swimwear/.

ASA (n.d.b). 'Choosing swimwear for men.' www.swimming.org/swimfit/mens-swimwear/.

Askwith, R. (2013). *Feet in the Clouds: The Classic Tale of Fell-running and Obsession*. Aurum Press (Kindle edition).

Atkinson, M. (2002). 'Pretty in ink: conformity, resistance and negotiation in women's tattooing.' *Sex Roles* 47(5–6): 219–235.

Atkinson, M. (2008). 'Triathlon, suffering and exciting significance.' *Leisure Studies* 27(2): 165–180.

Atkinson, M. (2010). 'Entering scapeland: yoga, fell and post-sport physical cultures.' *Sport in Society: Culture, Commerce, Media, Politics* 13(7–8): 1249–1267.

Ayo, N. (2012). 'Understanding health promotion in a neoliberal climate and the making of health conscious citizens.' *Critical Public Health* 22(1): 99–105.

Ayriss, C. (2012). *Hung Out to Dry: Swimming and British Culture*. Lulu.com.

Baldwin, C.K. (1999). 'Exploring the dimensions of serious leisure: "love me – love my dog!".' *Journal of Leisure Research* 31(1): 1–17.

Baron-Cohen, S. (2003). *The Essential Difference*. London, Penguin.

Bayers, P.L. (2003). *Imperial Ascent: Mountaineering, Masculinity and Empire*. Boulder, University Press of Colorado.

BBC (2006). 'Walliams completes Channel swim.' http://news.bbc.co.uk/sport1/hi/tv_and_radio/sport_relief/5256196.stm.

BBC (2008). 'Swimming the distance.' http://news.bbc.co.uk/1/hi/northern_ireland/foyle_and_west/7531544.stm.

BBC (2012). 'London 2012: Olympics women's boxing skirts still undecided.' www.bbc.co.uk/sport/0/boxing/16608826.

Beal, B. and C. Wilson (2004). '"Chicks dig scars": commercialisation and the transformations of skateboarders' identities.' In B. Wheaton (ed.) *Understanding Lifestyle Sports: Consumption, Identity and Difference*. London, Routledge: 31–54.

Beck, U. (1992). *Risk Society: Towards a New Modernity*. London, Sage.

Becker, H.S. (1963). *Outsiders: Studies in the Sociology of Deviance*. New York, Free Press.

Behar, R. (1996). *The Vulnerable Observer: Anthropology That Breaks Your Heart*. Boston, MA, Beacon Press.

Bell, K. and D. McNaughton (2007). 'Feminism and the Invisible Fat Man.' *Body & Society* 13: 107–131.

Bendelow, G.A. (2000). *Pain and Gender*. Harlow, Pearson Education.

Berlant, L. (2004). 'Introduction: compassion (and withholding).' In L. Berlant (ed.) *Compassion: The Culture and Politics of an Emotion*. London, Routledge: 1–14.

Bier, L. (2011). *Fighting the Current: The Rise of American Women's Swimming, 1870–1926*. London, McFarland & Company Inc.

References

Birke, L. (1999). *Feminism and the Biological Body*. Edinburgh, Edinburgh University Press.
Blackman, L. and C. Venn (2010). 'Affect.' *Body & Society* 16(1): 7–28.
Bogardus, L.M. (2011). 'The bolt wars: a social worlds perspective on rock climbing and intragroup conflict.' *Journal of Contemporary Ethnography* 41(3): 283–308.
Bolin, A. and J. Granskog (eds) (2003). *Athletic Intruders: Ethnographic Research on Women, Culture and Exercise*. SUNY Series on Sport, Culture and Social Relations. New York, State University of New York Press.
Booth, D. (2004). 'Surfing: from one (cultural) extreme to another.' In B. Wheaton (ed.) *Understanding Lifestyle Sports: Consumption, Identity and Difference*. London, Routledge: 94–109.
Bordo, S. (1993). *Unbearable Weight: Feminism, Western Culture and the Body*. Berkeley, University of California Press.
Bourdieu, P. (1992). *The Logic of Practice*. Cambridge, Polity Press.
Bourdieu, P. (2001). *Masculine Domination*. Cambridge, Polity Press.
Brabazon, T. (2006). 'Fitness is a feminist issue.' *Australian Feminist Studies* 21(49): 65–83.
Branningan, D. *et al.* (2009). 'Hypothermia is a significant medical risk of mass participation long-distance open water swimming.' *Wilderness and Environmental Medicine* 20: 14–18.
Bridel, W. and G. Rail (2007). 'Sport, sexuality and the production of (resistant) bodies: de-/re-constructing the meanings of gay male marathon corporeality.' *Sociology of Sport Journal* 24: 127–144.
Brown, D. (2006). 'Pierre Bourdieu's "Masculine Domination" thesis and the gendered body in sport and physical culture.' *Sociology of Sport Journal* 23: 162–188.
Bryant, J. (2005). *The London Marathon: The History of the Greatest Race on Earth*. London, Arrow Books.
Bunsell, T. (2013). *Strong and Hard Women: An Ethnography of Female Bodybuilding*. London, Routledge (Kindle edition).
Bury, M. (1982). 'Chronic illness as biographical disruption.' *Sociology of Health and Illness* 4(2): 167–182.
Butler, J. (1990). *Gender Trouble: Feminism and the Subversion of Identity*. New York, Abingdon, Routledge.
Byrne, C. and C. Lim (2007). 'The ingestible telemetric body core temperature sensor: a review of validity and exercise applications.' *British Journal of Sports Medicine* 41: 126–133.
Cahn, S.K. (1994). *Coming On Strong: Gender and Sexuality in Twentieth-century Women's Sport*. Cambridge, MA, Harvard University Press.
Callahan, J. (1993). *Menopause: A Midlife Passage*. Bloomington, Indiana University Press.
Campbell, A. (1999). *Childfree and Sterilized: Women's Decisions and Medical Responses*. London, New York, Cassell.
Carothers, P., M.P. Donnelly and J.J. Vaske (2001). 'Social values versus interpersonal conflict among hikers and mountain bikers.' *Leisure Sciences: An Interdisciplinary Journal* 23(1): 47–61.
Casey, S. (2010). *The Devil's Teeth*. London, Vintage.
CDC (2014). 'Unintentional drowning: get the facts.' www.cdc.gov/HomeandRecreational Safety/Water-Safety/waterinjuries-factsheet.html.
Chandler, E. (2007). 'Pride and shame: orienting towards a temporality of disability pride.' *Radical Psychology* 8(1): 2.
Chandler, E. (2010). 'Sidewalk stories: the troubling task of identification.' *Disability Studies Quarterly* 30(3/4).

Chapman, G.E. (1997). 'Making weight: lightweight rowing, technologies of power and technologies of the self.' *Sociology of Sport Journal* 14: 205–223.

Chase, L.F. (2008). 'Running bid: Clydesdale runners and technologies of the body.' *Sociology of Sport Journal* 25(1): 130–147.

Clare, E. (2003). 'Gawping, gaping, staring.' *GLQ: A Journal of Lesbian and Gay Studies* 9(1–2): 257–261.

Cleveland, M. (1999). *Dover Solo: Swimming the English Channel*, MMJ Press.

Coghlan, A. (2012). 'An autoethnographic account of a cycling charity challenge event: exploring manifest and latent aspects of the experience.' *Journal of Sport and Tourism* 17(2): 105–124.

Coghlan, A. and K.R. Filo (2013). 'Using constant comparison method and qualitative data to understand participants' experiences at the nexus of tourism, sport and charity events.' *Tourism Management* 35: 122–131.

Cohen, S. and L. Taylor (1992). *Escape Attempts: The Theory and Practice of Resistance to Everyday Life*. London, Routledge.

Comer, K. (2010). *Surfer Girls in the New World Order*. Durham, NC, Duke University Press (Kindle edition).

Connell, R.W. (1995). *Masculinities*. Cambridge, Polity Press.

Conrad, P. (1994). 'Wellness as virtue: morality and the pursuit of health.' *Culture, Medicine and Psychiatry* 18(3): 385–401.

Cooper, C. (2010). 'Fat studies: mapping the field.' *Sociological Compass* 4(12): 1020–1034.

Copelton, D.A. (2010). 'Output that counts: pedometers, sociability and the contested terrain of older fitness walking.' *Sociology of Health and Illness* 32(2): 304–318.

Cox, B. and S. Thompson (2000). 'Multiple bodies: sportswomen, soccer and sexuality.' *International Review for the Sociology of Sport* 35(1): 5–20.

Cox, L. (2006). *Swimming to Antarctica*. London, Orion.

Crawford, G. (2006). 'Health as a meaningful social practice.' *Health: An Interdisciplinary Journal for the Social Study of Health, Illness and Medicine* 10(4): 401–420.

Crawford, G. and V.K. Gosling (2004). 'The myth of the "puck bunny": female fans and men's ice hockey.' *Sociology* 38(3): 477–493.

Crosset, C. and B. Beal (1997). 'The use of "subculture" and "subworld" in ethnographic works on sport: a discussion of definitional distinctions.' *Sociology of Sport Journal* 14: 73–85.

Crossley, N. (2004). 'The circuit trainer's habitus: reflexive body techniques and the sociality of the workout.' *Body & Society* 10(1): 37–69.

Crossley, N. (2006). 'In the gym: motives, meaning and moral careers.' *Body & Society* 12(2): 23–50.

Crossley, N. (2007). 'Research embodiment by way of "body techniques".' In S. Shilling (ed.) *Embodying Sociology: Retrospect, Progress and Prospects*. Oxford, Blackwell: 80–94.

CS&PF (n.d.). 'Matthew Webb.' http://cspf.co.uk/matthew-webb.

CS&PF (2015). 'Solo swim statistics.' http://cspf.co.uk/solo-swims-statistics.

CSA (n.d.). 'About the CSA.' http://www.channelswimmingassociation.com/about/.

Curry, T.J. (1993). 'A little pain never hurt anyone: athletic career socialization and the normalization of sports injury.' *Symbolic Interaction* 16(3): 273–290.

Dahlberg, T. (2009). *America's Girl: The Incredible Story of How Swimmer Gertrude Ederle Changed the Nation*. New York, St. Martin's Press.

Dally, A. (1991). *Women Under the Knife: A History of Surgery*. London, Hutchinson Radius.

Davies, C. (2015). *Downstream: A History and Celebrationn of Swimming the River Thames*. London, Aurum Press.
Davis, K. (1995). *Reshaping the Female Body: The Dilemma of Cosmetic Surgery*. New York, London, Routledge.
Davis, K. (2007). 'Reclaiming women's bodies: colonialist trope or critical epistemology.' In C. Shilling (ed.) *Embodying Sociology: Retrospect, Progress and Prospects*. Oxford, Blackwell: 50–64.
Davis, W. (2012). *Into the Silence: The Great War, Mallory and the Conquest of Everest*. London, Vintage.
Dawson, K. (2006). 'Enslaved swimmers and divers in the Atlantic world.' *Journal of American History* 92(4): 1327–1355.
Dean, P. (2013). *Just Try One More*. London, Balboa Press.
Deem, R. (1987). 'Unleisured lives – sport in the context of women's leisure.' *Women's Studies International Forum* 10(4): 423–432.
Department for Culture, Media and Sport (2008). *Before, During and After: Making the Most of the 2012 Games*. London, Stationery Office: 88.
Department for Education (2014). *Behaviour and Discipline in Schools: Advice to Headteachers and School Staff*. London, Stationery Office.
Department of Health (2004). *Choosing Health: Making Healthy Choices Easier*. London, Stationery Office.
Dilley, R.E. and S.J. Scraton (2010). 'Women, climbing and serious leisure.' *Leisure Studies* 29(2): 125–141.
Dolan, A. (2011). '"You can't ask for a Dubonnet and lemonade!": working class masculinity and men's health practices.' *Sociology of Health and Illness* 33(4): 586–601.
Donnelly, P. and K. Young (1988). 'The construction and confirmation of identity in sport subcultures.' *Sociology of Sport Journal* 5: 223–240.
Dover.uk.com (2015). 'Successful swims.' www.dover.uk.com/channelswimming/swims/.
Downey, G. (2005). *Learning Capoeira: Lessons in Cunning from an Afro-Brazilian Art*. Oxford, Oxford University Press.
Driven (2014). 'About the film.' http://driven.vhx.tv/.
Dumit, J. (2012). *Drugs for Life: How Pharmaceutical Companies Define Our Health*. Durham, NC, Duke University Press.
Ebbeling, C.B., D.B. Pawlak and D.S. Ludwig (2002). 'Childhood obesity: public health crisis, common sense cure.' *The Lancet* 360: 473–482.
Eichenberg, E. *et al.* (2012). 'Best performances by men and women open-water swimmers during the "English Channel Swim" from 1900 to 2010.' *Journal of Sports Sciences* 30(12): 1295–1301.
Elias, N. and E. Dunning (1986). 'The quest for excitement in leisure.' In N. Elias and E. Dunning (eds) *Quest for Excitement: Sport and Leisure in the Civilising Process*. Dublin, University College Dublin Press: 44–72.
Ellis, C. (2004). *The Ethnographic I: A Methodological Novel about Autoethnography*. Walnut Creek, CA, Altamira Press.
Ellis, C. and A. Bochner (2006). 'Analyzing analytic autoethnography: an autopsy.' *Journal of Contemporary Ethnography* 35: 429–449.
Ericson, R., D. Barry and A. Doyle (2000). 'The moral hazards of neo-liberalism: lessons from the private insurance industry.' *Economy and Society* 29(4): 532–558.
Evans, B. (2006). '"Gluttony or sloth": critical geographies of bodies and morality in (anti)obesity policy.' *Area* 38(3): 259–267.

Evers, C. (2009). 'The Point: surfing, geography and a sensual life of men and masculinity on the Gold Coast, Australia.' *Social and Cultural Geography* 10(8): 893–908.

Ewald, K. and R.M. Jiobu (1985). 'Explaining positive deviance: Becker's model and the case of runners and bodybuilders.' *Sociology of Sport Journal* 2: 144–156.

Farred, G. (2012). 'The uncanny of Olympic time: Michael Phelps and the end of neoliberalism.' In D.L. Andrews and M.L. Silk (eds) *Sport and Neoliberalism: Politics, Consumption and Culture*. Philadelphia, PA, Temple University Press: 109–123.

Fausto-Sterling, A. (1992). *Myths of Gender: Biological Theories about Men and Women*. New York, Basic Books.

Faux, M. (1984). *Childless by Choice: Choosing Childlessness in the Eighties*. New York, Anchor Press, Doubleday.

Featherstone, M. (2010). 'Body, image and affect in consumer culture.' *Body & Society* 16(1): 193–221.

Fine, C. (2010). *Delusions of Gender: The Real Science Behind Sex Differences*. London, Icon.

Fine, G.A. (1998). *Morel Tales: The Culture of Mushrooming*. Cambridge, MA, London, Harvard University Press.

Fisher, J. (2002). 'Tattooing the body, marking culture.' *Body & Society* 8(4): 91–107.

Fitzpatrick, M. (2001). *The Tyranny of Health: Doctors and the Regulation of Lifestyle*. London, Routledge.

Fong, K. (2013) *Extremes: Life and Death and the Limits of the Human Body*. London, Hodder & Stoughton.

Ford, N. and D. Brown (2006). *Surfing and Social Theory*. London, Routledge.

Foresight (2007). *Tackling Obesity: Future Choices – Project Report*. London, Government Office for Science.

Foucault, M. (1976). *The History of Sexuality: An Introduction*. London, Penguin.

Foucault, M. (1977). *Discipline and Punish: The Birth of the Prison*. London, Penguin.

Foucault, M. (2008). *The Birth of Biopolitics: Lectures at the College de France, 1978–79*. London, Palgrave.

Francombe, J.M. and M.L. Silk (2012). 'Pedagogies of fat: the social currency of slenderness.' In D.L. Andrews and M.L. Silk (eds) *Sport and Neoliberalism: Politics, Consumption and Culture*. Philadelphia, PA, Temple University Press: 225–241.

Frank, A.W. (1995). *The Wounded Storyteller: Body, Illness and Ethics*. Chicago, London, University of Chicago Press.

Fusco, C. (2006). 'Spatializing the (im)proper subject: the geographies of abjection in sport and physical activity space.' *Journal of Sport and Social Issues* 30: 5–28.

Game, A. (2001). 'Riding: embodying the centaur.' *Body & Society* 7(4): 1–12.

Gard, M. and J. Wright (2005). *The Obesity Epidemic: Science, Morality and Ideology*. London, Routledge.

George, M. (2005). 'Making sense of muscle: the body experiences of collegiate women athletes.' *Sociological Inquiry* 75(3): 317–345.

Geurts, K.L. (2005). 'Consciousness as "feeling in the body": a West African theory of embodiment, emotion and the making of the mind.' In D. Howes (ed.) *Empire of the Senses: The Sensual Culture Reader*. Oxford, Berg: 164–178.

Giddens, A. (1991). *Modernity and Self-identity: Self and Society in the Late Modern Age*. Cambridge, Polity Press.

Giddens, A. (1999). 'Risk and responsibility.' *Modern Law Review* 62(1): 1–10.

Gill, R. (1996). 'Discourse analysis: practical implementation.' In J.T.E. Richardson (ed.) *Handbook of Qualitative Research Methods for Psychology and the Social Sciences*. Leicester, BPS Books: 141–158.

References

Gill, R. (2000). 'Discourse analysis.' In M.W. Bauer and G. Gaskell (eds) *Qualitative Researching with Text, Image and Sound: A Practical Handbook*. London, Sage: 172–190.

Gill, R., K. Henwood and C. McLean (2005). 'Body projects and the regulation of normative masculinity.' *Body & Society* 11: 37–62.

Gillespie, D.L., A. Leffler and E. Lerner (2002). 'If it weren't for my hobby, I'd have a life: dog sports, serious leisure and boundary negotiations.' *Leisure Studies* 21(3–4): 285–304.

Goffman, E. (1963). *Behaviour in Public Places: Notes on the Social Organisation of Gatherings*. London, Collier-Macmillan.

Grosz, E. (1994). *Volatile Bodies: Toward a Corporeal Feminism*. Bloomington, IN, Indiana University Press.

Guerandel, C. and C. Mennesson (2007). 'Gender construction in judo interactions.' *International Review for the Sociology of Sport* 42(2): 167–186.

Hahn, T. (2007). *Sensation Knowledge: Embodying Culture through Japanese Dance*. Middletown, CT, Wesleyan University Press.

Hanold, M.T. (2010). 'Beyond the marathon: (de)construction of female ultrarunning bodies.' *Sociology of Sport Journal* 27: 1601–1177.

Hansen, E. and G. Easthope (2007). *Lifestyle in Medicine*. London, Routledge.

Hardy, K.A. (2013). 'The education of affect: anatomical replicas and "feeling fat".' *Body & Society* 19(1): 1–24.

Hargreaves, J. (1994). *Sporting Females: Critical Issues in the History and Sociology of Women's Sports*. London, Routledge.

Hargreaves, J. (2000). *Heroines of Sport: The Politics of Difference and Identity*. London, Routledge.

Harte, A.R. (2008). 'Swimmer's sea record claim sunk.' *The Mirror*, 20 August. www.thefreelibrary.com/Swimmer's+sea+record+claim+sunk%3B+CHANNEL.-a0183341446.

Harvey, D. (2005). *A Brief History of Neoliberalism*. Oxford, Oxford University Press.

Hemmings, C. (2005). 'Invoking affect.' *Cultural Studies* 19(5): 548–567.

Herndon, A.M. (2005). 'Collateral damage from friendly fire? Race, nation, class and the "war against obesity".' *Social Semiotics* 15(2): 127–141.

Heyes, C.J. (2006). 'Foucault goes to Weight Watchers.' *Hypatia* 21(2): 126–149.

Heywood, I. (1994). 'Urgent dreams: climbing, rationalization and ambivalence.' *Leisure Studies* 13(3): 179–194.

Hills, A. (2012). 'Interview with Leroy Moore.' https://disabilityrightnow.wordpress.com/2012/05/14/interview-with-leroy-moore-2/.

Hoberman, J. (1997). *Darwin's Athletes: How Sport has Damaged Black America and Preserved the Myth of Race*. New York, Houghton Mifflin.

Hockey, J. (2005a). 'Injured distance runners: a case of identity work as self-help.' *Sociology of Sport Journal* 21: 38–58.

Hockey, J. (2005b). 'Sensing the run: the senses and distance running.' *Senses and Society* 1(2): 183–202.

Hodkinson, P. (2002). *Goth: Identity, Style and Subculture*. Oxford, Berg.

Hong, S., D.W. Rennie and Y.S. Park (1987). 'Humans can acclimatize to cold: a lesson from Korean women divers.' *Physiology* 2(3): 79–82.

Horwood, C. (2000). '"Girls who arouse dangerous passions": women and bathing, 1900–39.' *Women's History Review* 9(4): 653–673.

Howe, D. (2001). 'An ethnography of pain and injury in professional rugby union: the case of Pontypridd RFC.' *International Review for the Sociology of Sport* 36(3): 289–303.

Howe, D. (2004). *Sport, Professionalism and Pain: Ethnographies of Injury and Risk*. London, Routledge: 5349 (Kindle edition).

Howes, D. (2005). 'Introduction: empire of the senses.' In D. Howes (ed.) *The Empire of the Senses: The Sensual Culture Reader*. Oxford, Berg: 1–17.

Hughes, R. and J. Coakley (1991). 'Positive deviance among athletes: the implications of overconformity to the sport ethic.' *Sociology of Sport Journal* 8: 307–325.

Humberstone, B. (2011). 'Embodiment and social and environmental action in nature-based sport: spiritual spaces.' *Leisure Studies* 30(4): 495–512.

Humphreys, M. (2013). *In Cold Water*. AuthorHouse.

Hunter, J. and M. Csikszentmihalyi (2000). 'The phenomenology of body–mind: the contrasting cases of flow in sports and contemplation.' *Anthropology of Consciousness* 11(3/4): 5–24.

Ingold, T. (2000). *The Perception of the Environment: Essays on Livelihood, Dwelling and Skill*. London, Routledge.

Irwin, R. et al. (2008). *Constraints Impacting Minority Swimming Participation*. Memphis, TN, University of Memphis.

James, K. (2000). '"You can feel them looking at you": the experiences of adolescent girls at swimming pools.' *Journal of Leisure Research* 32(2): 262–280.

Jamieson, K.M., S. Stringer and M.B. Andrews (2008). 'Athletic fatness: forgiving corpulence in elite bodies.' *Sociology of Sport Journal* 25(1): 148–163.

Jutel, A. (2005). 'Weighing health: the moral burden of obesity.' *Social Semiotics* 15(2): 113–125.

Jutel, A. (2006). 'The emergence of overweight as a disease entity: measuring up normality.' *Social Science and Medicine* 63: 2268–2276.

Kane, M.J. and R. Zink (2004). 'Package adventure tours: markers in serious leisure careers.' *Leisure Studies* 23(4): 329–345.

Karnazes, D. (2005). *Ultramarathon Man: Confessions of an All-night Runner*. New York, Tarcher/Penguin.

Kay, J. and S. Laberge (2004). '"Mandatory equipment": women in adventure racing'. In B. Wheaton (ed.) *Understanding Lifestyle Sports: Consumption, Identity and Difference*. London, Routledge: 154–174.

Keatinge, W.R. et al. (2001). 'Hypothermia during sports swimming in water below 11 degrees C.' *British Journal of Sports Medicine* 35: 352–253.

Kiewa, J. (2001). 'Control over self and space in rockclimbing.' *Journal of Leisure Research* 33(4): 363–382.

Kiewa, J. (2002). 'Traditional climbing: metaphor of resistance or metanarrative of oppression.' *Leisure Studies* 21(2): 145–161.

King, B. (2012). 'Swimming across the English Channel.' www.swimvet.blogspot.co.uk/2012/09/swimming-across-english-channel.html.

King, S. (2001). 'An all-consuming cause: breast cancer, corporate philanthropy and the market for generosity.' *Social Text* 19(4): 115–143.

King, S. (2006). *Pink Ribbons, Inc: Breast Cancer and the Politics of Philanthropy*. Minneapolis, London, University of Minnesota Press.

Klawiter, M. (1999). 'Racing for the cure, walking women, and toxic touring: mapping cultures of action within the Bay Area terrain of breast cancer.' *Social Problems* 46(1): 104–126.

Knechtle, B et al. (2014). 'Women outperform men in ultra-distance swimming – the "Manhattan Island Marathon Swim" from 1983–2013.' *International Journal of Sports Physiology and Performance* 9(6): 913–924.

Kortaba, A. (1983). *Chronic Pain: Its Social Dimension*. London, Sage.

Ladd-Taylor, M. and L. Umansky (eds) (1998). *'Bad' Mothers: The Politics of Blame in Twentieth Century America*. New York, London, New York University Press.

References

Larsen, J. (2014). '(Auto)ethnography and cycling.' *International Journal of Social Research Methodology* 17(1): 59–71.
Laurendeau, J. and N. Sharara (2008). '"Women could be every bit as good as guys": reproductive and resistant agency in two "action" sports.' *Journal of Sport and Social Issues* 32(1): 24–47.
Laurier, E. (2003). *Field Report 1: The Basics of Becoming a Barista*. Glasgow, University of Glasgow.
Laviolette, P. (2011). *Extreme Landscapes of Leisure*. London, Ashgate.
Laws, S. (1990). *Issues of Blood: The Politics of Menstruation*. London, Macmillan.
Lazzarato, M. (2009). 'Neoliberalism in action: inequality, insecurity and the reconstitution of the social.' *Theory, Culture and Society* 26(6): 109–133.
Lea, J. (2009). 'Becoming skilled: the cultural and corporeal geographies of teaching and learning Thai Yoga massage.' *Geoforum* 40: 465–474.
LeBesco, K. (2005). 'Situating fat suits: blackface, drag and the politics of performance.' *Women & Performance: A Journal of Feminist Theory* 15(2): 231–242.
Leder, D. (1990). *The Absent Body*. Chicago, IL, University of Chicago Press.
Lewis, N. (2000). 'The climbing body, nature and the experience of modernity.' *Body & Society* 6(3): 58–80.
Lewis, N. (2004). 'Sustainable adventure: embodied experiences and ecological practices within British climbing.' In B. Wheaton (ed.) *Understanding Lifestyle Sports: Consumption, Identity and Difference*. London, Routledge: 70–93.
Light, R. and T. Rockwell (2005). 'The cultural origins of competitive swimming in Australia.' *Sporting Traditions* 22(1): 21–37.
Little, D.E. (2002). 'Women and adventure recreation: reconstructing leisure constraints and adventure experiences to negotiate continuing participation.' *Journal of Leisure Research* 34(2): 157–177.
Lorimer, H. and K. Lund (2003). 'Performing facts: finding a way over Scotland's mountains.' *Sociological Review* 52(1): 130–144.
Love, C. (2007a). 'Swimming and gender in the Victorian world.' *International Journal of the History of Sport* 24(5): 586–602.
Love, C. (2007b). 'Social class and the swimming world: amateur and professional.' *International Journal of the History of Sport* 24(5): 603–619.
Lupton, D. (1995). *The Imperative of Health: Public Health and the Regulated Body*. London, Sage.
Lupton, D. (1996). *Food, the Body and the Self*. London, Sage.
Lupton, D. (2013a). 'Quantifying the body: monitoring and measuring health in the age of mHealth technologies.' *Critical Public Health* 23(4): 393–403.
Lupton, D. (2013b). 'Understanding the human machine.' *IEEE Technology and Society Magazine* Winter: 25–30.
Lyng, S. (2005). 'Edgework and the risk-taking experience.' In S. Lyng (ed.) *Edgework: The Sociology of Risk-taking*. London, Routledge: 3–16.
Lyons, A.C. and S. Willott (1999). 'From suet pudding to superhero: representations of men's health for women.' *Health* 3(3): 283–302.
Magdalinski, T. (2009). *Sport, Technology and the Body: The Nature of Performance*. Abingdon, Routledge.
Maguire, J. (2002). 'Body lessons: fitness publishing and the cultural production of the fitness consumer.' *International Review for the Sociology of Sport* 37(3/4): 449–464.
Maguire, J. and L. Mansfield (1998). '"No-body's perfect": women, aerobics and the body beautiful.' *Sociology of Sport Journal* 15: 109–137.

Makinen, T.M. (2010). 'Different types of cold adaptation in humans.' *Frontiers in Bioscience* S2: 1047–1067.

Mann, T. *et al.* (2007). 'Medicare's search for effective obesity treatments.' *American Psychologist* 62(3): 220–233.

Mansfield, L. (2011). 'Fit, fat and feminine: the stigmatization of fat women in fitness gyms.' In E. Kennedy and P. Markula (eds) *Women and Exercise: The Body, Health and Consumerism.* London, Routledge: 81–100.

Markula, P. (1995). 'Firm but shapely, fit but sexy, strong but thin: the postmodern aerobicizing female bodies.' *Sociology of Sport Journal* 12(4): 424–453.

Markula, P. (2013). '(Im)mobile bodies: contemporary semi-professional dancers' experiences with injuries.' *International Review for the Sociology of Sport*: 1–25.

Mauss, M. (1973). 'Techniques of the body.' *Economy and Society* 2(1): 70–88.

McCardel, C. (2012). 'Cuba–USA world record 2013.' www.chloemccardel.com/cuba-usa-world-record-2013/.

McEwen, K. and K. Young (2011). 'Ballet and pain: reflections on a risk-dance culture.' *Qualitative Research in Sport, Exercise and Health* 3(2): 152–173.

McKibben, B. (2010). *Long Distance: Testing the Limits of Body and Spirit in a Year of Living Strenuously.* New York, Rodale.

McNay, L. (1999). 'Gender, habitus and the field: Pierre Bourdieu and the limits of reflexivity.' *Theory, Culture and Society* (16): 1.

McNay, L. (2009). 'Self as enterprise: dilemmas of control and resistance in Foucault's *The Birth of Biopolitics*.' *Theory, Culture and Society* 26(6): 55–77.

Mekky, S. (2014). *Wearable Computing and the Hype of Tracking Personal Activity.* Stockholm, Sweden, Royal Institute of Technology.

Mendoza, K.R. (2009). 'Seeing through the layers: fat suits and thin bodies in The Nutty Professor and Shallow Hal.' In E. Rothblum and S. Solovay (eds) *The Fat Studies Reader.* New York, New York University Press: 280–288.

Mennesson, C. (2000). '"Hard" women and "soft" women: the social construction of identities among female boxers.' *International Review for the Sociology of Sport* 35(1): 21–33.

Merchant, S. (2011). 'Negotiating underwater space: the sensorium, the body and the practice of scuba-diving.' *Tourist Studies* 11(3): 215–234.

Merleau-Ponty, M. (1962). *Phenomenology of Perception.* London, Routledge.

Messner, M. (1988). 'Sports and male domination: the female athlete as contested ideological terrain.' *Sociology of Sport Journal* 5: 197–211.

Miami News (1927). 'Channel swim hoax admitted by prize winner.' https://news.google.com/newspapers?nid=2206&dat=19271016&id=BUEuAAAAIBAJ&sjid=gNgFAAAAIBAJ&pg=5908,3836016&hl=en.

Miller, T. (2012). 'A distorted playing field: neoliberalism and sport through the lens of economic citizenship.' In D.L. Andrews and M.L. Silk (eds) *Sport and Neoliberalism: Politics, Consumption and Culture.* Philadelphia, PA, Temple University Press: 23–37.

Mitchell, R.G. (1983). *Mountain Experience: The Psychology and Sociology of Adventure.* Chicago, London, University of Chicago Press.

Moir, A. and D. Jessel (1991). *Brain Sex: The Real Difference Between Men and Women.* London, Mandarin.

Mol, A. (2009). 'Living with diabetes: care beyond choice and control.' *The Lancet* 373: 1756–1757.

Monaghan, L.F. (2007a). 'Body Mass Index, masculinities and moral worth: men's critical understandings of "appropriate" weight-for-height.' *Sociology of Health and Illness* 29(4): 584–609.

Monaghan, L.F. (2007b). 'McDonaldizing men's bodies? Slimming, associated (ir)rationalities and resistances.' *Body & Society* 7(13): 67–93.

Monaghan, L.F. (2008). *Men and the War on Obesity: A Sociological Study*. London, Routledge.

Moore, S.E.H. (2008). *Ribbon Culture: Charity, Compassion and Public Awareness*. Houndmills, Palgrave Macmillan.

Morell, C. (2000). 'Saying no: women's experiences with reproductive refusal.' *Feminism and Psychology* 10(3): 313–322.

Morell, M.M. (1994). *Unwomanly Conduct: The Challenges of Intentional Childlessness*. London, Routledge.

Moreno-Black, B. and H. Vallianatos (2005). 'Young women's experiences of menstruation and athletics.' *Women's Studies Quarterly* 33(1/2): 50–67.

Morrison, E. (2011). 'On wetsuits in marathon swimming.' http://marathonswimmers.org/blog/2011/09/wetsuits-in-marathon-swimming/.

Mortimer, G. (2008). *The Great Swim*. London, Short Books.

Mostafanezhad, M. (2014). *Volunteer Tourism: Popular Humanitarianism in Neoliberal Times*. Farnham, Ashgate (Kindle edition).

MSF (2012a). 'Diana Nyad's directional "streamer".' http://marathonswimmers.org/forum/discussion/211/diana-nyad-s-directional-streamer/p1.

MSF (2012b). 'No more cold water training required! What next?!' http://marathonswimmers.org/forum/discussion/178/no-more-cold-water-training-required-what-next/p1.

MSF (2013a). 'Who earns the title "Channel Swimmer"?' http://marathonswimmers.org/forum/discussion/344/who-earns-the-title-channel-swimmer/p1.

MSF (2013b). '110 miles, 53 hours: questions for Diana Nyad.' http://marathonswimmers.org/forum/discussion/606/110-miles-53-hours-questions-for-diana-nyad/p1.

MSF (2013c). 'Janet Manning Lake Tahoe swim'. http://marathonswimmers.org/forum/discussion/571/janet-manning-lake-tahoe-swim/p1.

MSF (2014a). 'Rules of marathon swimming.' http://marathonswimmers.org/rules/.

MSF (2014b). 'Do you wear a wrist watch in marathon swims?' http://marathonswimmers.org/forum/discussion/732/do-you-wear-a-wristwatch-in-marathon-swims/p1.

Munatones, S. (2013a). 'Fit for a king, but not for the channel community.' http://dailynews.openwaterswimming.com/2013/01/fit-for-king-but-not-for-channel.html.

Munatones, S (2013b). 'Darren Jaundrill, an unlikely swimmer setting the bar.' http://dailynews.openwaterswimming.com/2013/02/darren-jaundrill-unlikely-swimmer.html.

Murray, S. (2005). '(Un/be)coming out? Rethinking fat politics.' *Social Semiotics* 15(2): 153–163.

Murray, S. (2008). *The 'Fat' Female Body*. Houndmills, Routledge.

Nettleton, S. (2013). 'Cementing relations within a sporting field: fell running in the English Lake District and the acquisition of existential capital.' *Cultural Sociology* 7(2): 196–210.

Nettleton, S. and J. Green (2014). 'Thinking about changing mobility practices: how a social practice approach can help.' *Sociology of Health and Illness* 36(2): 239–251.

Nettleton, S. and J. Hardey (2006). 'Running away with health: the urban marathon and the construction of "charitable bodies".' *Health* 10(4): 441–460.

NHS (2013). 'Exercise to relieve stress.' www.nhs.uk/conditions/stress-anxiety-depression/pages/stress-relief-exercise.aspx.

Niedzviecki, H. (2006). *I'm Special: How Individuality Became the New Conformity*. San Francisco, CA, City Lights.

Nixon, H. (1992). 'A social network analysis of influences on athletes to play with pain and injuries.' *Journal of Sport and Social Issues* 16(2): 127–135.

Nuñez, A. (2012). 'Motivation Monday: meet the woman who swam the English Channel.' http://www.shape.com/blogs/shape-your-life/motivation-monday-meet-woman-who-swam-english-channel.

Nyad, D. (2012a). 'Official: total number of hours swum.' http://web.archive.org/web/20120828090100/http://www.diananyad.com/blog/total-hours-swum.

Nyad, D. (2012b). 'Response to heat drip dialogue.' https://web.archive.org/web/20120728073836/http://diananyad.com/response-to-heat-drip-dialogue/.

O'Connor, E. (2007). 'Embodied knowledge in glassblowing: the experience of meaning and the struggle towards proficiency.' *Sociological Review* 55(May): 126–141.

Ogilvie, D. and N. Hamlet (2005). 'Obesity: the elephant in the corner.' *British Medical Journal* 331: 1545–1548.

Orend, A. and P. Gagne (2009). 'Corporate logo tattoos and the commodification of the body.' *Journal of Contemporary Ethnography* 38: 493–517.

Ortner, S.B. (1999). *Life and Death on Mt Everest: Sherpas and Himalayan Mountaineering.* Princeton, Oxford, Princeton University Press.

Osmond, G. and M. Phillips (2004). '"The bloke with a stroke": Alick Wickham, the "crawl" and social memory.' *Journal of Pacific History* 39(3): 309–342.

Palfrey, P. (2012). 'Cuba 2012 – What an aventure we had ... some great times and some heartache....' http://pennypalfreyproject.blogspot.com.au/2012/07/cuba2012-what-adventure-we-hadsome.html.

Palmer, C. (2004). 'Death, danger and the selling of risk in adventure sports.' In B. Wheaton (ed.) *Understanding Lifestyle Sports: Consumption, Identity and Difference.* London, Routledge: 55–69.

Palmer, C. and K. Thompson (2010). 'Everyday risks and professional dilemmas: fieldwork with alcohol-based (sporting) subcultures.' *Qualitative Research* 10: 421–440.

Pantzar, M. and M. Ruckenstein (2014). 'The heart of everyday analytics: emotional, material and practical extensions in self-tracking market.' *Consumption Markets and Culture* 18(1): 92–109.

Parker, C. (2010). 'Swimming: the "ideal" sport for nineteenth-century British women.' *International Journal of the History of Sport* 27(4): 675–689.

Parr, S. (2011). *The Story of Swimming.* Stockport, Dewi Lewis Media.

Pike, E. (2005). 'Doctors just say "rest and take ibuprofen": a critical examination of the role of "non-orthodox" health care in women's sport.' *International Review for the Sociology of Sport* 40(2): 201–219.

Pike, E. and J. Maguire (2003). 'Injury in women's sport: classifying key elements of "risk encounters".' *Sociology of Sport Journal* 20: 232–251.

Pitterle, B. and B. Hall (2014). *Driven.* Carpentaria, Element 8 Productions.

Pitts, V. (2003). *In the Flesh: The Cultural Politics of Body Modification.* New York, Houndmills, Palgrave Macmillan.

Pitts-Taylor, V. (2007). *Surgery Junkies: Wellness and Pathology in Cosmetic Culture.* New Brunswick, NJ, Rutgers University Press.

Potter, C. (2008). 'Sense of motion, senses of self: becoming a dancer.' *Ethnos* 73(4): 444–465.

Potter, J. and M. Wetherell (1987). *Discourse and Social Psychology: Beyond Attitudes and Behaviour.* London, Sage.

Pringle, R. and P. Markula (2005). 'No pain is sane after all: a Foucauldian analysis of masculinities and men's experiences in rugby.' *Sociology of Sport Journal* 22(4): 472–497.

Pugh, L. (2009). 'How I swam the North Pole.' www.ted.com/talks/lewis_pugh_swims_the_north_pole.

References

Pugh, L. (2010a). 'My mind-shifting Everest swim.' www.ted.com/talks/lewis_pugh_s_mind_shifting_mt_everest_swim?language=en.
Pugh, L. (2010b) *Achieving the Impossible*. London, Simon & Schuster.
Raisborough, J. (2006). 'Getting onboard: women, access and serious leisure.' *Sociological Review* 54(2): 242–262.
Raisborough, J. (2007). 'Gender and serious leisure careers: a case study of women sea cadets.' *Journal of Leisure Research* 39(4): 686–704.
Rapp, R. (1999). *Testing Women, Testing the Fetus: The Social Impact of Amniocentesis in America*. New York, Routledge.
Reed-Danahay, D.E. (1997). 'Introduction.' In D.E. Reed-Danahay (ed.) *Auto/Ethnography: Rewriting the Self and the Social (Explorations in Anthropology)*. Oxford, Berg: 1–17.
Reischer, E.L. (2001). 'Running to the moon: the articulation and the construction of self in marathon runners.' *Anthropology of Consciousness* 12(2): 19–35.
Rew, K. (2009). *Wild Swim: River, Lake, Lido and Sea: The Best Places to Swim Outdoors in Britain*. London, Guardian Books.
Rinehart, R. and S. Sydnor (eds) (2003). *To The Extreme: Alternative Sports, Inside and Out*. Albany, SUNY Press.
Ritzer, G. (2004). *The McDonaldization of Society, Revised New Century Edition*. London, Sage.
Roberts, D. (2001). *Great Exploration Hoaxes*. New York, Modern Library.
Robinson, V. (2008). *Everyday Masculinities and Extreme Sport: Male Identity and Rock Climbing*. Oxford, Berg.
Roderick, M., I. Waddington and G. Parker (2000). 'Playing hurt: managing injuries in English professional football.' *International Review for the Sociology of Sport* 35(2): 165–180.
Rodgers, T. (1999). 'Resurfacing.' *San Diego Union Tribune*, 15 August. www.doversolo.com/carolsing.htm.
Rothblum, E. and S. Solovay (eds) (2009). *The Fat Studies Reader*. New York, New York University Press.
Rowe, N. and Champion, R. (2000). *Sports Participation and Ethnicity in England*. London, Sport England.
Rust, C., et al. (2014a). 'Will women soon outperform men in open-water ultra-distance swimming in the "Maratona del Golfo Capri–Napoli"?' *SpringerPlus* 3: 86.
Rust, C. T. Rosemann and B. Knechtle (2014b). 'Performance and sex difference in ultra-triathlon performance from Ironman to Double Deca Iron ultra-triathlon between 1978 and 2013.' *SpringerPlus* 3: 219.
Sandford, E.S. (2006). 'My shoe size stayed the same: maintaining a positive sense of identity with achondroplasia and limb-lengthening surgeries.' In E. Parens (ed.) *Surgically Shaping Children: Technology, Ethics and the Pursuit of Normality*. Baltimore, MD, Johns Hopkins University Press: 29–42.
Sassatelli, R. (1999). 'Fitness gyms and the local organization of experience.' *Sociological Research Online* 4(3).
Schumacher, J. (2012). 'English Channel – Part I.' http://jenschumacher.org/blog/comments/english-channel-part-1/.
Scott, B. and J. Derry (2005). 'Women in their bodies: challenging objectification through experiential learning.' *Women's Studies Quarterly* 33(1/2): 188–209.
Scott, S. (2010). 'How to look good (nearly) naked: the performative regulation of the swimmer's body.' *Body & Society* 16(2): 143–168.

Sheridan, M. (2012). 'Take all your chances while you can….' http://reminiscencesofalongdistanceswimmer.blogspot.co.uk/2012_11_01_archive.html.
Sheridan, M. (2013). '2 Swim 4 Life 2013.' http://reminiscencesofalongdistanceswimmer.blogspot.co.uk/2013/04/2-swim-4-life-2013.html.
Shildrick, M. (1997). *Leaky Bodies and Boundaries: Feminism, Postmodernism and (Bio) Ethics*. London, New York, Routledge.
Shilling, C. (1993). *The Body and Social Theory*. London, Sage.
Shilling, C. (2007). 'Sociology and the body: classical traditions and new agendas.' In C. Shilling (ed.) *Embodying Sociology: Retrospect, Progress and Prospects*. Oxford, Blackwell: 1–18.
Shilling, C. (2010). 'Exploring the society–body–school nexus: theoretical and methodology issues in the study of body pedagogics.' *Sport, Education and Society* 15(2): 151–167.
Shogan, D. (1999). *The Making of High-performance Athletes: Discipline, Diversity and Ethics*. Toronto, University of Toronto Press.
Silk, M.L. and D.L. Andrews (2012). 'Sport and the neoliberal conjuncture: complicating the consensus.' In D.L. Andrews and M.L. Silk (eds) *Sport and Neoliberalism: Politics, Consumption and Culture*. Philadelphia, PA, Temple University Press: 1–22.
Sisjord, M.K. and E. Kristiansen (2009). 'Elite women wrestlers' muscles: physical strength and a social burden.' *International Review for the Sociology of Sport* 44(2–3): 231–246.
Skeggs, B. (1997). *Formations of Class and Gender: Becoming Respectable*. London, Sage.
Sloop, J. (2012). '"This is not natural": Caster Semenya's gender threats.' *Critical Studies in Media Communication* 29(2): 81–96.
Smith, B. and A. Sparkes (2008). 'Changing bodies, changing narratives and the consequences of tellability: a case study of becoming disabled through sport.' *Sociology of Health and Illness* 30(2): 217–236.
Smith, R.T. (2008). 'Pain in the act: the meanings of pain among professional wrestlers.' *Qualitative Sociology* 31: 129–148.
Smith, S.L. (2000). 'British nonelite road running and masculinity: a case of "running repairs".' *Men and Masculinities* 3(2): 187–208.
Snee, S. (2014). 'Doing something "worthwhile": intersubjectivity and morality in gap year narratives.' *Sociological Review* 62: 843–861.
Snelgrove, R. and L. Wood (2010). 'Attracting and leveraging visitors at a charity cycling event.' *Journal of Sport and Tourism* 15(4): 269–285.
Sparkes, A. (1996). 'The fatal flaw: a narrative of the fragile body-self.' *Qualitative Inquiry* 2: 463–494.
Sparkes, A. (2000). 'Autoethnography and narratives of self: reflections on criteria in action.' *Sociology of Sport Journal* 17(1): 21–43.
Spelman, E.V. (2010). 'Woman as body: ancient and contemporary views.' In P. Davis and C. Weaving (eds) *Philosophical Perspectives on Gender in Sport and Physical Activity*. London, Routledge.
Spencer, D.C. (2009). 'Habit(us), body techniques and body callusing: an ethnography of mixed martial arts.' *Body & Society* 15(4): 119–143.
Spinney, J. (2006). 'A place of sense: a kinaesthetic ethnography of cyclists on Mont Ventoux.' *Environment and Planning D: Society and Space* 24: 709–732.
Sprawson, C. (1992). *Haunts of the Black Masseur: The Swimmer as Hero*. London, Vintage.
St. Pierre, J. (2012). 'The construction of the disabled speaker: locating stuttering in disability studies.' *Canadian Journal of Disability Studies* 1(3).
Stacey, J. (1988). 'Can there be a feminist ethnography?' *Women's Studies International Forum* 11(1): 21–27.

References

Stalp, M.C. (2007). *Quilting: The Fabric of Everyday Life*. Oxford, Berg.

Stanhope, N. (2005). *Blood, Sweat and Charity: The Ultimate Charity Challenge Handbook*. Bridgnorth, Eye Books.

Stearns, P.N. (2002). *Fat History: Bodies and Beauty in the Modern West*. New York, New York University Press.

Stebbins, R.A. (2007). *Serious Leisure: A Perspective for our Time*. New Brunswick, NJ, Transaction Publishers.

Stevenson, C.L. (2002). 'Seeking identities: towards an understanding of the athletic careers of master swimmers.' *International Review for the Sociology of Sport* 37(2): 131–146.

Stout, G. (2009). *Young Woman and the Sea: How Trudy Ederle Conquered the English Channel*. Boston, MA, Houghton Miffin Harcourt.

Straughan, E.R. (2012). 'Touched by water: the body in scuba diving.' *Emotion, Space and Society* 5: 19–26.

Strauss, A. (1978). 'A social world perspective.' *Studies in Symbolic Interactionism* 1: 119–128.

Strauss, A. (1982). 'Social worlds and legitimation processes.' *Studies in Symbolic Interactionism* 4: 171–190.

Strauss, A. (1984). 'Social worlds and their segmentation processes.' *Studies in Symbolic Interactionism* 5: 123–139.

Sudnow, D. (2001). *Ways of the Hand: A Rewritten Account*. Cambridge, MA, MIT Press.

Swan, M. (2012). 'Sensor mania! The internet of things, wearable computing, objective metrics and the quantified self 2.0.' *Journal of Sensor and Actuator Networks* 1: 217–253.

Synne Groven, K., K.N. Solbrække and G. Engelsrud. (2011). Large women's experiences of exercise. In E. Kennedy and P. Markula (eds) *Women and Exercise: The Body, Health and Consumerism*. London, Routledge: 121–137.

Tabor, J.M. (2007). *Forever on the Mountain: The Truth Behind One of Mountaineering's Most Controversial and Mysterious Disasters*. New York, W. W. Norton & Company.

Taylor, K. (2009). 'Channel swim becomes a Dover marathon.' http://kyletaylor.com/blog/2009/7/7/channel-swim-becomes-a-dover-marathon.html.

Theberge, N. (2000). *Higher Goals: Women's Ice Hockey and the Politics of Gender*. Albany, State University of New York Press.

Theberge, N. (2008). '"Just a normal bad part of what I do": elite athletes' accounts of the relationship between health and sport.' *Sociology of Sport Journal* 25: 206–222.

Thorpe, H. (2011). *Snowboarding Bodies in Theory and Practice*. Houndmills, Palgrave Macmillan.

Throsby, K. (2007). '"How could you let yourself get like that?" Stories of the origins of obesity in accounts of weight loss surgery.' *Social Science and Medicine* 65: 1561–1571.

Throsby, K. (2008). 'Happy re-birthday: weight loss surgery and the "new me".' *Body & Society* 14(1): 117–133.

Throsby, K. (2009). 'The war on obesity as a moral project: weight loss drugs, obesity surgery and negotiating failure.' *Science as Culture* 18(2): 201–216.

Throsby, K. (2012). 'Obesity surgery and the management of excess: exploring the body multiple.' *Sociology of Health and Illness* 34(1): 1–15.

Throsby, K. (2013a). '"If I go in like a cranky sea-lion, I come out like a smiling dolphin": marathon swimming and the unexpected pleasures of being a body in water.' *Feminist Review* 103: 5–22.

Throsby, K. (2013b). 'Decisions, decisions….' http://thelongswim.blogspot.co.uk/2013/06/decisions-decisions.html.

Throsby, K. (2013c). '"You can't be too vain to gain if you want to swim the Channel": marathon swimming and the construction of heroic fatness.' *International Review for the Sociology of Sport*. DOI: 10.1177/1012690213494080.

Throsby, K. (2015a). 'Unlikely becomings: passion, swimming and learning to love the sea.' In M. Brown and B. Humberstone (eds) *Seascapes: Shaped by the Sea: Embodied Narratives and Fluid Geographies*. Farnham, Ashgate: 155–172.

Throsby, K. (2015b). '"This girl can" … or why this woman won't….' http://thelongswim.blogspot.co.uk/2015/01/this-girl-canor-why-this-woman-wont.html.

Throsby, K. and B. Evans (2013). '"Must I seize every opportunity?" Complicity, confrontation and the problem of researching (anti-) fatness.' *Critical Public Health* 23(3): 331–344.

Throsby, K. and D. Gimlin (2009). 'Critiquing thinness and wanting to be thin.' In R. Flood and R. Gill (eds) *Secrecy and Silence in the Research Process: Feminist Reflections*. London, Routledge: 105–116.

Till, C. (2014). 'Exercise as labour: quantified self and the transformation of exercise into labour.' *Societies* 4: 446–462.

Titmuss, R.M. (1971). *The Gift Relationship: From Human Blood to Social Policy*. New York, Vintage Books.

Tomrley, C. and A. Kaloski Naylor (eds) (2009). *Fat Studies in the UK*. York, Raw Nerve Books.

Tulle, E. (2007). 'Running to run: embodiment, structure and agency amongst veteran elite runners.' *Sociology* 41(2): 329–346.

Tullis, J. (1986). *Clouds from Both Sides*. London, Grafton.

Turkle, S. (ed.) (2007a). *Evocative Objects: Things We Think With*. Cambridge, MA, MIT Press (Kindle edition).

Turkle, S. (2007b). 'Introduction: the things that matter.' In S. Turkle (ed.) *Evocative Objects: Things We Think With*. Cambridge, MA, MIT Press (Kindle edition): 34–115.

Turner, B.S. and S.P. Wainwright (2003). 'Corps de Ballet: the case of the injured ballet dancer.' *Sociology of Health and Illness* 25(4): 269–288.

Tyler, I. (2013). *Revolting Subjects: Social Abjection and Resistance in Neoliberal Britain*. London, Zed Books: 6651.

Unruh, D.R. (1980). 'The nature of social worlds.' *Pacific Sociology Review* 23(3): 271–296.

Vrasti, W. (2013). *Volunteer Tourism in the Global South: Giving Back in Neoliberal Times*. London, Routledge.

Vybiral, S. et al. (2000). 'Thermoregulation in winter swimmers and physiological significance of human catecholamine thermogenesis.' *Experimental Physiology* 85(3): 321–326.

Wackwitz, L. (2003). 'Verifying the myth: Olympic sex testing and the category "woman".' *Women's Studies International Forum* 26: 553–560.

Wacquant, L. (2004). *Body & Soul: Notebooks of an Apprentice Boxer*. Oxford, Oxford University Press.

Waddington, I. (2000). *Sport, Health and Drugs: A Critical Sociological Perspective*. London, E. and FN Spon.

Wainwright, S. and B.S. Turner (2004). 'Epiphanies of embodiment: injury, identity and the balletic body.' *Qualitative Research* 4(3): 311–337.

Wainwright, S.P., C. Williams and B.S. Turner (2005). 'Fractured identities: injury and the balletic body.' *Health: An Interdisciplinary Journal for the Social Study of Health, Illness and Medicine* 9(1): 49–66.

Walsh, D. (2013). *Seven Deadly Sins: My Pursuit of Lance Armstrong*. London, Simon & Schuster.

References

Watson, K. (2000). *The Crossing: The Curious Story of the First Man to Swim the English Channel*. London, Headline.
Webb, M. ([1876] 1999). *The Art of Swimming*. Whitstable, Pryor Publications.
Wetherell, M. (2012). *Affect and Emotion: A New Social Science Understanding*. London, Sage.
Wheaton, B. (2003). 'Windsurfing: a subculture of commitment.' In R.E. Rinehart and S. Sydnor (eds) *To the Extreme: Alternative Sports, Inside and Out*. New York: State University of New York: 75–101.
Wheaton, B. (2004a). 'Introduction: mapping the lifestyle sport-scape.' In B. Wheaton (ed.) *Understanding Lifestyle Sports: Consumption, Identity and Difference*. London, Routledge: 1–28.
Wheaton, B. (2004b). '"New lads"? Competing masculinities in the windsurfing culture.' In B. Wheaton (ed.) *Understanding Lifestyle Sports: Consumption, Identity and Difference*. London, Routledge: 131–153.
Wheaton, B. (ed.) (2004c). *Understanding Lifestyle Sports: Consumption, Identity and Difference*. Routledge Critical Studies in Sport. London, Routledge.
Wheaton, B. (2013). *The Cultural Politics of Lifestyle Sport*. Abingdon, Routledge (Kindle edition).
Wheaton, B. and A. Tomlinson (1998). 'The changing gender order in sport? The case of windsurfing subculture.' *Journal of Sport and Social Issues* 22(3): 252–274.
Whitson, J.R. (2013). 'Gaming the quantified self.' *Surveillance and Society* 11(1/2): 163–176.
WHO (2000). Obesity: preventing and managing the global epidemic: Report of a WHO consultation. *WHO Technical Report Series*. Geneva, World Health Organization.
Willig, C. (2008). 'A phenomenological investigation of the experience of taking part in "extreme sports".' *Journal of Health Psychology* 13(5): 690–702.
Wiltse, J. (2007). *Contested Waters: A Social History of Swimming Pools in America*. Chapel Hill, University of North Carolina.
Wolkowitz, C. (2006). *Bodies at Work*. London, Sage.
Wood, L.A. and R.O. Kroger (2000). *Doing Discourse Analysis: Methods for Studying Action in Talk and Texts*. London, Sage.
Young, I.M. (2005). *On Female Body Experience: 'Throwing like a girl' and other essays*. Oxford, Oxford University Press.
Young, I.M. (2010). 'The exclusion of women from sport: conceptual and existential dimensions.' In P. Davis and C. Weaving (eds) *Philosophical Perspectives on Gender in Sport and Physical Activity*. London, Routledge: 1320.
Young, K. and P. White (1995). 'Sport, physical danger and injury: the experiences of elite women athletes.' *Journal of Sport and Social Issues* 19(1): 45–61.
Zanker, C. and M. Gard (2008). 'Fatness, fitness and the moral universe of sport and physical activity.' *Sociology of Sport Journal* 25(1): 48–65.
Zornig, S. (2011a). 'What's wrong with marathon swimming?' http://www.icontact-archive.com/9BwG8tBcsCV_QYleE0UgK960z1Zfecew?w=2.
Zornig, S. (2011b). 'What's wrong with marathon swimming II?' http://dailynews.openwaterswimming.com/2011/09/whats-wrong-with-marathon-swimming-ii.html.

Index

Note: 'n.' after a page reference indicates the number of a note on that page.

8 Bridges Hudson River Swim 3, 19, 22n.1

abjection 51, 145, 178
actively absent 49–50, 62, 160, 162
Adams, Nick 66, 78
alliances of suffering 102, 109, 111, 115
altruism 109
   creative 108
   see also altruistic
altruistic 104, 108, 109
   see also altruism
amateur sport 158–159
Amateur Swimming Association 122
amateurism 65–67
apolitical gloss 6, 21, 120, 127, 134, 175
aquatic
   environment 9, 19, 41–42, 57, 65, 173–175
   sociologist 18
   sociology 13, 19
   wildlife 29, 58, 60–61
   see also sharks; wildlife
Aquatic Park 30, 64
   see also San Francisco
Armstrong, Lance 142
ASA *see* Amateur Swimming Assocation
athletic intruder 13
Atkinson, Michael 53, 110, 157, 175
authentic marathon swimming 62–67, 79, 94, 166
(auto)ethnography 15
autotelic pleasures 20, 57, 61–62

biographical disruption 155–156
bioprene 142
body fat 21, 124–125, 130, 137–138, 140, 142, 144, 146, 150, 151n.1
   see also dieting; fat phobic; Fat Studies; obesity epidemic; war on obesity
Bogardus, Lisa 63, 74
boundary work 65, 79–80
Boyton, Paul 7
Bruce, James 86
Butler, Judith 65, 124

Cabrera Channel 166
capital 13, 17, 20, 56, 116, 142, 157, 171
   cultural 145
   existential 20, 56–57, 61–62, 79, 175
   physical 145, 157
   social 13, 22, 79, 116
   symbolic 88
Catalina Channel 3, 48, 56, 58, 82, 96, 117n.3, 165
Chadwick, Florence 7
Channel rules 9, 63, 65, 68–69, 71–72, 74–75, 77
Channel Swimming and Piloting Federation 6, 66, 69, 74, 78, 80n.2, 85, 102
charitable fund-raising 6, 20–21, 41, 77, 101–103, 105–107, 110–111, 114, 116, 159
   see also charitable swimming; charity challenge; philanthropy; swimming for…
charitable swimming 21, 88, 102–107, 109, 114–116, 120, 168
   see also charitable fund-raising; charity challenge; philanthropy; swimming for…

Index

charity challenge(s) 30, 101–102, 104–105, 107, 109–110
  see also charitable fund-raising; charitable swimming; philanthropy; swimming for...
chavs 145
  see also middle-class; working-class
civil inattention 123, 127, 134
climbing 55, 63, 68, 71, 74–76
compassion 101, 107, 109, 111, 114–116
Cork 17, 53
Cox, Lynne 93
Crossley, Nick 33–34, 49
CS&PF see Channel Swimming and Piloting Federation
culture of risk 156, 158, 163–165

Did Not Finish 156, 166–167, 170
dieting 106, 132, 138, 147
  see also body fat; fat phobic; Fat Studies; obesity epidemic; war on obesity
disgust 29, 45, 64, 127, 133, 141–142, 145, 147
disrespect 75, 78
  see also disrespectful; respect
disrespectful 37, 77, 160
  see also disrespect; respect
DNF see Did Not Finish
domestic labour 130, 134
  see also reproductive labour
Dover 7, 17, 36–37, 69, 76–77, 110, 122, 144, 146
  harbour 1–2, 17, 36–37, 44n.4, 64, 66, 76, 118–119
dys-appearance 50, 62, 161, 165

Edborg, Cherie 126
Ederle, Gertrude 7, 11, 95
edgework 10, 156, 174
empowerment 133–135, 178
escape attempts 52, 54, 71, 176
Everest 71, 75–76
evocative objects 84, 96–97
exciting significance 21, 52, 109, 116, 165, 170–171
extreme 10, 17, 19, 38, 52, 112

fat phobic 16, 142, 147–148
  see also body fat; dieting; Fat Studies; obesity epidemic; war on obesity

Fat Studies 138, 148, 150–151
  see also body fat; dieting; fat phobic; obesity epidemic; war on obesity
Fédération Internationale de Natation 69
femininity 125, 128, 130, 134, 149, 177
  normative 38, 114, 129, 133, 146
feminist 120, 124, 132–135, 177
FINA see Fédération Internationale de Natation

gamification 91, 94–95, 97
Gleitze, Mercedes 85
Goh, Fiona 126
Gove, Michael 45
Gozo 17, 31, 38, 40, 50, 126
grease 8, 31, 46, 54
  see also Vaseline
Grimsey, Trent 9
Grosz, Elizabeth 62, 174

health 11, 20, 89–94, 103–106, 109, 121, 136, 139, 141, 147, 150, 156–157, 162–163, 165–166, 169–171, 174, 177–178
  charities 107
  holiday 165
  ill 21, 102, 107, 147, 149
    see also healthy, unhealthy
  healthy 104, 106, 107, 141, 156–157, 161–165, 171
    see also health; unhealthy
heroes 75, 78, 126, 135, 175, 177
  see also heroism
heroism 65, 126
  narratives of 13, 19, 43, 65
  see also heroes
heterosexuality 39, 145
homophobic 16, 39, 130, 145
homosocial 39, 130, 144–146
hypothermia 50, 66, 93, 98n.7, 137

ILDSA see Irish Long Distance Swimming Association
ingestible thermometer 92–93, 98n.5
Irish Long Distance Swimming Association 86

Jaundrill, Darren 86–87
Jersey-France 3

Karnazes, Dean 111–112
Kellerman, Annette 121
King, Brittany 66, 72, 76

La Jolla Cove 17, 59, 64
Lake Tahoe 78
leisure 12, 19, 36, 53, 65, 116, 127, 129–130, 136, 145–146, 172n.3, 176
   activity 11, 29, 53, 65, 174
   see also serious leisure
lifestyle sports 9–10, 45, 69, 123, 178
Logan, Dorothy 85

Manhattan Island Marathon Swim 23n.5, 47, 124, 153–154, 156, 158, 161, 172n.1
Marathon Swimmers Federation 23n.4, 68–69, 71, 74, 76, 78, 98n.2
masculinity 7, 10, 39, 120, 145–149
   normative 39, 94
Mauss, Marcel 32–34
McKibben, Bill 53, 165
menstruation 123, 126–127, 135n.2
middle-class 9–10, 18, 145, 155
   see also working-class; chavs
MIMS see Manhattan Island Marathon Swim
mind-body split 6, 41, 62, 125, 174
Möbius strip 62, 174
modernity 20, 70–71, 78–79, 88, 104, 173–174
Morrison, Evan 69–70, 126
MSF see Marathon Swimmers Federation
Munatones, Steven 66–67, 72, 117n.3

no-pain, no-gain 16, 47–48, 160, 165
North Channel 86, 117n.3
Nyad, Diana 67–68, 70–72, 77, 79, 87, 98n.2

obesity epidemic 136, 147
   see also body fat; dieting; fat phobic; Fat Studies; war on obesity
O'Donnell, Henry 86

pain
   bad 49, 157, 160–161, 164
   and discomfort 48–49, 109, 115, 156
   good 49–50, 157, 164–165
   Zatopekian 157
Palfrey, Penny 67
Peary, Robert 84

Phelps, Michael 142
philanthropy 22, 104, 108–109, 116
   adventure 101–102
   see also charitable fund-raising; charitable swimming; charity challenge; swimming for…
physical activity 46, 102, 136–137, 151, 157, 162
pleasures of swimming 14, 16, 41, 47, 58, 62, 82, 129, 156, 175
professional athletes 53, 156, 161, 165
publicity-seeking 67, 77
Pugh, Lewis 93, 112–114
purity 63–65, 79, 173

quantification 20, 88–89, 91, 94–96, 98
   self- 89–91, 94

rationalisation 20, 65, 71, 74, 78–79
reproductive labour 12, 128–130
   see also domestic labour
respect 17, 66, 75, 78–79, 141, 143, 175
   see also disrespect; disrespectful
Rottnest Channel 47
Round Jersey 3, 82, 96
Ruiz, Rosie 84

Sandycove Island 53, 56
San Francisco 17, 30, 58, 64, 95, 109, 114, 130
   see also Aquatic Park
Santa Barbara Channel Swimming Association 73
SBCSA see Santa Barbara Channel Swimming Association
seasickness 55, 57, 62
sensorium 40–42
   shifted 41–42, 62, 174
sensory deprivation 41, 55
   see also sensorium
serious leisure 9, 29
   see also leisure
sharks 54, 59–60, 127
   see also aquatic wildlife; wildlife
shivering 40, 50–51, 76, 145, 167
social inequalities 21, 102, 111, 113
social media 3, 51, 61, 64, 67, 88–89, 92, 96
social worlds 4, 63–64, 69, 74, 76
Solo Swims of Ontario 93

Index

SSO *see* Solo Swims of Ontario
Straits of Gibraltar 117n.3
Streeter, Freda 37
stroke correction 32, 34, 39, 44n.2, 155, 161, 165
swim charts 82, 96
swimming for... 21, 101–103, 108–110, 112, 114, 117

tattoos 96–97
Taylor, Kyle 76
techniques of the body 19, 30, 32, 38–39, 42–43, 46–47
technology 20, 28, 69, 84, 88, 91–94, 97–98
  see also technologies
technologies 10, 28, 70, 72, 79–80, 84, 87, 89–90, 91–92, 94–95, 97–98
  see also technology
This Girl Can 177
Titmuss, Richard 102, 108
tradition-oriented 20, 64, 69, 84, 88, 97, 173–175
triathlon 6, 14, 29, 63, 72, 74, 133, 141, 149

unhealthy 103, 144, 177

Vaseline 2, 31, 36, 54, 118, 123, 145
  see also grease
volunteer tourism 5, 102–103

Walker, Adam 113–114
war on obesity 21, 103, 136–137, 139, 142–143, 147, 150, 162
  see also body fat; dieting; fat phobic; Fat Studies; obesity epidemic
Webb, Matthew 7–9, 69, 75, 96
wetsuits 7, 63, 71–72
whiteness 12–13, 125
wildlife 8, 17, 58–61, 87, 107, 113
  see also aquatic wildlife; sharks
working-class 145, 155
  see also chavs; middle-class

Young, Iris Marion 39, 125, 127–128, 132

Zornig, Scott 73–75, 78–79

Lightning Source UK Ltd.
Milton Keynes UK
UKHW021820170321
380525UK00006B/1503